CVE

D1631577

NO SUBSTITUTE
Keith Peacock

First published in 2004 by Charlton Athletic Football Company Limited,
The Valley, Floyd Road, London SE7 8BL.
Telephone: 020-8333 4000. Website: www.cafc.co.uk.

Printed and bound by Antony Rowe Limited, Bumpers Farm,
Chippenham, Wiltshire SN14 6LH.

ISBN 0 9529668 2 4

Production and marketing by Corinna Huxley (votv@btinternet.com).

To my wife, Lesley, my very best friend, who has shared my journey from the day I signed for Charlton as a 17-year-old. From girlfriend to wife, mother and grandmother, the way you have fulfilled each role has my total admiration. Thank you for being the wind beneath this Peacock's wings. For you, there is No Substitute.

ACKNOWLEDGEMENTS

My special thanks go to my collaborator, Rick Everitt, without whom this book would not have been written. He has worked tirelessly to ensure that more than 40 years of my life have been clearly and accurately documented, and his ability to put down my thoughts and experiences in an orderly fashion has been quite remarkable. Working with Rick over these past months, his devotion to Charlton Athletic has shone through, while his knowledge of the club and background involvement with it is extraordinary. I am grateful to Rick and his partner Corinna Huxley – who has been responsible for the production and marketing of the book – for their time, patience and expertise.

Thanks are also due to my wife, Lesley, and to club historian Colin Cameron and Charlton assistant communications manager Matt Wright for their help and advice to Rick and myself during the drafting of the text, especially at the proof-reading stage. Tony Hudd, of the Kent Messenger, kindly read the Gillingham and Maidstone chapters. Nevertheless, Rick and I take full responsibility for any errors or omissions that have crept in despite our best efforts.

I thank club photographer Tom Morris for his assistance with Charlton pictures, including several on the cover, and Jon Mason of the club's communications team, who designed the latter.

Chief executive Peter Varney deserves a special mention for his support and encouragement of the project. I regret that this has restrained me from revealing too many stories about him from the veterans' tours. Mind you, Peter, there's always the sequel!

I would also like to acknowledge all the current staff at Charlton for the work they do to make my job so much easier.

Finally, I would like to thank my family and all my friends and colleagues over the years at Charlton, the Columbus Magic, the Tampa Bay Rowdies, Gillingham, Maidstone United and Queens Park Rangers. This is my story, but it would be very different without you.   KP

CONTENTS

Rick Everitt, who collaborated with Keith on this book, covered Charlton Athletic from 1989-98 for the *SE London & Kentish Mercury* and was the paper's sports editor from 1993 until appointed to establish the club's communications department in 1998. He also founded *Voice of The Valley* fanzine, which he edited from 1988-2001, and was secretary of Charlton Athletic Supporters' Club from 1991-98. Rick is the author of *Battle for The Valley* (1991) and co-publisher of Colin Cameron's *Home & Away with Charlton Athletic 1920-2004*. He gave up his full-time post as the club's communications director in 2003 to concentrate on writing and his role as a Bexley councillor, having been elected to represent East Wickham ward in Welling the previous year. Rick and his partner Corinna have one daughter, Natasha (6), whose favourite Charlton player is now Keith Peacock.

INTRODUCTION

I've been lucky enough to travel through football from Sheffield to Shanghai, Luton to Las Vegas. My entire playing career in England was spent at Charlton. I learnt the management trade in two challenging and exciting years in the United States, fell in love with Gillingham, flirted with Queens Park Rangers and Maidstone, then returned to the warm embrace of the very happy Valley – my true home.

I have survived a lifetime in the beautiful game of football and it has lifted me to some heady heights. I can still remember scoring on my home debut as if it were yesterday, and the pain of missing the promotion game in 1975. Then there was the heartbreak of taking Gillingham to within 11 minutes of promotion and Maidstone to the brink of Wembley, and, of course, the 1998 play-off final, the game of all games. These are just a few of the memories that have lain dormant in my mind, but which have been evoked during the writing of this book. Whether they are good or bad, happy or sad, I am so very fortunate to have them all.

The former Charlton player Steve Jones once said to me that he would rather score a hat-trick in one game at Wembley than play in 600 League matches. That was his vision.

For me there is nothing equal to a lifetime in football, being paid to do something that is thrilling and rewarding. To walk out on the training field each day is literally a breath of fresh air. In life, people look to different forms of entertainment to make them laugh, cry, be very happy or extremely sad. Well, I've had that on a weekly basis.

Some people have said that I was unlucky not to play in the top division or not to get promotion with Gillingham or Maidstone. Don't you believe it! I am the fortunate one just to have been in the game, and especially with Charlton for all these years.

I have met a host of colourful characters along the way, with whom I've shared laughter and tears. I have brushed shoulders with the great and good, but I like to think that I'll always remain one of the lads.

Mine is just the story of a boy from Barnehurst – far from being the best player in the world – who had a dream. There are many thousands out there with the same ambitions I had as a youngster. I would say to them: have self-belief, never stop working at it, and above all retain your humility. The ups and downs come fast and furious, so no matter what, pick yourself up and get back in the race, because that's life!

As my 43rd season begins to unfold, I'm hoping there is still a chapter or two to be written before I take off my coaching cap for good. Who knows, perhaps a cup final?

Whatever happens, I'll have few regrets.

As I began to cast my mind back over half a century, my problem was to know where I could possibly begin . . .

Keith Peacock
October 2004

Chapter One
THE GLORY GAME

I grabbed hold of the man to my left. He had his eyes firmly closed and his hands were over his face. I yelled into his ear: "We're in the Premiership!" For a split second he stared at me. Then it all went crazy.

Sasa Ilic had just saved Michael Gray's penalty and half the stadium had erupted in celebration. The other half had been stunned into complete and utter silence. If you were relying on the noise alone, there was a moment or two before it was clear who was responsible. But it was the Roker roar that had died, Charlton who had just won promotion. Top-flight football would be played at The Valley again for the first time in 41 years.

Eighteen or so hours earlier, Alan Curbishley, Les Reed, Jimmy Hendry and I had been sitting in a hotel lounge having a late-night glass of red wine. There was the usual chat about the impending match, but nothing too heavy. Les and Alan's preparation had left nothing to chance. It was bound to be tight and seemed likely just one goal would be enough to decide the outcome. We just hoped it would be ours. The players were already in bed and we soon went off to our own rooms. I was to realise in the following months that this would be the last time that Alan could sit in a public place without being continually interrupted by strangers. He was hours away from becoming a nationally recognised face.

Monday, May 25th, 1998, dawned bright, although the air was sticky. Some of the players came down for breakfast and then had a pre-match meal at 11.45, while others combined the two. Curbs had haddock and poached eggs. He was a braver man than I.

Soon we were all wearing our new beige suits, looking for all the world as if we were going to a wedding. Players were milling around the hotel grounds and the nearby village, but nobody was talking about what lay ahead of us that afternoon. The whole of the senior squad was there. Everyone had played a part, big or small.

My heart went out to those players who were going to miss out, such as Anthony Barness, Phil Chapple and Paul Mortimer. They had put on brave faces and seemed to be enjoying themselves, but I knew they would be hurting inside. John Robinson hadn't made the starting line-up and I was certain that beneath the surface he was heartbroken. Curbs had been right to leave John out, because he hadn't had the correct build-up due to injury.

Alan had made a point of naming the team two or three days earlier so that those who were omitted would not have to deal with the disappointment on the day. He knew from bitter experience how that could feel. Charlton had been to Wembley in 1987 for the Full Members' Cup final and manager Lennie Lawrence had told him late on that he would not be playing. Curbs was determined not to make the same mistake.

As we drew close to Wembley, the assembling crowd seemed to consist entirely of Sunderland supporters. It was like arriving at an away fixture. For a moment I wondered if there had been a hitch with the tickets. Maybe their fans had arrived early because they had further to come or perhaps they just knew, from experience, that it was preferable to be able to linger on such occasions.

When the teams came down the tunnel together and strode into the stadium, it was very different. We had 35,000 there to cheer us on. It was a far cry from so many afternoons at The Valley in my playing days, and in the intervening years as well.

I'd seen just as many Addicks supporters before, but perhaps not since a grim afternoon 40 years earlier. These were the children and grandchildren of fans whose crushing disappointment had fired my own passion for the club.

For a while we had been delighted just to get to the play-off final, which was an achievement in itself, but on the day we became very focused on winning. Sunderland were favourites. They had finished above us, but we were the in-form team, which made the contest difficult to predict.

There were no big stars in the Charlton side, but we did have a dedicated group of players. Mark Kinsella was our Captain Courageous play-maker – fast making a name for himself in the midfield. Central defender Richard Rufus was one of the quickest and most ruthless tacklers in the division. And the predatory Clive Mendonca had already scored 25 times in his first season at the club – he was about to become a legend. Danny Mills had just come into the club at right-back. He was aggressive and full of energy. Eddie Youds was a powerful, accomplished defender, very solid. Mark Bowen was a two-footed, classy and highly experienced left-back. Keith Jones, a gutsy little destroyer, blended well with Kinsella in midfield. Shaun Newton provided pace and power on the right flank. Loan signing Neil Heaney, on the left, was the one we couldn't be entirely sure about, but only because we didn't know him so well. Up front, Mark Bright was the consummate professional, powerful in the air and providing all the right touches and nudges.

And then there was Sasa Ilic, who had started the season in non-League football and kept nine consecutive clean sheets to help get us this far. If he could keep a tenth we would surely win the game. A single Mendonca goal would be enough. He scored in the 23rd minute. The finish was sublime.

Half-time came and went in a blur, but Sunderland scored twice in quick succession at the beginning of the second half and now we had it all to do. Mendonca netted again to equalise, with an even better goal than his first. I was relieved, but the script had now been thrown out of the window. Sasa no longer looked formidable. He'd been beaten by both Niall Quinn and Kevin Phillips, and both those dangerous strikers looked capable of adding to their tally. With 17 minutes of normal time left, Quinn did.

Doubts were now beginning to creep into my mind, but the spirit in the Charlton side somehow kept us going. Rufus equalised with his first-ever goal, but some of the credit belonged to Bright for his wily blocking of goalkeeper Lionel Perez. It was the slightest of interventions but it was all about experience. Mark knew how to prevent Perez getting near the ball, leaving Rufus to head into an unguarded net. That moment and the way Bright unsettled Jody Craddock were vital to our eventual success.

It is unusual for there to be any interaction between the benches during matches, particularly when there is so much at stake, but this was an exception. "Can you believe this game?" shouted across Sunderland manager Peter Reid. We were all aware that we were watching something extraordinary. It was hard to know where to begin to analyse it tactically or how to stop the goals going in. Players were tiring, so substitutions were being made on each side, but now it was a case of finding the men for the occasion rather than trying to change the shape of the game. Enter striker Steve Jones and then, in extra-time, the ever-reliable Steve Brown.

Nicky Summerbee put Sunderland ahead once more nine

minutes into the first additional period, but Mendonca would not be denied. Brown played his part by winning the ball for fellow substitute Jones, who had fresh enough legs to run to the byline and get his cross in. Any player in the history of the game would have been proud of Clive's touch and finish for the equaliser.

At 4-4 fatigue finally overcame the teams and the players no longer had the energy to run the extra yard or hit the ball any harder. The play-off final had reached stalemate and would have to be decided by the lottery of penalties. When I had walked out on to the pitch prior to the game I'd thought to myself how much I'd have loved to be taking part. Suddenly, I didn't envy the players their job one bit.

In my career I'd taken seven penalties, scored five and had two saved. I was always willing to have a go, but I wasn't an expert, as Mendonca, Paolo Di Canio or Bob Curtis had been in different eras for Charlton. The problem with this shoot-out was that we had to use players who were not penalty-takers at all. One by one, they came forward. The club's fate lay at their feet.

Mendonca was a safe bet. I felt confident about Brown, even though he didn't himself, but nervous for him too. Keith Jones, who took the third, worried me. I think he'd missed when we'd staged a mock shoot-out in training on the Friday. Kinsella was a good striker of the ball and a man in form. Sure-footed Bowen used his cool head. About Robinson, I didn't have a clue. At least he was centre stage, after all. I wasn't completely convinced about Newton, either, but he too showed his mettle. Their courage shone through.

Sasa had only got near one of the Sunderland kicks, but there had been a brief cry of hope from the Charlton supporters. Curbs had been looking away and for an instant wasn't sure what had happened. He watched the next one beat Ilic and then put his head in his hands as Gray stepped up.

I was thinking what a great left foot Gray had. He had the ability to put the ball within an inch of where he wanted, but on this day it was more about nerve. He scuffed his shot. Sasa dived to his left. He saved. Charlton were promoted.

It wasn't easy for Curbs to tell from which side the noise was coming, so when the roar went up there was a moment before he knew what had happened. Then we were all on the pitch, embracing one another and shaking hands. In that moment, Charlton were transformed.

I looked up into the crowd and spotted Lesley, my wife, with our children, Gavin and Lauren, and their respective partners, Amanda and Andy, all with their faces lit up, like the thousands around them.

The next 40 minutes of celebration were gone in a flash and as I finally neared the tunnel, I turned to have one last look at the emptying arena. All the relegation battles I had endured, all the years of promise that had ended in disappointment, had ceased to matter. We had won promotion to the top division and I had been part of it, not as a player and not as manager, but I was there.

After four decades – and in the most dramatic manner conceivable – my ambition had been realised . . .

Chapter Two
FINDING MY FEET

My father, Tom Peacock, was fond of saying that "bread and jam at home tastes much better than fillet steak anywhere else in the world". As I got older I grew to realise that this wasn't literally true. Most people prefer fillet steak wherever they are. What he meant was that family life is more important than anything that happens elsewhere. It's an opinion that I very much hold dear.

Although I grew up in and have always lived within a few miles of Barnehurst, my parents originally came from South Shields. They were forced to come south by my father's search for work before the war, but if they'd had the choice they would have remained in the North East of England.

Dad was a wiry five-foot eight-and-a-half, with blue eyes and brown hair. My sister Valerie, who was older than me by three years, took after him. I had more of the look of my mother, Lydia.

My father was an affable man, well liked and respected, and with a stubborn streak that prevented him being anybody's fool. He had been in the merchant navy before the outbreak of hostilities, so it was natural that he joined the Royal Navy when the war came, serving on the minesweepers. Afterwards, he was employed at the Ford plant in Dagenham – and later Woolwich – for 20 years.

I was born in May 1945, just as the war in Europe was coming to an end, and in my early years we lived in a terraced house in Parkside Avenue, Barnehurst. Dad worked long hours and was often on the nightshift, but he spent as much time as he possibly could with his wife and children. Indeed, he gave his time unstintingly to his family, right up to his death at the age of 81.

He had been quite a good footballer himself at school level and it was evident when we kicked a ball around over the park that he had two good feet. On one occasion we even got him to play for a Barnehurst Primary School parents' team.

Due to the way his life had panned out, he'd probably only ever been to St James' Park once or twice, but for all that Newcastle United were very much his team. As I grew up, he would occasionally take me to The Valley to see Charlton, who were now our local side, but we would travel all over London to see Newcastle. First and foremost he was a family man. His other passion was certainly football, but he worked hard for a living and wouldn't have felt able to justify going to Charlton every week.

I always think of the 1950s, in which I grew up, as days of sublime freedom. Ironically, this is because there was discipline on all fronts. If you got into trouble at school or with the police, you knew your parents would back the authorities up without question and you would have to face the music. Having that structure to your life allowed you to develop in other ways.

Even within the little gang of youngsters around Parkside Avenue, you knew where you stood. There would be various things you had to do to win the respect of your contemporaries. You had to be able to spit ten feet, walk on your hands for ten yards, take up a handstand position against a wall for a minute and a half, smoke at least half a cigarette and be able to swear. Then, if you could run right round the block, you were in. I was six when I joined the gang and I was one of the youngest, because most of the members were Valerie's age. I was allowed to join because I passed all the tests. They sound silly now, but it gave you a sense of belonging.

There were very few cars on the road in those days and we would spend hours playing with the youngsters from the neighbouring houses, never straying from the immediate vicinity. There was a level of self-organisation within the group and we looked after each other. We all knew that we had to go in when our parents called us and if we didn't then we'd probably get a good hiding or wouldn't be allowed out the next night.

It may be that these days some kids get away with more or money is more available for them to buy their entertainment at the cinema or the bowling alley, but the supervision and sense of responsibility has been lost as a consequence.

When I was eight we moved about a mile to a semi-detached house in Merewood Road. Perhaps to help meet the increased expense, my mother went to work at a factory in Thames Road, Erith, which was a 15-minute bicycle ride away. During the school holidays she would spend half her lunch-hour cycling home from work and back again to make sure that Valerie and I had a proper meal. It was a measure of her dedication to her family, although as children her presence was something we took for granted.

Another stroke of good fortune was that we lived right next to Barnehurst golf course. It had a fairly large section of spare land that became a gigantic playground for us. A doodle-bug had fallen there during the war and left a huge chasm in the ground. There we were able to mix with other kids, play sport and learn to organise ourselves. Naturally, football became a big part of that.

At first I went across with my dad, but later I would go with my mates after school and during the holidays. Of course, it was a great advantage if you owned a football, as I did. In those days it would be well dubbined and had to be laced up, so you'd spend a fair amount of time getting the ball ready, never mind your boots.

Our games were never organised, not even to the extent of everybody arriving at the same time. You'd start out with just a couple of mates, and then a few more lads would turn up and you might play four versus four. As time went on the older boys would come along on their way home from work. What had started as two-a-side might have become 12-a-side by now, and with the bigger lads involved you might well not be getting a kick.

That was part of my football education in itself. As one of the better players in your own age group you had the opportunity to linger on the ball, but if you did that against the older lads they'd quickly knock you out of the way. Without ever being coached, you soon realised that the way to succeed was to limit yourself to one or two touches and adapted your game accordingly.

Peter Reeves, who later played alongside me at Charlton and was a few years younger than me, used to say something similar. He was always one of the smallest boys when he was growing up, so he learned that he had to make daring tackles to get the ball. They then became his trademark as a professional.

In the 1950s there was very little football on television, so you weren't exposed to the constant repetition and analysis of moves that there is today. Even if you were lucky enough to attend a professional match, everything happened too quickly for you to be able to study it in detail. So it transpired that the tricks you learned in the playground became your game. If you had any aptitude for football, you learned from each other. I believe that the top players today still learn their skills intuitively in the playground. The difference now is that they have developed exceptional levels of power and fitness compared to the heroes of my youth.

I carried on going over to the golf course until I was about 14, but certainly I was a regular visitor while I was at junior school. That was Barnehurst Primary School, which had the reputation of being very sound. The headmistress was Mrs Mumford, who became quite a local legend. However, it was the sports master, John Attwood, who was a huge influence on me. He was a young, all-round sportsman, who loved his football and was a useful centre-forward himself. I still see him to this day.

I remember him taking me aside when I was about eight and asking me what I wanted to be when I grew up. He then told me that I'd never make a footballer unless I could kick with both feet. Such was the respect for authority in those days that his words made a big impression on me. I spent the next few months smacking the ball against a small wall in our back garden. By the time I was nine, I could kick with both feet.

My respect for John's advice had been total. It served me well, too. When my career did develop at Charlton I could play on either wing. Indeed, the 107 goals that I scored were evenly divided between each foot, with a few headers on top.

While I was at Barnehurst Primary, I had my first success as a player, captaining the school team as we won our league and representing the district. It was probably because I was a good player that I was given the captaincy, but I have a feeling that it was also because I was looked upon as something of a leader, who fostered team spirit and encouraged the weaker players.

Football didn't distract me from my studies, however, and in my last year at junior school I passed the 11-plus exam and was accepted at Erith Grammar School, as it then was. This was an important event, but it had implications for my sporting ambitions. At Erith, they only played football in the spring term. The period from September to Christmas was dedicated to rugby and the summer, naturally, to cricket. In addition to that, the headmaster, and most of the teachers who were involved in sport, preferred rugby to "soccer", as they called it.

Even so, the fact that Erith played football at all was enough to persuade me that it was a better option than Dartford Grammar School. My uncle had gone to the Dartford school many years before, so it might have been seen as the logical choice on those grounds alone, but crucially they only played rugby there.

I wasn't great at rugby, but I was always in the side, either at scrum-half or inside-centre, and would captain the team at my age group. I even got as far as the Kent trials at U15 level.

There was no organised junior football outside of the school and representative structure, so my opportunities to play in formal matches were limited to the spring term. This did put my football development back. With such a short season, bad weather in January could easily mean that I might only play eight games all year. I would still go to district trials and I did play a few times for North Kent, but I was beginning to lose ground. Others would be playing regularly all winter and also going to trials in the autumn.

I was half-decent at cricket and again I found myself captain of the side. In athletics I tended to be more of a distance runner than anything else.

I wasn't a high-flyer intellectually, but given that it was a grammar school I think after a few years it was assumed that I would become a sports master and I was being guided that way. I was harbouring the dream of becoming a footballer, but from the school's perspective the focus was more on academic work and all-round character development.

With hindsight, I don't think I would have had it any other way. Playing regularly for a rugby team taught me about a different culture, and together my educational and sporting upbringing gave me a wide appreciation of most sports and activities.

As for Charlton, they had yet to win my affections in those early days at Erith. Unsurprisingly I'd taken up my father's allegiance to Newcastle and in 1955, when I was ten, I saw them play in the FA Cup final at Wembley against Manchester City on the television. They won 3-1, Jackie Milburn scoring the first goal with a great header. Of course, you couldn't buy replica kit back then, but I remember getting a pair of Newcastle socks when I was 12. Either they made things to last in those days or my mum allowed for growth, because I was still wearing them when I was 16.

Football support locally was quite mixed. My best mates tended to be Charlton fans, but the Munich air disaster in 1956 captured the hearts of the country and turned a lot of people into Manchester United fans. It affected me too. They were in the middle of a Cup run and the aftermath of the accident was on the news every night, with the survivors struggling for life and the patched-up team battling on against the odds.

I would go wherever there was a professional match, but Charlton were the nearest big club, so naturally I went there often. It was the Blackburn game in 1958 that really changed my attitude.

It was a big game for both clubs, with Charlton needing just a draw to reclaim the First Division place that they had lost 12 months earlier, and Rovers needing to win to edge them out. There were only two clubs promoted from the Second Division in those days.

I went there with my dad and some friends, aware that it was a big game but not really caring too much about the result. Newcastle were still my team. I remember being to the right of the halfway line, opposite the players' tunnel. I wasn't as high up the bank as usual, because of the size of the crowd. The record books tell me that there were 56,435 in the ground that afternoon. Charlton went 4-1 down. They pulled it back to 4-3 but just couldn't manage the equaliser.

The scoreline tells its own story of a thrilling match, but my abiding memory is the journey away from the ground. The Blackburn fans were obviously quite happy, but there was no hostility towards them. There were no recriminations or criticism of the Charlton players either. Instead, it was like coming away from a funeral. It was deathly quiet, with everybody lined up on the platform at Charlton Station, shuffling forward each time a train came in. I just remember feeling so sad for the Charlton fans. Almost out of respect for them, I was being quieter than usual, and my dad was sympathetic to the local side, even though they weren't his team.

It was in that moment that I realised I wanted to play for Charlton and one day take them back into the First Division. It was just the schoolboy dream of scoring the winning goal to win promotion, but the emotion of that day tied me to the club. After that, Charlton were my team. I was just turning 13 and believed I could make it happen. I wanted to do something about the way those people were feeling. As you get older your dreams fade and you realise your own limitations, but as it turned out my dream did come true many years later, albeit not in quite the way I expected.

I started going to Charlton whenever possible. Occasionally, this would be with my dad, but often I'd go on my own or with a friend. My dad would grab an hour's nap when he came off the nightshift on a Saturday morning and then get up again to watch me play, but after that he'd go back to bed to catch up on his sleep. In those later years I do remember him starting to take more notice of Charlton's results. He wanted them to do well and liked the fact that I was taking an interest in the club.

My mother never went to matches. It wasn't even conceivable and she'd have laughed had it been suggested. There were women at games, but they were very few in number.

Charlton were always quite entertaining to watch in those years after they dropped out of the First Division. They had players like Stuart Leary, Sam Lawrie and Johnny Summers, who all scored goals for fun, and I remember seeing the 6-6 draw with Middlesbrough, in 1960, in particular. I was becoming a proper supporter in that period, although I had a lot of other things going on around my school life and in terms of playing myself. Heaven knows where I got the energy!

One clear memory I have from when I was about 14 and a half is of looking at the school noticeboard to check the different activities in which I was involved in that particular week. My name was there under a number of different headings – the school drama rehearsal, football practice, basketball and a gym meeting.

John Graham, the sports master, came past and joked that I was a "jack of all trades". Of course, the conclusion of that little saying, although he didn't continue it, is "and master of none". I decided there and then that this wasn't what I wanted. As far as I could be, I wanted to be the master of one – and that was football.

It was clear that my football development was suffering as I threw my energies into so many other aspects of school life. My prospects did not look good. Indeed, this was underlined for me by another sports master, Phil Moore. He had shown an interest in me, but pointed out how far I was behind the boys who were playing for their county or country. Time was running out and I might have to face the fact that being a professional was an ambition that many youngsters had but were never able to fulfil. I left the sports field that day dejected, feeling that I no longer had a dream to chase.

However, when I told my dad what Mr Moore had said, he lifted my spirits by replying encouragingly: "Keep plugging away, son. You'll be OK." He gave me a dozen reasons to be grateful for everything that I had, and I set off for my beloved golf course with my ball feeling more determined than ever to play for Charlton.

I broke my private record that evening, keeping the ball in the air 3,330 times. This feat took me nearly 40 minutes of sheer concentration to complete, combining skill and mental determination. Other people could give up on me, I thought, but I was not about to give up on myself.

My dad arranged for me to join a team from Woolwich Arsenal called ROFSA, but this was short-lived. When I did manage to get some regular football it came, strangely enough, through a contact of my mother. She was working at Cutters, a local hairdresser's owned by a Mrs Hanks, whose son was running a men's side called Embassy Royals. They played at Bourne Road, in Bexley. The facilities were horrendous. I can remember there being big troughs of water outside the changing rooms that we used to clean the mud off our hands.

This was a poor team and it was a good day if we kept the scoreline under double figures. I remember a week when we lost 21-1. The goalkeeper was massive and everything seemed to go through his legs. However, I kept turning up, and if I got one goal myself every now and again then that was something. I was a boy among men, but I think going there and getting hammered every week taught me a sort of discipline. No matter how badly things were going, you never let the rest of the team down. You showed up on time no matter what.

One Sunday John Attwood played alongside me at Bourne Road. He was still quite a good player and he put us 1-0 up with a goal from about 30 yards. We eventually lost 2-1, but I can still remember the euphoria we felt in holding a lead for about an hour. Afterwards he promised that he would get me into another team of a better standard, but the season was drawing to an end and nothing materialised at that time.

At this stage there wasn't a lot my parents could do to help me progress my football career. They had given me everything they could, and my dad was very wise in the ways of the world. His support was ever present during the little spare time he had. He was also a great believer in fate, which did indeed intervene – through him – to give me my first contact with Charlton, in 1960.

My dad was now working on the belt system for Ford at Woolwich and one of his workmates was Eric Lancelotte, a former Charlton forward who'd played 41 games for the club in the seasons either side of the war. I don't know how the conversation came about, but my dad evidently asked him how I could go about getting a trial with a professional club. Eric agreed to contact Charlton and ask them to take a look at me on his recommendation.

They agreed and I was summoned to The Valley. It was a warm May night and there were maybe 30 or more boys present, with the trial taking the form of a series of teams coming on and off. Some of the boys were already with the club. Others, like me, were there by recommendation, but mainly that would have come through their school and they would have already been playing for their district or county. In any event I played well and was asked to come back for the Tuesday and Thursday training sessions at the start of the following season. I had just turned 15, and it was my first break.

Unfortunately, it was almost a case of one door opening and another slamming in my face, as I suffered an immediate setback. I'd seen a doctor about a pain I was getting in my left knee, but he was very dismissive about it. It wasn't the done thing to question medical advice, so although it ached I just carried on. My sister's boyfriend, Pete Woollard, then noticed that my left leg had become thinner than my right one. When I measured this I found there was a one-inch difference. In fact, it is still thinner to this day. I saw John Buck, a specialist who was connected with Charlton for many years, and it transpired that the problem was a piece of bone floating behind the kneecap.

I'd been due to go to the Rome Olympics that summer with the school, but instead I found myself entering hospital for an operation that left me in plaster for eight weeks. Worse still were the strict instructions that I wasn't to kick another ball for six months.

In that time, I wasn't allowed to participate in any sport, I could only work with weights. So for my first six months with Charlton, all I could do was go along once a week to the old wooden gymnasium behind the west stand and do exercises. This was as much about showing my face and being part of the club as for any practical benefit. It was a hard knock so soon after being invited to train at The Valley.

At least it was the rugby term I was missing at Erith. And the remainder of the football season was far from wasted. At the turn of the year, I joined a Sunday team called Witton United, which was John Attwood's side. Pete, who would marry Valerie in 1962, was in goal. I just arrived with my boots on New Year's Day, hoping someone would be hungover and not turn up. I got my wish and ended up playing, scored a goal, and soon became a regular in the team.

Witton played in the Metropolitan League, which was a good standard. The side included a number of players from the lower ranks of the semi-professional game, who would turn out for the likes of Erith and Belvedere on a Saturday. This experience was important, because it got me back into playing football regularly after the long absence and it gave me a real kick-on.

By April I had progressed sufficiently to make my debut for the Charlton colts, in a 5-1 win over Luton Town at New Eltham, although I had to wait for the return fixture three weeks later to get on the scoresheet. By the end of the season I had played five times for them in all, and netted four goals.

During term-time I now had a hectic schedule. Often I would spend the day at school, take part in circuit training at the end of lessons, then jump on a bus to Erith Station, take the railway to Charlton and run down the hill to train at The Valley. Going back I had the choice of catching a bus from Erith to Barnehurst or using the fare to buy a bar of chocolate and running and walking home. Invariably, I'd do the latter!

I was studying for my O-levels at the time, so even when I got home I would still have mountains of homework to do. This was twice a week, so looking back it was quite a stiff programme.

By the start of 1961/62, when I entered the sixth form, I was playing for the colts on a Saturday morning, rugby for the school in the afternoon and then football on Sunday for Witton United. I was 16 that summer and Charlton signed me as an amateur. This showed I had made certain progress and enabled me to play for the A team and the reserves. I felt I was doing all right with Charlton, but nothing sensational. I was holding my own at best.

One thing I would do at school whenever I had the time was practise striking the ball. I had remembered reading an article about Bobby Charlton that said whenever he was having a poor run of form he would go and work in a shooting box, with walls on either side. The object was to be able to strike the ball accurately first time. It's common sense that the less time you give a goalkeeper to think, the less chance there is of him making a save.

I had found that diving headers could be very effective in games, but first-time finishing – volleys with either foot – was my particular speciality and that is what I kept practising. I could do this on my own, as long as I had a wall either side of me and another in front. This was available in the gym at school. There was also a dilapidated wooden shooting box at The Valley, and I used this at every opportunity.

Witton had a good striker called Derek Mann. He recommended me to Erith and Belvedere, so I was asked to play in their reserves in a midweek game at the beginning of 1961/62. It didn't lead anywhere, because I was committed to Charlton, but soon I became a key player in the Sunday side and of course that did a lot for my confidence. I played inside-forward on either side and just lived for goals. We won promotion and by now I was in the first team at school, where the goals were also flying in.

I started to shine in the colts as well and towards the end of March I was asked to play for the reserves. I got a couple of goals for them on my debut against Queens Park Rangers and it was the fact that I could score at that level that really established me at Charlton. I could control the ball pretty well and make reasonable use of it, but my ability to put half-chances away from any angle was the clincher.

I played for the colts whenever I could, but was limited because school sport came first – even if the school game was rugby. If one match was in the morning and the other in the afternoon then I would dash between the two. I had little energy left for the second game and wasn't doing myself any favours, but there was no thought of Charlton being the priority. The reserves played in the evenings, so there was no conflict there. And once I got into the reserves for the first time, I had realistic prospects of becoming a professional.

I was now alongside people like Don Townsend, father of Republic of Ireland international Andy, who had been a first-team regular for a number of years. I played in his last two games for the club before he moved to Crystal Palace. Both were against Swindon, which was his neck of the woods. I scored in the away match and he also got one, from about 30 yards.

Gordon Jago was often in the reserve side, as was Freddie Lucas. They were both seasoned professionals. But this was an era when the Charlton first-team squad had become a bit smaller to suit its new Second Division status. There was a fairly tight-knit core of 16 getting into the first team, with the South African-born Stuart Leary, who also played cricket for Kent, as the star man.

I had no contact with the first team at all when I trained on Tuesdays and Thursdays, although there was an intermediary group of part-time professionals and they would come in and train with us. Some pros were on about £14 a week, the part-timers would get £8 in the season and £4 in the summer. They played mainly in the reserves, but now and again they could get a game in the first team. They would invariably be apprentices in other jobs, not earning very much for it, but with the part-time money they got from Charlton making up a viable wage.

I'd see them on Tuesdays and Thursdays, although they tended to train apart from us most of the time. It was a real buzz just going to the ground on those evenings, particularly if you were one of the first to arrive or last to leave and were virtually alone in that vast arena. We'd do skill drills and then finish up with a game in the car park. It was very poorly lit and these days no youngster would be allowed to train in such conditions, although your eyes would gradually adjust. There were no real lines and just a few cones, the wall of the gym and the toilets made up one of the sides of the pitch. It was part of the game to play off the wall. We would have some terrific matches on what seemed to be coaldust. In some ways it was quite a good surface to play on, but it was very fast and initially I found it very hard to adapt.

A lot of the other players had experience at district and county level, and had been toughened up in the more competitive environment of inner London schools. I had the fitness as I'd always worked hard on that, but I was physically smaller and surprised by the pace of the sessions.

Joe Guymer was one of the people who took our training, but Peter Croker – one of the 1947 FA Cup final winning team and still an active supporter of the club – was involved in getting the schoolboys down. The assistant manager, George Robinson, would often oversee a few things, and Jock Basford, the first-team coach, might be about. The one person that you never saw was Frank "Tiger" Hill, who took over from Jimmy Trotter as manager in November 1961. The first time I ever saw him was the day I signed my professional contract.

I knew a choice was looming in the spring of 1962 and it wasn't a hard one to make. But that isn't to say it was an obvious decision to other people, especially my headmaster, Mr Sumner. The maximum wage for footballers had only recently been removed and the game wasn't seen as particularly lucrative. You might earn £20 a week and that would be more than the average schoolteacher, but a football career was likely to be short and unpredictable. Indeed, there was no guarantee that you would make the grade at all.

My father had left school at 14 and was largely self-educated. He pushed me in every way that he could. I was always taught to do my best. But he also said that I should be sure not to have any regrets. If I had a chance in life, I should take it.

My own feeling was that if I went into football and failed then I would still have the opportunity to resume my education. It was harder, but at least it was possible. The other way would have been to go to college and then come back into football when I was 21 or

22, but that seemed a lifetime away. It was also quite uncommon for someone to be successful in the game by following that route.

Charlton's Second Division season ended in a flourish, with a sequence of five wins and two draws in the space of seven games hauling them clear of relegation danger. Amazingly, they fielded outfield player John Hewie in goal for four of them. But they lost their two final away matches and there can't have been too much enthusiasm in the camp for the traditional end of season Kent Cup game against Millwall.

Much to my astonishment, I was asked to play. I'd only just got used to appearing alongside some of the reserve players and now I was being asked to report to The Den with the full first team, including Hewie, Brian Kinsey, Sam Lawrie and Mike Bailey. I was the only amateur on the field. But Stuart Leary wasn't available, and that's how I got in.

We lost 3-0, in front of a crowd of just under 7,000, although it didn't help that Lawrie was off the field injured for most of the first half. I don't think I did particularly well, and the game must have been the last thing that the senior players wanted at the end of a season in which they had only just managed to stay up.

More important than the result was the fact that Jock Basford took the opportunity to approach my dad, who had taken me to The Den, to see if I was interested in turning professional. I was just 17 but more independent than the boys Charlton sign of that age today. In fact, it was the first contact the club had made with my father. Nowadays we're in regular touch with parents of boys from the age of 12.

If a 16-year-old who was still at school was scoring in the reserves today and then breaking into the first team, the local papers would be full of it. But things were different then. The school's assumption was no doubt that I would continue as an amateur, play occasionally for the reserves, and pursue my education.

I informed the headmaster that Charlton had offered me a year's apprenticeship – I'd already missed the first 12 months – on £7 a week and £5 appearance money, compared to £10-12 a week plus appearance money for a full professional. It was clear he felt that I was wasting my education and my head had been turned by the lure of celebrity.

With all the enthusiasm of youth, I had no misgivings. I left school on July 19th and went to The Valley to deal with the formalities the same day. There was no great ceremony about it, I just sat down with George Robinson to complete the paperwork. To my surprise, Frank Hill said that I might as well sign as a full professional straight away. This meant that I didn't have to take on the menial tasks of an apprentice and was able to spend one and a half days a week at college in Woolwich studying accountancy. However, my wages remained at £7 a week.

There was no scope for negotiation. You were just told what you were getting, and you were so pleased to sign that you didn't worry about it. In all fairness, I played about 30 times in that first season and they more or less gave me the appearance money all the time. The business is so competitive today that promising youngsters coming to clubs as trainees are often able to secure deals that guarantee them one or two years as a professional. Back then, you had to wait until the end of the season to find out, through the post, whether you would get a new contract. You took nothing for granted.

Such worries were a long way from my mind as I joined my new colleagues for pre-season training in the summer of 1962. Little did I know how soon I would be called upon to join them on the field.

Chapter Three
ONE OF THE LADS

Although I had the advantage of living locally and knowing some of the personalities at Charlton, at least from the terraces, I had no reason to expect a smooth introduction to the professional set-up. For a start I was 17, when most youngsters would be a year into their apprenticeship. Going to grammar school had also set me slightly apart from the background of most of the other players, even though both my parents were factory workers. Charlton was a strongly working-class environment. There was a lot more industrial language for a start. Altogether, it was a harsher way of life and my education didn't count for much there in the early years.

Lenny Glover was 18 months older than me. He had signed in May, but this was also his first taste of full-time training and together we learned to cope with the rigours of our first pre-season. We soon became firm friends. Lenny lived in a world that was alien to me. He was from Camberwell and had worked at Covent Garden market as a porter from the age of 15. He was always ducking and diving. He frequented the pubs of the East End and the Old Kent Road, and was always dressed in the latest fashion, which he tried to get me to follow too. I must have seemed like a country bumpkin to him, but I found him funny and his stories made compulsive listening. His life made mine seem mundane and boring by comparison. I liked him a lot.

After training we would soak in the big bath at The Valley for ages then walk up the hill together to Charlton Station. He'd wait on the London platform and I'd be on the other side going to Erith. We'd chat across the tracks until our respective trains arrived. I often thought how our lives away from the club were so completely different.

Lenny and I were based in the reserve dressing room, with the other young pros and a few who were into their 20s but hadn't succeeded in establishing themselves in the first team.

People outside the game probably don't realise that dressing-room acceptance is a big thing in terms of a new player's confidence and can have a huge effect on his achievements on the field. Joining the football fraternity is all about giving and taking stick to just the right level. As a youngster, you can't allow yourself to be trampled on, but at the same time there is a line of respect that you mustn't cross. It's a difficult balancing act. I think I handled it reasonably well, but I probably took a few things to heart after a verbal hammering from the senior players when I'd made a mistake in training or in a match. It's just something that you have to learn to deal with when you start at a new club.

One indication I was becoming one of the lads came when I was given the nickname "Snatch" by Roy Matthews. It was based on my habit of stealing unexpected goals in our training matches, using the first-time techniques I had honed in my practice sessions over the previous years. The title lapsed as my role in the team and the players around me changed, although it was still being used in the local press years later.

A falling-out between Stuart Leary and the manager was to play a big part in getting me an early debut. The South African forward had been at Charlton for 11 years and was, by then, the club's all-time record goalscorer. He had also carved out a formidable career as a Kent cricketer during the summer months.

Leary was influential not only on the field but also in the dressing room. At the centre of his dispute with Frank Hill was his wish to miss the first three months of the 1962/63 season to recuperate from both his sporting exertions over many years and the death that summer of his former teammate and great friend Johnny Summers. Leary didn't come back as instructed for the start of the season and Hill announced that the South African would never play for Charlton again. These days such a situation would be the talking point all around the club, but as a 17-year-old just starting out I was barely aware of it. I certainly didn't realise the dramatic effect the row would have on my own prospects of first-team football.

I was part of the senior side that took part in a pre-season friendly against Aldershot on August 8th that year, scoring the Charlton goal at The Valley in a 1-1 draw. On the opening Saturday of the 1962/63 season a fortnight later, though, I turned out for the youth team against Crystal Palace. That was a great feeling in itself now that I'd been taken on as a professional and was being paid. I scored a hat-trick, and even at that level earned a win bonus of £1.

The first team drew the opening Second Division match of the season 2-2 at home to Swansea, with Brian Tocknell getting a late equaliser. Like Charlton, Swansea had only just avoided relegation the previous season, so it was looked upon as a poor result.

The next first-team game was in midweek away to Sunderland. It was still only August, five weeks after I'd left school. When my name was posted to travel, I just thought that it was very generous to take me as reserve to the North East, where my roots lay. The introduction of substitutes was three years away, but the manager would take 12 players on such trips, with the extra man as cover in case someone was taken ill or failed a fitness test. My name was at the bottom of the list to go.

We travelled up by train on the day and had a pre-match meal at the Roker Park Hotel, near Sunderland. It was just a matter of months since I'd been watching the Charlton players from the terraces and I was still pretty much in awe of them. It was only when the manager started to discuss how he wanted the team to play that it became apparent I would be starting the match, alongside Dennis Edwards up front.

No sooner was that over than we were on the coach to Roker Park. I was nervous now, but there wasn't time for the significance of the situation to really get to me. I'd have lost a lot of nervous energy if I'd known 24 hours earlier, so on the whole I think it was good management. All I was told was to be aware of Sunderland legends Stan Anderson and Charlie Hurley.

One unfortunate consequence of the lack of notice is that it deprived my dad of the chance to see my League debut. He would definitely have taken time off to travel up. There wasn't even time for me to phone and break the news personally, but I did see some of my family from the North East at the ground when I arrived and managed to get them a few tickets.

In those days you'd typically arrive only an hour before kick-off and sometimes it could be even later if you had been held up. Some players, such as Roy Matthews and Marvin Hinton, would still be fully dressed 20 minutes before kick-off. The warm-up was derisory. I remember my hands trembling as I did up my bootlaces, but somehow when I went up the tunnel I knew it was going to be all right. As soon as I stepped on the pitch, I felt confident. I wanted the ball.

We lost 1-0. They had the late Brian Clough in their side, although he didn't score. I had one shot that Jim Montgomery saved and overall had done OK. Frank Hill evidently thought so too. His private note of my performance in the Charlton archives says simply: "First game – played well." I retained my place for the next match, at Chelsea.

Manager Tommy Docherty had assembled a young squad at Stamford Bridge and they became a great side, with people like Bobby Tambling, Terry Venables, Eddie McCreadie and Peter Bonetti in their line-up. They eventually won promotion that season as runners-up to Stoke City.

The Doc knew John Hewie through playing alongside him for Scotland, and he came into our dressing room about half an hour before kick-off. He was cracking jokes, as ever, and had us all laughing. Then, just as he was going out, he turned and said that his team were in a different class to us and they were going to give us a terrible hammering. He wasn't wrong, either. They beat us 5-0, and the fact that Brian Kinsey got an injury didn't help our cause.

I lost my place for the return fixture in midweek against Sunderland, which ended 2-2, with Hill giving a debut to a young Scot called John Henderson. The next match was at home to Luton. I was told to report at 2pm and didn't have much expectation of being included, but when I arrived I was told to get my boots as I would be making my Valley debut on the left wing in place of Kinsey.

I'd only ever played at inside-forward, certainly while I was at Charlton, so it was a bit of a shock. In fact, I hated being out on the wing. I was instructed to play in Kinsey's position and I did quite well there, cutting inside and having a few shots, all of which produced a ripple of appreciation from the crowd. We went 1-0 up through Henderson and then, with about eight minutes to go, Sam Lawrie got the ball on the right and chipped it to the far post at the north end. I was already there and sprang up to head it back past the former England goalkeeper Ron Baynham and into the opposite corner.

At school it had been frowned upon to celebrate goals in the same way as professionals. We just used to run back and take up our positions, so that's what I did when I scored. But Mike Bailey came up and hugged me and I remember momentarily putting my arms around him in response and being struck by the sheer size of his chest.

I also recall going down with cramp in both calves. It was a problem that plagued me throughout my playing career. I sweat profusely and could lose seven pounds in an average game on a cool day. It affected me badly late in matches. Our intake of fluids at half-time would be limited to a cup of tea or a glass of orange squash. Nowadays players are encouraged to take on plenty of liquid.

I would never trade my playing days for those of the modern era, even with the financial benefits on offer now, but the lack of knowledge about fluid intake was most definitely detrimental to my performances. If only I'd had access to today's facilities and medical expertise, especially regarding rehydration.

We won 2-0 against Luton and I vividly recall the beaming faces of my parents as I walked off the pitch. It was a great day all round. I always think that a player's home debut, when the pressure is on, can tell you a lot about which way he will go. Often it's the ones who pull something off in that first game who prove to have the ability to cope.

My next game was a midweek fixture away to Stoke City. We were waiting in the lobby of the hotel where we had our pre-match meal when in walked the legendary winger Stanley Matthews, who had just returned to our opponents from Blackpool at the grand age of 47. He knew Hewie from the international scene, as well as one or two of the other Charlton lads, and had come in search of complimentary tickets for friends or family, knowing that there would be little demand from our own followers for a midweek match so far from home.

I was thrilled just to be in the same room as Matthews, never mind run out on the same pitch as him that evening. He played the game in short bursts, which is understandable given his age, and each time he touched the ball you could sense the excitement in the crowd. He also did something that I had never seen before, refusing a pass from his full-back by turning away with a shake of the head. Apparently he needed more recovery time from recent exertions. I never really came up against him directly that night, but his influence on the game was unquestionable and Stoke ran out 6-3 winners, with the former Manchester United star Dennis Viollet scoring four times.

I had the opportunity to study Matthews at even closer quarters a week later when Stoke came to The Valley for the return fixture. It used to be said that his appearance put 5,000 on a crowd. There must have been something in that, because the 13,000 who had turned out for our weekend win over Scunthorpe United was swollen by almost 5,000 for this midweek game. The players of his generation received little financial reward for such celebrity as they were all on similar contracts to their teammates.

This time I did find Matthews bearing down on me at one point, as Brian Kinsey and I did our best to protect Hewie at full-back. The Stoke man was three decades my senior, while Brian was at his peak and even John must have been a dozen years younger. If nothing else, I thought, we must be able to prevent him running past us. I don't know if Matthews' reputation was already so powerfully implanted in my mind that it affected my reaction, but he seemed to twitch his neck, there was a little shimmy and he was gone. Brian and I were left for dead. Matthews pushed the ball past Hewie and crossed for goal. Nothing came of the move, but his skills were mesmerising. He'd returned to Stoke from Blackpool to get the Potteries club back into the First Division after a ten-year absence and did so at the first attempt. It was a privilege to have been able to play against him just weeks after leaving school, even though Stoke's 3-0 win was demoralising.

As if to remind me of how quickly my life had changed I found myself being urged on by a group of my former Erith schoolmates late on in the game when I ran over to take a throw-in at the north-west corner of the pitch. I glanced up and found myself looking straight at Paul McKeough, who was prominent in the school rugby team. Forty years later I had a moment of deja-vu, when I picked out Paul in the east stand during the warm-up before a Premiership game. He is now a season-ticket holder at The Valley.

Another early highlight was the second-round League Cup trip to Leicester City at the end of September. The competition was only in its third season and the final had yet to move to Wembley. Perhaps the big clubs weren't taking it that seriously, but this was the first time that I had come up against First Division opposition and the match at Filbert Street was only my eighth senior appearance. The fixture evidently didn't mean too much to the locals. The crowd was only just over 8,000 at a time when the home side was averaging more than 25,000 in the League.

Leicester would go on to finish fourth in the table, so they represented formidable opponents to a side that had been struggling in the Second Division, but I was quite oblivious to the array of talent I was up against that day. In goal Gordon Banks must have been on the fringes of the England squad, but he had yet to make his international debut, while Frank McLintock, who was a few years older than me, was in a similar position with Scotland.

We didn't make an auspicious start. At half-time we were 4-0 down and being totally murdered. Very unusually, Frank Hill decided to make some tactical changes. It was rare that he or any other manager would do this at the break in those days. Usually the most that happened would be that a centre-half was thrown up front for the last 15 minutes. We had been playing with a forward line of Mike Kenning, myself, Lenny Glover and Roy Matthews. In the second half, he put Matthews down the middle for the first time.

My main thought at the interval had been to hope that Leicester didn't go on and get ten. Brian Kinsey pulled a goal back quite quickly and then I scored twice. The first was a left-foot chip. The full-back was bringing the ball out and I managed to get a block on it as the defence was coming out, leaving me faced with Banks. My second was a good example of my one-touch finishing. Banks parried a shot and I slid the ball home from a tight angle. Fred Lucas then got the equaliser with a 25-yard stinger. I can't remember a comparable comeback during my time as a player. It was fantastic to be part of it, and to score a couple of goals was the icing on the cake. Years later my sense of achievement was further enhanced when Banks went on to become one of the greatest goalkeepers ever.

We won the replay at The Valley 2-1 a week later and the League Cup proved to be something of a relief in what was a tough inaugural season. I think there was something of a hangover from losing Leary, although from a personal point of view that was why I had got my break.

The win over Leicester gave the side a boost and we went on to play Bradford Park Avenue in the next round. I didn't feature in the 2-2 draw up there, but I was involved again when we won the replay at The Valley, getting the only goal after managing to intercept a slightly soft back pass. Bradford had Jimmy Scoular, the old Newcastle star, as player-manager. It was only a few years earlier that I had watched him play in a shock FA Cup defeat at Millwall. The Geordie crowd had spilled out of the terracing at the old Den and I'd ended up sitting along the touchline, so I had a clear memory of him coming over and taking the throw-ins. Scoular was a tough player – the Millwall fans called him "Scoular the Fouler". Now here I was playing against him.

In the fourth round we were drawn away to Leyton Orient, who had been promoted as Second Division runners-up the previous season, the first and only time the O's have reached the top flight. They would finish ten points adrift at the bottom of the First Division table and I got on the scoresheet for the third consecutive round with the final goal of the game, but it wasn't enough to stave off a 3-2 defeat.

The old "WM" formation was being phased out around this time and we were playing what would now be considered 4-2-4, with myself as one of the strikers. I was really an attacking midfielder, but now had to play a bit further up the field and off the main striker.

I was still very much a boy among men. Senior professionals Tocknell and Hewie, both South Africans, were especially friendly and helpful towards me during my early days. Hewie seemed to have legs that went on forever. You could jump up to head a ball and he'd put his foot above you. He would even kick balls that had come to rest on the roof of the net. He was nearing the end of his career by then, but I never knew how old he was because he'd give me a different answer each time I asked him. To this day I don't know what age he was when he finished. He was a terrific team player. He didn't have some skills that you might expect in an international, but he was very adaptable and a tremendous asset to Charlton.

Someone nearer my own age who made a big impression on me was Mike Bailey. He was only 20 when I made my debut. He set a strong example and was very serious in his approach. I looked up to him as a role model and he encouraged me to do the right things. When he eventually left for First Division football with Wolverhampton Wanderers in February 1966 it was a big blow to me personally. It seemed he was the rock on which the team was based.

The manager was a figurehead and much more remote than it is possible to imagine today. Hill would come out to watch the training, and occasionally he'd join in, even though he was in his late 50s by then. For the most part, however, training was about fitness rather than tactical work.

On one occasion I clearly recall, he came out wearing his suit to watch us playing five-a-side on the old black gravel training area. He suddenly shouted "bring the ball down!" and stepped into the game. It is the only time I can remember him trying to coach me. I'd laid the ball off first time and obviously it hadn't gone where I wanted. He took off his jacket, hung it on the fence, then asked for the ball to be chipped up to him, chested it down and laid it off, leaving a big black mark on the front of his otherwise immaculate white shirt, before snapping: "That's what you do!" He then put his jacket back on and watched for a while longer, before disappearing off to his office. I was dumbfounded.

In the afternoons, he would invariably take on the apprentices – and anybody else who was interested – on the snooker table. This was located just outside the dressing room and was covered over on matchdays to form a refreshment table. It was about three-quarter size and had a decided slope. Hill knew every little eccentricity about the make-up of that table and probably earned himself a tidy bonus on it during the course of a week. I can see him now, standing there hands in pockets with a cigarette in his mouth.

The whole senior squad would train together for about two and a half hours in the mornings. There were odd times when Jock Basford might keep one or two of us back for extra shooting practice, but things weren't as fragmented as they are today. Now I might take a shooting session, Curbs could be with the midfielders and the back four might be working with Mervyn Day. That sort of thing never took place in the early 1960s. For a start we didn't have the facilities or the staff to oversee it, but in any case the thinking about the game wasn't that advanced.

As if things weren't difficult enough for Charlton, that winter produced some of the worst weather on record. It was so bad that we only managed to complete one League game from just before Christmas until the first week of March. Our third-round FA Cup tie with Cardiff City was postponed ten times before it was finally played in the middle of February. We won 1-0 and then went out 3-0 at home to Chelsea in the next round, but I had to wait another couple of years for my own FA Cup debut.

Throughout that bleak winter we continued to train at The Valley, which seems remarkable now. We went up to Blackheath for the odd run, but mostly we used a part of the terracing that had been cleared, or played on snow in the car park. We would also do a circuit inside the old west stand, running up the stairs, along the bar area, down again and through the little corridors outside the players' dressing rooms.

Today we have access to indoor facilities, such as the inflatable dome at Sparrows Lane, or if we have enough notice, go off for a week to Spain. Even in the latter stages of my career we would have contacted a local leisure centre and gone there. As it was we would train and run hard, and work with medicine balls – something that has now come back into fashion. Maintaining match fitness would be the big issue if we had that kind of enforced break today, but most clubs were in the same predicament during that winter of 1963.

When football finally did resume, Charlton still had 18 Second Division matches left to play. The season was extended well into May, but in April alone we played nine times. I was in and out of the side throughout the campaign, perhaps being rested because of my relative youth, and it was something I accepted without complaint. Given my success it was surprising that Frank Hill didn't make more use of me in the closing months, but maybe I'd been showing signs of tiredness in my first full year.

The two matches against Plymouth, either side of that winter break, were eventful. I scored very early on in the game at Home Park in October. I was quite excited about it, although I shouldn't have been because the clubs had a history of high-scoring matches. On this occasion, Plymouth went on to lead 4-1 at half-time and eventually racked up six goals without any further reply.

We had our revenge at The Valley in March, however, when we beat them 6-3. There was a mix-up in the goalmouth that resulted in me nudging their centre-half in the back. He collided with the goalkeeper and I slotted the ball home for the second goal. Bailey also scored twice that day. Plymouth turned out to be among my favourite opponents and I got my only hat-trick against them a couple of years later.

One disappointment was that I missed both the games against Newcastle. From my earliest schooldays, my greatest wish had been to play for – and now, of course, against – my father's team, but this eluded me right until the end of my career. They weren't in Charlton's division for most of that period. Whenever they were, it always seemed that I was injured or rested. Ironically, I did play a number of times down the road at Sunderland, including my debut. We lost 5-3 when I eventually got to St James' Park, in what was almost my final match.

Over the years at Charlton, I'd have to admit that my interest in Newcastle waned. I wasn't a player who found it easy to go and watch other games, except on the big occasions. There was always the family influence in the background, however, and my father continued to look for their result. I did get to play against former Newcastle players, such as a little striker and hero of mine called Lennie White, when he turned out against us for Huddersfield.

We were still in trouble at the end of the 1962/63 season. Another South African, Cliff Durandt, who was skilful but somewhat overweight, had arrived from Wolves at the end of March. He could score great goals, although his most important one didn't necessarily fit into that category. His big moment came in the 89th minute of the penultimate game of the season, at home to Southampton. We were drawing 1-1 and if the score had stayed like that we would have been relegated to the Third Division. Many people had given up hope of a reprieve and were already on their way home from the ground. Then Durandt cut inside from the left and shot. He didn't really connect with the ball properly and it was bouncing along towards the north goal. I ran in, as I always did, in the hope of converting any rebound, but it was an easy take for the keeper. Somehow, though, the ball bobbled over him as he went down and ended up in the bottom corner of the goal.

It was an unbelievable break, but even then we had to win the last game, away to Walsall, to stay up on goal average. They would then be relegated instead. We travelled up to Fellows Park on a sweltering Tuesday and ran out to play on a field with a bone-hard surface and a pronounced slope. Half-time came with no score, but I was on song. We then went out to start the second half and the skies suddenly opened up. There wasn't much grass on the pitch at that time of year and the water was gushing down the slope at a tremendous rate. There was nothing the referee could do but abandon the match.

As it was the end of the season, the game had to be replayed just three days later. It seems crazy now, but I can remember that we reported to The Valley at 11am, did some training, and then were given a short time to go off and get something to eat. This would be at places like Len's Shack, a transport café just across from the Antigallican pub on the Woolwich Road, or the Hole in the Wall, near the bottom of Charlton Church Lane. The proprietor, Don, was about 25 stone. He did mouth-watering sausage sandwiches, and the players used to love going down there. The café was below ground level and a popular haunt for the local roadsweepers and workmen. These days you wouldn't travel on the day of a game, especially for such a big match. But that is what we did.

We didn't play well in the second game. Just before half-time, centre-forward Jim Ryan smashed into the Walsall goalkeeper and broke the latter's cheekbone. This was a dreadful handicap for them, especially as another of their players had already damaged his knee ligaments. So they had ten men on the field, but one of them could only limp about and provide nuisance value.

It was 0-0 at half-time, which would have meant we were relegated. Ten minutes after half-time I put us in front, firing into the roof of the net from just on the edge of the penalty box, then Mike Kenning scored a second. But with 18 minutes to go, Walsall pulled a goal back and we had it all to do against nine fit men just to hang on. At one point, our keeper Peter Wakeham was bouncing the ball prior to kicking it out and John Sewell, who had been covering back, ran past him to rejoin the play and clipped the ball with his heel, sending it just past the post for a corner. It would have been the most ridiculous own goal of all time, but thankfully the gods were with us that night.

I recall sitting in the bath afterwards and being ecstatic that we had stayed up. I had played all right, but we had been on the back foot for most of the game so I hadn't seen that much of the ball. I asked Frank Hill if there was any champagne and he barked back: "You don't deserve any champagne, the way you played!" It certainly dampened the moment of glory for me, although clearly not everyone was subdued by the reproof. I can remember Bailey, who was injured but had travelled with the team, ribbing the manager by singing and dancing on the coach home, and growling at the old Tiger each time he passed him.

I had made 30 first-team appearances in my first season, mostly in my favourite inside-forward role. In fact, I ended up top scorer that year with 11 goals. It wasn't a huge tally, but it was a good return for a 17-year-old in his first season. The fact that Charlton were caught up in a relegation battle inevitably affected the number of chances that came my way as a forward. Overall, I had reason to be satisfied with myself, but just as the departure of one Charlton legend had given me my big break, so the return of another was to set me back.

In the pre-season of 1963 we were training at the Stone's sports ground over the road from The Valley when I saw a majestic figure of a man arrive. It was Eddie Firmani, who had left The Valley for Sampdoria in 1955. He had evidently come down to work out for a couple of days while he was in the country.

As we took a short break from our session, Eddie was going through a continental-style warm-up routine. I just couldn't take my eyes off this magnificent sight. Wearing a tight, blue Italian-style training shirt, five-foot-eleven tall and with powerful thighs and calves the size of grapefruits, he bounced over the grass like a panther waiting to pounce upon its prey. I had watched him play once when I was younger, but then he had been a rough and ready centre-forward. Now he was 30 and you could see as he knocked the ball about that he had matured into the perfect striker.

Unbeknown to me, plans were evidently being laid for him to come back to Charlton, which duly happened at the beginning of October. Although I played in the opening two Second Division matches, a 6-1 drubbing at Southampton and a 3-1 defeat at Preston North End, I then lost my place. With Firmani's return and the team moving up the table, there was no reason to recall me.

With hindsight, it was no bad thing. I continued to score regularly in the reserves in midweek and for the A team on Saturday, so I was getting two games a week. This was a period of learning my trade after being thrown in at the deep end. When I did break back into the side at the end of the season I hit five goals in nine games, so the campaign wasn't a total loss. It was also great to be around someone like Firmani, to see what a perfectionist he was and how he disciplined and looked after himself.

His return created a buzz around The Valley and I remember the news coming through that he had scored two goals in his first match back at Manchester City. Had Charlton also spent money on another top player that might have even been enough to take them back into the First Division, but whenever the club had a good side they never followed up with the crucial next step. Even if Frank Hill had settled his differences with Leary that might have done the trick. Leary had no pace at that stage, as I had discovered when he did briefly return for training before being sold to Queens Park Rangers the previous December, but just playing with him in one five-a-side match had shown me the quality of his football brain. The passes that he could deliver were better than those of anybody else at the club. Perhaps putting the two South Africans together could have been the trigger to achieve promotion.

Charlton eventually finished fourth, but 13 points adrift of second-placed Sunderland, who were promoted with champions Leeds United. At least that was a big improvement on recent seasons and the best since that near miss in 1957/58. It also saw the average home crowd rise by nearly 50 per cent, to more than 18,000, but personally I had started only 11 matches, which would be the least of any season in my whole career.

On the domestic front, I was still living with my parents. I had met my future wife Lesley at school in Erith, and we'd started going out together just before I left. She wasn't impressed by the so-called glamour surrounding football and footballers. This was always good from my point of view, because when we were together the conversation would be about anything but the game. I have always treasured the opportunity to have a private life away from my job.

Lesley came to the odd match, but for six months we had been aware that she and her parents were on a waiting list to be considered for emigration to Australia. At Christmas 1963, news finally came through that the application had been successful. Her parents paid the £25-a-head fee and began making the arrangements.

It was an awkward situation. Lesley and I had been together for about two years by now, but were still very young. I was 18 and a half and she was a year younger. Had we been a couple of years older things may have been different, but she reached an agreement with her parents to go with them to Australia for a year. Then, if we still felt the same way about each other, she would return. So in April 1964 I waved her off from Southampton docks, not knowing if we would see each other again as she set sail on her 12,000-mile journey aboard the Canberra.

The good news was that she couldn't wait a year and after four months she wrote asking me to send her the £300 it would cost to come back. That was a lot of money in those days, but I raised it and she returned. As it turned out, her parents followed a couple of months later. She had never really given Australia a chance, she just wanted to come home so we could be together. In the meantime, however, we'd had some interesting conversations about me going out there instead, including the prospect that I could play for the Newcastle club over there. Obviously, I didn't buy that idea!

No sooner had Lesley set off for home than I went down with glandular fever, which sidelined me for the opening part of the 1964/65 season. We were married in July 1965, with David Stocks as best man. He and I had become good friends during my second season, when we were mostly in the reserves together. Stocksy was a left-back from Dulwich and a couple of years older than me. He'd made his debut at Anfield at the end of 1961/62 as a part-time professional and he also worked as a draughtsman.

We would play tennis and golf together. It was hard to keep in touch with my mates from school, because they had either gone off to university or they would want to be out enjoying themselves on a Friday night. It was wise to keep away from that environment. I wasn't much of a drinker anyway, as was proven by my stag night. Stocksy took me up the Old Kent Road. I remember very little of what happened, but I know we got back in the early hours of the morning. The following day I couldn't eat or drink anything. Fortunately, Lesley was none the wiser and put anything odd about my behaviour down to wedding-day nerves. I've always thought that the modern practice of having such celebrations well in advance of the big day has a lot to be said for it.

The club owned a number of houses, mostly in Blackheath and Kidbrooke, and Lesley and I were able to get a three-bedroom mid-terrace in Ankerdine Crescent, Shooters Hill, for £1.50 a week, which included the rates and decoration. Most couples our age would have had to wait a few years to get a place of their own, so it was a huge perk and enabled us to save up to buy a property.

At the time I was on £25 a week, with £10 appearance money and a £4 win bonus We also received gate money of £1 for every thousand spectators over 8,000. Win, lose or draw, you could earn a healthy bonus for playing against attractive opposition. The players would have a good look around the ground before kick-off to see what pay-out they might get.

My own playing fortunes were looking up to the extent that I played in 23 games in the 1964/65 season, scoring six times. However, three of those goals, as previously mentioned, came in the away match at Plymouth. We'd beaten Ipswich 4-0 at The Valley the week before and Firmani had got a hat-trick. I got the other goal, a rebound from the keeper's chest, which I snapped up with a diving header before he had time to react.

I'd twisted my ankle, so I had a late fitness test before the Plymouth game on a local army pitch. Firmani was again up front alongside me that day, but this time it was my turn for the hat-trick. I was even carried off the pitch by the travelling Charlton fans. Afterwards I went timidly to the home dressing room to ask for the match ball. The reply was very short and sharp, consisting of two words. Needless to say, I beat a hasty retreat. Today, the opposition kit man would ensure you left with the ball.

Those two wins more or less sealed Charlton's Second Division safety, which was just as well. We picked up only three points from the remaining five games to complete another unsatisfactory season for the club. Firmani was about to make his second exit from The Valley, this time to Third Division Southend United, and by the time the new season came around, the club would have a new manager and I would have a new role to play on the field – as well as a new wife.

Chapter Four
A CLAIM TO FAME

Frank Hill was sacked in August 1965 and replaced as manager by Bob Stokoe. In contrast to his predecessor, who was less than a year short of his 60th birthday when he left The Valley, Stokoe was 35. He had been player-manager at Bury and still wanted to be actively involved with the squad. He was full of enthusiasm and keen that players should put themselves about physically. Although I would still be in and out of the side over the next two years, the new manager liked me and I was always involved.

Bob was the type of manager who valued organisation and wanted things to be done the right way. He was also very passionate about the game. There were limits to what a manager was allowed to do during a match in those days, but he would often shout and scream from the dugout and his eyes seemed almost to bulge out of their sockets. Such antics were new to me. Tiger Hill had always watched from the stand. I had never seen a manager on the bench during a game.

It was Stokoe who gave me a place in football history – or at least in football trivia. I had expected to be in the starting line-up when we travelled to Bolton on the opening day of the season, but we also took a 17-and-a-half-year-old Scot called Alan Campbell. He had yet to make his senior debut, but he had evidently impressed Stokoe in pre-season. The new manager called me in before the game to say that after a lot of thought he'd decided to go with Campbell at inside-forward and make me substitute.

That season was the first time that the Football League had allowed a replacement to be used, the initial thinking being that substitutions would only be made to replace injured men. As time wore on, however, it was apparent that players could feign injury in order to allow the manager to freshen up the side and so this convention lapsed. There was also a feeling that to withdraw a man during a match for reasons other than an injury was a blow to his reputation. Mentally, it took English players a long while to get used to the idea that this was simply a tactical part of the game.

Naturally, I was very disappointed not to be in the starting line-up that afternoon. It was an odd experience, having to get changed with the others but with no expectation of playing. Until then the word "substitute" wasn't even in the English football vocabulary, never mind the rulebook. I just thought of it as being reserve, as we'd had up until then, with the only difference being that you had to put your kit on.

I didn't have to wait very long to be put straight. After 11 minutes our goalkeeper Mike Rose was unable to continue and John Hewie took over from him. I was called on to become the first-ever substitute in the Football League. Hewie was a useful deputy, but the fact that we were able to continue with 11 players didn't do us much good as Bolton went on to win 4-2.

At first I was just pleased to have had the opportunity to play in the game and it was only when we were coming back on the train that I realised I'd been the first replacement to come on that day. We found out from a brief mention in a Saturday evening football paper we were able to buy at one of the stations. It was only in later years that it became a talking point. It's an oddity, because in a way I'm most famous for not being selected for the starting XI that day, rather than anything I achieved. But I suppose I can take some consolation from the fact that no one can ever take the distinction away from me.

Another development in Stokoe's first season was the rapid emergence of Billy Bonds, a local lad who had made his debut in Hill's last year. I can remember going on a short break to Blackpool with the team and Bonds hiding away in a five-a-side game, in a bid to avoid incurring the wrath of the Tiger. The old man could have that effect on younger players. Bill was a year younger than me. When he'd been playing wing-half in the reserves there had been doubts about whether he would make the grade, but he came on in leaps and bounds once Hill had left the club.

Bill was a quiet personality off the field, but on it things were different. He was such a powerful runner. When I played on the right in those years he would come pounding through on the overlap as soon as I got the ball. You just got out of the way. What was equally impressive was that he could get back so quickly. It was an incredible sight. However it was too early for me to judge how successful he would become in his long career with West Ham, where he was still a first-team regular at the age of 41.

Although we made a solid start to the campaign, we went out of the League Cup with a 4-3 defeat at Third Division Peterborough United in mid-October and didn't manage to win another game until February. By Christmas we were only being kept off the bottom of the table by Leyton Orient and Stokoe brought in Dick Graham – until very recently manager at Crystal Palace – to take over training. This was seen as a brave move. If we did well Graham would surely get the credit, and even if we didn't he would be well placed to succeed Stokoe.

Among the first things that Graham did was to put a television set, flowers and fruit in the dressing room. All that it had ever had in the past was the occasional coat of paint. He also took us to train at the Crystal Palace athletics stadium twice a week, which involved trampolining, five-a-side and then a session on the running track. Some lads would be physically sick from the exertion and this could be on a Friday, the day before a game. One of those who suffered particularly was Ron Saunders, who had been one of Stokoe's first signings, as replacement for the departed Firmani.

Some of the things that Graham did were outrageous. In one particular exercise, you had to put your legs either side of two benches and jump. If you were tall it wasn't so bad, but if you were five-foot-eight or less then you would land on your toes and end up bruising the inside of your thighs.

If you didn't do that properly, he would make you pair up with another player and jump over some long sticks. You had to whack the other fellow's ankles with your stick. If you didn't, you would get a merciless tongue-lashing from Graham. He was like a stereotypical sergeant-major and would give you a tremendous verbal hammering. It was the hardest training I ever experienced and every day was a challenge, from the warm-up onwards.

In February 1966 we signed 37-year-old Cliff Holton, known as "Doc" Holton, from Watford. He'd made his name at Arsenal and had enjoyed a tremendous career at centre forward and centre half, but in his latter years he had gained a reputation for rescuing clubs in trouble. His goals were lifesavers for ailing teams – hence his nickname. He had also been Graham's first signing as manager of Crystal Palace, and possessed a phenomenal shot. Graham used to slaughter him in training, but looking back that must have been a bit of an act to ensure that we thought he was treated like the rest of us.

What Holton did for us was to finish everything off, scoring seven goals in the 18 games he played. There were also other ex-Crystal Palace players like Brian Whitehouse and Peter Burridge who arrived at the same time, obviously on Graham's recommendations.

The men Graham brought in were presumably familiar with his unorthodox methods, but some of the other older pros like Saunders thought them absolutely crazy. Our legs were tired before we went out on to the pitch on a Saturday, and yet we felt that we could run forever. It was a strange situation because Graham himself never even went to our games. He was away watching the next opponents. On matchdays, Stokoe was always back in charge. He was also about during the week and would take part in the five-a-sides. Dick would put up £25 for the winning team and as a result there were some blood-curdling tackles in these games, which took place in an indoor arena.

This vigorous training only lasted four months and was just something you had to get through. Slowly but surely we pulled out of trouble. Graham was instrumental in that turnaround, because love him or hate him he rattled everyone's cage. He brought something different. One day we might play some squash and on another we would be jumping through different coloured hoops. The intensity of his sessions was probably too great, but it struck me at the time that the variation he introduced, even something as simple as changing the environment, helped us get through the week. His use of psychology, albeit in an unusual way, and the extra competitiveness in training was transferred to matches. We became a braver team, with a never-say-die approach, which paid off.

He had us defending 12 yards out with Holton, Burridge and Kenning – three of the hardest hitters – smashing balls in. Every player had to hold his ground and be prepared to take the impact full on. The result was that no wall ever broke and no one shirked a penalty-box block. Players may have been winded, but no one ever got injured.

At the beginning of February we finally got another victory, winning 4-1 at Ipswich, where I got a couple of goals and Holton scored on his debut. I was also on target as we beat Birmingham 2-1 at The Valley in the next match and again the following week at Leyton Orient, where we won by the same scoreline. We seemed to have turned a corner, but around it was another disappointment.

Less than 48 hours after the Orient game, club captain Mike Bailey was sold to First Division Wolverhampton Wanderers for

£35,000. He had just turned 24. I had watched Mike from the terracing before being taken on by the club. For me, he was the mainstay of the team. He was so focused on the job and determined to succeed, more so perhaps than some of the senior men, who had ability but were never prepared to be as professional. At the time he was one of only two Charlton players to have been capped by England since the war, which even then was a colossal achievement for a Second Division player.

Our next match was away to Bury, Stokoe's old club, and despite Holton being called into service to fill the gap at the back we lost 3-0. Stokoe's response was to make three new signings. Ian King came in from Leicester City to shore up the defence, along with midfielder Whitehouse from Palace. But the most significant new face and the one who would provide a measure of compensation to the disappointed Charlton fans was goalkeeper Charlie Wright, an £8,000 signing from Grimsby.

Charlie was one of the game's entertainers and very good-hearted. He was a character and someone to whom the fans could relate. He was also a good goalkeeper, the best the club had had since the legendary Sam Bartram retired and better than those who immediately followed him, but when he had a bad game he could make quite drastic mistakes.

In recent years the goalkeeper has become more of a specialist. Back then they had to do all the running and gym work that the other players did. Often this became a bone of contention, because they were usually bigger and heavier than the outfield players, and found it more difficult. Now the keepers might spend half or all of a training session working together as a separate group. John Burridge was the first keeper that I knew who held out against doing the general work. They could also end up being cannon fodder for the other players, in shooting sessions, rather than doing quality training that was of more value to them.

We finished the season in 16th, five places and five points above relegated Middlesbrough, in 21st, with Leyton Orient ten points adrift of them. In Charlton terms it was a relatively comfortable mid-table spot.

England won the World Cup in the summer of 1966 and they famously did it without wingers, which at the time was a real novelty. It had a knock-on effect in club football, with more concentration on strengthening the midfield area and from now on teams were more likely to line up with just one wide man. That trend wasn't particularly good news for me, especially as Charlton had Mike Kenning to play on the right and Lenny Glover on the left. I'd broken into the side a month before Len, but he was slightly older than me and it wasn't really a surprise that after that first season he established himself and became almost a permanent fixture in the team, certainly over the next three years. I would be used anywhere up front during this period, but I could quite often be the one who made way as well, so I was only featuring in about half the games.

The World Cup was great for the country and nationally it triggered a boom in interest in football, but it didn't seem to make too much difference at The Valley – 1966/67 turned out to be another season of struggle for the club.

Early on in the campaign we had to play newly-promoted Millwall at The Den. It wasn't exactly unfamiliar territory for us. We'd played there most years in the Kent Cup, but it was the first time the teams had met in the League for more than 30 years. They were also in the middle of their record-breaking run of 59 home League matches without defeat, so the goalless draw that gave us our first point of the season was quite a welcome result. It would be the same scoreline when we met at The Valley in December.

To be honest we probably had a bit of a snobbish attitude towards Millwall. We looked upon them as an inferior club who shouldn't be mentioned in the same breath as Charlton. When they came up, however, they had a good team and over the following years we went on a few pre-season trips with them, so we became friendly with people like Barry Kitchener, Derek Possee and Keith Weller. There were no big vendettas, although Harry Cripps was one Millwall player you were never going to invite back for tea. It was always a question of how soon he kicked or thumped you.

One one occasion I took the ball up to Cripps and he just punched me straight in the solar plexus as I went past. He didn't even attempt to get the ball. "Sorry, ref, first game back from injury, you know how it is," said Harry. "Just got my timing wrong." Of course, he got away with a warning. By the time he was in any danger of being booked, you'd be carrying so many knocks that it inevitably affected your performance. You'd have had to be a lunatic to take him on again.

There was no doubt that the crowd at The Den gave Millwall an advantage. Referees were intimidated. It was understandable, but that didn't make it right. It must have been in the back of their mind that at the end of the game they had to go back down that tunnel at

Left: We were too young to join the gang in Parkside Avenue, but Valerie (5) had already learned to keep a tight hold of her two-year-old brother

Above: Mum and I shake a leg on party night during a holiday in Jersey in 1955

Above: My father, Tom Peacock, in naval uniform during the Second World War

Right: Valerie and I feeding the Trafalgar Square pigeons in about 1950

Above: Barnehurst Primary School were district champions in 1955/56, with me (front row, third from right) as captain. Sports master John Attwood and headmistress Mrs Mumford are pictured with the proud team

As a sixth-former at Erith Grammar School in 1962, I set a pole-vault record that apparently stood for many years – there can't have been much competition!

Two of my best mates at Erith, Chris Hanman (first left) and Dave Robinson (second right) joined me (with ball) in the front row of this school football team picture in 1957/58

Right: We played rugby in the autumn term at Erith. Here I am as skipper of the colts XV in 1959. Charlton fan Paul McKeough is behind my left shoulder

Below: Frank Hill became the first of my five Charlton managers in July 1962 – just weeks later I was in the first team playing at Roker Park

Left: My first photoshoot after signing as a professional for Charlton at the start of 1962/63

All action pictures in this section by Tom Morris

Above: Farewell to Firmani – although I got the better of Leicester City's David Nish here, this was the disastrous 5-0 home defeat in March 1970 that cost the Charlton manager his job. Top: I'm seen in hot pursuit of the ball at The Valley a few years earlier

Left: Manager Theo Foley helps Charlie Wright and I cool off during pre-season training – no showers then!

Above: In action during the club's golden jubilee match against Watford in 1971

Below: A rare headed goal for me in the 2-1 win at Luton Town in November 1971. Bobby Hunt and Cyril Davies look on in surprise

Right: Bob Stokoe, my second Charlton manager, was delighted when his Blackpool side sent us down in 1972

Far right: Eddie Firmani had three spells with Charlton as a player and a brief but memorable period as manager from 1967-70

Above: A splashing time at Brighton in March 1975, with Derek Hales (8) awaiting my pass

Theo Foley (far left) couldn't get Charlton back to the Second Division, but did sign the players Andy Nelson (left) moulded into a promotion side

Above: This header versus Hull City in October 1976 was over-shadowed by Derek Hales' hat-trick

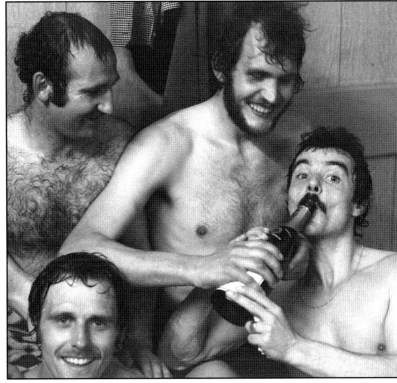

Success of a sort: Alan Dugdale (left), Dave Shipperley and Phil Warman (front) help celebrate yet another relegation escape, this time at Orient in 1978

Family portrait: Lauren, Gavin and Lesley join me in front of the camera in the mid-1970s. We were living in Okehampton Crescent, Welling, at the time

A day's golf at Frinton was a popular mid-season treat. Pictured (from left) are players Harry Cripps, Richie Bowman, Colin Powell, Jimmy Giles, myself, Phil Warman, Jeff Wood, Mike Flanagan, Peter Hunt and manager Andy Nelson

Right: Any goal against Millwall is worth celebrating. Here my penalty has just made it 2-2 at The Valley in April 1977. We went on to win the match 3-2

the Cold Blow Lane end. They would definitely change their view of decisions if under pressure from the crowd. On one occasion I was blatantly shoved into the back of the goal when I was about to head into an empty net. The referee didn't give anything and I never had any doubt that he'd bottled out.

Once I went to take a corner and was whacked over the head with an umbrella by a woman in the crowd – and I was one of those the Millwall fans treated relatively well, being someone who got kicked rather than handed it out! I don't think it was anything personal with the woman with the brolly. I just happened to be the unfortunate player wearing a Charlton shirt who came into range.

Many years later, my son Gavin went to take a throw-in at The Den and a voice from the crowd shouted out: "Oi, Peacock! You're not as good as your dad!" Like any good professional, Gavin affected not to have heard. He had to smile, however, when another Millwall fan chipped in: "Never mind *his* dad – he's not as good as mine!"

Personally, I liked the atmosphere at The Den. There was a buzz about the place, even if the crowd was hostile to the visitors. The atmosphere was a problem at The Valley once the big crowds had dwindled away, because of the sheer size of the place. Rodney Stone, who was general manager later on, memorably said that the night games were better because you couldn't see the spaces on the terraces – and he was right. Nevertheless, some players were intimidated going to Millwall and that did have an effect.

From the perspective of the dressing room it was always more important to beat Crystal Palace, who had reached the Second Division two years earlier. They seemed to think they were a cut above us. Millwall knew their limitations when they came up. They were a team that would dig in and tough it out. They were developing as a side, but they knew their roots and didn't have any pretensions to be something they weren't.

Palace were another club we hadn't played for 30 years. They finished above us in both 1964/65 and 1965/66, winning the first three meetings between the sides, and no doubt felt they had left us behind. They thought we were standing still and they were a team of the future, and in fairness that's what happened in the following few years. We did at least have the satisfaction of beating them in March 1966, which was the first time I played against them. Mike Kenning converted from the penalty spot at The Valley for the only goal after keeper John Jackson had brought me down.

I enjoyed the derby games in particular. There was nothing quite like going out there and having two sets of rival supporters roaring encouragement to their respective teams. There was no proper segregation of the fans and it was possible to have 10,000-plus away supporters at these games. This created an extra level of atmosphere and the players generally rose to the occasion.

The arrival of Millwall and Palace in the division certainly added interest for the supporters, but there were other changes afoot in the Second Division. Coventry City won the title that season, under Jimmy Hill, and they did it using some very tough tactics, stretching the laws of the game to the limit. Teams would go to Highfield Road and find that the heating was on full blast in the away dressing room on a hot day, or that it wouldn't work at all on a cold day. Then you would find that the balls you had been given to use in the warm-up were much heavier than the one used for the match. Invariably, they would make sure that the away team ran out first, so they would witness the thunderous reception the home side received. This was gamesmanship in the extreme.

Jimmy Hill was a visionary. As chairman of the Professional Footballers' Association he had been instrumental in the abolition of the maximum wage and what he did for the players will never be forgotten. However, there was no doubt that he used every trick in the book to secure promotion for the Sky Blues.

These kinds of methods were starting to creep into the game in the late 1960s. Leeds United were becoming practised at time-wasting. Players were beginning to feign injury to break up the rhythm of the game if things were going against them. At Charlton we were relatively innocent of these tricks and it wasn't until Andy Nelson took over in the mid-70s that we had a manager who really seemed to put any thought into the psychology of the game.

The reason these methods were shocking was that the majority of players were generally honest. The practice of diving to try to earn free-kicks and penalties was much less prevalent, whereas it's gone over the top now. There were always players who had perfected the technique of provoking a foul from a defender. Rodney Marsh was the master of it. I would often take the ball up to a defender and make my run, knowing that his outsretched leg would bring me down. I never considered that this was bending the rules, because in the 60s if you took the ball up to a defender and then went past him you invariably got kicked. A winger had to be brave enough to accept that pain in order to win a free-kick or a penalty.

Referees were different, too. Some would enjoy a bit of banter with you, others would take no nonsense and use the book if you so much as looked sideways at them. But heavy tackles, particularly from behind, were accepted as part of the game and players got away with outrageous fouls that seriously hindered skilful football. Players would mete out their own punishments and referees allowed some of that to go on. You'd get a couple of warnings before being booked, never mind sent off.

I once met Willie Bell, the Leeds full-back, on holiday in Majorca and as he hobbled towards the beach he told me about the injury he'd received in the last game of the season when the ball fell between him and Northampton Town's Theo Foley and both men went over the top. Despite his reputation, Theo was a good passer of the ball, but the Cobblers back four would intimidate the opposition and they were allowed to get away with it much more than today. It was the first time I had heard Theo's name. Little did I know how much he was going to figure in my career.

We played Coventry at The Valley in February and took a physical battering. I replaced the injured Rodney Green halfway through the first half and Matt Tees, a striker we'd only recently signed from Grimsby, was smashed all over the park. Hill believed that this was the way to get promotion and that he would worry about playing more attractive football when they reached the top division. I have to admit that it worked out for Coventry. As everyone knows, once they did get up they stayed there for 34 years.

We went into the penultimate game needing to beat Northampton at The Valley in order to be sure of staying up. I was directly up against Foley and we won 3-0, which gave us the rare luxury of a meaningless final match against Birmingham City.

Eddie Firmani bagged two of the goals against Northampton, having returned from Southend in March for his third spell at the club. In fact, he scored six goals in nine games, a number of them crucial. The Cobblers' relegation, meanwhile, had another consequence for Charlton – Foley signed for us at the start of the following season.

Those survival battles were so tense and there was so much at stake as a player. As long as you were only one step from the top division you could always persuade yourself that next year would be the one. Oddly, of course, when you survive you finish the season on a high, even if it's been a year of struggle that has landed you in the predicament in the first place.

During this period I was still developing as a player and leaving the club had never crossed my mind. There was little movement in the game generally and less of a disparity in wages, so there was no great financial incentive to look for a transfer. When players did go, it received much less public attention. It wouldn't have been unusual to report for training at the start of a new season and find a couple of faces in the squad that you hadn't heard about, even if they were reasonably significant signings. They wouldn't necessarily be reported in the national press and there was no Teletext or Sky Sports, so the only place you might have read about them would be the local press. How all that has changed!

Of course, Charlton weren't known for making major signings in this era, but from my perspective the club's priority ought to have been to hold on to the best players. Bailey's departure had been the biggest blow, but we also lost Kenning to Norwich in December 1966 and then Bonds to West Ham in the 1967 close season.

Not long into the 1967/68 campaign, Lenny Glover left for Leicester City, with the £80,000 fee a Football League record, at the time, for a winger. My two friends from the early days had both now departed. David Stocks had left on a free transfer in 1965. He subsequently enjoyed a long career at Bournemouth and Torquay. Glover was in my opinion the best winger Charlton had during my playing days at The Valley, and he was sorely missed.

The only positive from the situation was that the club continued to produce youngsters to fill the gaps, with Bob Curtis, Peter Reeves and Campbell all coming through in this period.

The sales didn't suggest that the club was ambitious, but the directors were evidently sufficiently dissatisfied with what Stokoe had achieved to sack him five matches into his third season in charge.

My first reaction on hearing the news was one of guilt. We had played Cardiff City at The Valley ten days earlier. Half an hour into the first period, with the score still 0-0, we were awarded a penalty. I had volunteered to take them, so I grabbed the ball and placed it on the spot. We were attacking the south goal and a gale-force wind was blowing into my face as I stepped back to take the kick. This was my first penalty in a League match and as I looked up at Bob Wilson, the Cardiff keeper, he appeared to fill most of the goal.

"I must keep it low," I kept saying to myself. The wind seemed to grow stronger. I was getting very nervous. I ran up and in my determination not to lift the ball over the bar, I only connected with the top half. It trickled slightly towards the keeper's left at an embarrassingly slow pace. By the time Wilson fell on the ball – after what I remember as the fourth bounce – my head was already in my hands. "Stokoe will kill me," I thought. I didn't dare to look at the bench, but I could feel his eyes springing out of his face and hitting the back of my neck!

Worse was to follow – within two minutes Cardiff went 1-0 up. Just then joining the teaching profession appeared most appealing. In fact, enlisting in the Foreign Legion seemed an even better idea. At half-time I crept into the dressing-room, waiting for all hell to break loose.

"Bad luck, son. Keep going!" said Bob. What a relief. I went our for the second half hoping to make amends, but I was having an absolute nightmare. With four minutes to go, central defender Paul Went took advantage of the wind to smash a shot fully 40 yards into the top corner of the north goal. I'd never kissed a fellow pro, but that night I came close as I jumped on his back in sheer delight.

My mate Wenty had not only rescued a point but saved my skin – or so I thought. As I walked through the dressing-room door after the final whistle, Stokoe jumped down my throat and let me know in no uncertain terms that I'd taken my last penalty for the club while he was in charge. Little did I realise that he'd be gone before our next home game.

His last match was a 3-0 defeat at Crystal Palace, when he named Firmani as substitute, a rare indignity for Eddie, I'm sure. By the time we took on and beat Aston Villa 3-0 the following week, Firmani had hung up his boots and was picking the team.

Chapter Five
RISE AND FALL

Bob Stokoe's departure from Charlton was acrimonious and in due course there turned out to be a sting in the tale. The dismissal was probably triggered as much by Eddie Firmani's presence waiting in the wings as the outgoing manager's failings, however. Chairman Michael Gliksten would have watched Firmani play as a youngster and then seen the effect that he had on the team and the fans when he returned to Charlton in 1963, and to a lesser extent again earlier that year. He was bound to see Firmani as an inspirational figure and want to capitalise on that after several years in the doldrums.

I received a phone call on the Sunday from one of the other players to say that Stokoe had gone. Then, when I went in on the Monday, Eddie was in charge. Seemingly he had been asked to take the job the previous day and at first refused. However, after several hours of persuasive argument from the chairman, he had eventually agreed. Maybe because I was still relatively young and Eddie was such a senior figure, it wasn't like having one of your teammates take over. He had my respect from the start, although perhaps he had to work to gain it from the more experienced men.

The team responded to his appointment well and we won our next match, at home to Aston Villa 3-0. It was particularly memorable for me. I scored the third goal at the south end with an overhead kick – the only such goal of my career. I never saw the ball go in and I've always wished that the match had been televised. I'd love to see it again. An old friend and supporter, Ted Randall, came over for dinner recently and reminded me of that goal. Poor bloke, I made him describe it in detail at least half a dozen times.

The fans were chanting Eddie's name outside the dressing room that afternoon against Villa and he went up to Harry Gregory and said: "They'll be chanting your name before the end of the season." Harry had come from Leyton Orient in the summer of

1966 and was a free-running centre forward with bags of energy. He didn't score a lot of goals, but some of those he did were spectacular. He was a real favourite of Eddie's, and the new manager got the best out of him over the next couple of seasons.

Theo Foley became assistant manager in December and he would often take charge of training, with Eddie keeping a watching brief. For his first two seasons, Firmani seemed to get the balance right. He was hands-on and very definitely the manager, but he would then withdraw and let Theo take over to create that necessary bit of distance. Players need a bit of a break from the man in charge and it was something I tried to do when I became a manager, just to give them a rest from my voice and presence. Theo loved being on the coaching field and generally had a good eye for players. He was able to help me immensely. As a former full-back, he knew exactly what a winger needed to do to make life difficult for his opponent.

After Lennie Glover left, in November, Gregory would often play wide on the right and I became the main winger. I thrived under Eddie, and Theo's influence was important to that. Whether it was because I'd played directly against him and made a good impression I don't know, but he just wanted me to have the ball as much as possible. It's important to have someone who believes in you as a player and at this point in my career Theo did exactly that for me. It gave me real confidence. I knew that even if I made a mistake I need have no fear. I was the number one in terms of the team's forward play. Between the two of them, they gave me just the lift that I needed.

It helped that we soon had a pair of strikers, Matt Tees and Ray Treacy, as good as any in the division. Tees was brave as a lion and could rise in the air higher than anyone I had ever played alongside. I knew that if I delivered the ball into the box then one of them would be about. There might not always be a goal scored, but there was a good chance something would come out of it.

The autumn of 1967 was a special time for me for another reason. Early on the morning of November 18th, I became a father for the first time when my son Gavin was born in the Memorial Hospital, Shooters Hill. My family has always been the prime consideration to me, but having a child is one of the major events in your life and I was lucky enough to be present at the birth, as Lesley had wanted. That feeling of having created another human being must rank as one of the best experiences of all and it certainly put the highs and lows of football into a different perspective for me.

Appropriately enough, Gavin arrived on a Saturday, which meant that I had to go without sleep on the night before a game. I'm not sure what would have happened if we had been playing away. It would have been unheard of then to have asked for permission to miss a game in order to stay with your wife and I probably wouldn't have had the temerity even to make that suggestion. I think in the prevailing atmosphere they'd have thought I was mad.

Lesley was two weeks overdue and each day for the previous fortnight the lads had asked me: "Hasn't she had it yet?" I arrived at the ground, bursting with pride and grinning like a Cheshire cat, expecting the usual enquiry. But nobody said a word!

Although we didn't play particularly well against Blackpool, I didn't look out of place. Fortunately, when my daughter Lauren arrived in June 1970, the only football going on was in Mexico, where England were defending the World Cup.

Years later, when I was at Queens Park Rangers, I saw the same situation from another perspective. Martin Allen wanted to stay with his wife rather than travel to an away game at Newcastle and Trevor Francis, the manager, refused to agree. In the event she went into labour, so he just got on a plane and headed back to London without Trevor's permission. This led to a bust-up and the media took it up as a major debate. The episode showed inexperience on Trevor's part, because it was an argument that he couldn't win. Sometimes discretion is the better part of valour.

Around the time that Gavin was born I grew a moustache. It doesn't sound too dramatic an event, but it went on to become very much part of my identity as far as everyone else was concerned. I like to think I was a trendsetter, because it was just before facial hair became really fashionable. In one close season I even experimented with a beard, but I decided against inflicting that on the Charlton public. Nobody could have competed with Derek Hales on that score anyway.

Although I did shave the moustache off from time to time over the years, I have only really dispensed with it since it started looking like a Newcastle United scarf, with as much white as black hair. Even my closest family struggled to get used to my new clean-shaven look and when I travel up north I often find that people whom I played against and who have known me for years will take a second look before they are entirely sure it's me.

The 1967/68 season wasn't a classic by any means, but there was a growing confidence about the place and if we hadn't fallen away in the last few weeks, we'd have finished a lot higher than the 15th we eventually managed. I missed only two League matches and scored nine goals, despite being out on the wing, which was a good return.

I also tasted success for the first time when we won the London and national five-a-side tournaments at Wembley's Empire Pool in May 1968. The capital tournament was sponsored by the Evening Standard and took place in the run-up to the FA Cup final. It was always a great night, with a vibrant 8,000 crowd and a good mix of supporters. We played small-sided games most days in training and I would always walk off the field with a bounce in my step if my side had won.

Harry Gregory captained the team, with Charlie Wright, Brian Kinsey, Alan Campbell, Gordon Bolland and myself making up the squad. I was in my element and managed to score four of our six goals, including the winner in the final. Following a bye in the first round, we squeezed past Arsenal 5-4 on penalties after drawing 2-2, then beat Fulham 2-0 in the semi-final. Crystal Palace were our final opponents and we won 2-1, with Alan Campbell getting the first goal and my former teammate John Sewell scoring for them.

This meant we qualified to take part in the national competition, sponsored by the Standard's then sister paper, the Daily Express, six days later. The Charlton squad was unchanged. We met Morton in the first round and won 4-3 on penalties. I scored the clinching fourth penalty. There were no goals in the semi-final against Grimsby Town, but again we went through on spot-kicks, this time 5-4. We faced Gillingham in the final and I managed to score the only goal of the game two minutes from the end. It was great to be part of a Charlton team winning a trophy.

A potentially successful squad was coming together on the full-size pitch as well. Ray Treacy had joined us from West Bromwich Albion in February 1968. He was an outgoing character, full of confidence. He scored nine goals in the final 18 games, which given that Tees was already making a big impression up front was a good omen for the future. Tees notched 14 goals that year, while Campbell got ten as the playmaker in midfield. He could run all day.

We also had Graham Moore, a stylish midfielder signed in the 1967 close season from relegated Northampton. A Welsh international, with First Division experience at Chelsea and Manchester United, he had little pace but could spray the ball around. Big Paul Went had also come from Orient the previous summer, so the elements of a successful team were beginning to come together. There was a level of expectation when we came back the following year for what would prove one of the most significant campaigns of my playing career.

The sense of anticipation was one reason I gave no serious consideration to an opportunity that arose unexpectedly that summer. Under the contract arrangements that existed then, the club was obliged to write to each player every year to tell them whether they were being retained for the following season. If the letter failed to arrive then you were entitled to a free transfer – even if this was the result of an administrative error.

That is exactly what happened to me in the summer of 1968. For whatever reason, no letter arrived. I would have had a reasonable value in the transfer marker by then and could have used the situation to get a sizeable signing-on fee, much as players do now under the Bosman ruling. Charlie Wright was the union representative at the time and his advice was quite clear that I could look for another club if that was what I wanted.

It was one of the only occasions during my playing career when Michael Gliksten was involved in contract negotiations with me. I had got to know the chairman slightly in the summer of 1965 when working in his offices as part of my accountancy studies. In general, however, players had minimal contact with directors and there was little or no negotiation about salaries, so this was a rarity. I was eventually summoned to the boardroom for talks. The chairman sat me down on one of those big leather sofas that seem to swallow you up, leaving me looking up at him behind his desk. It was quite a good ploy from his point of view as I felt at a disadvantage before the discussion had even started.

In the end, I accepted an extra £5 a week as a result of the error. It was still early in my career and I was enjoying myself at Charlton, so I didn't really have any desire to go. The chairman told me years later that it was the one and only time he was worried about me leaving. Modern agents would be much more ruthless in exploiting such a situation, but I would have no regrets about being part of the season that was about to unfold.

What happened in 1968/69 was built on the combination of Firmani and Foley, which is often the case with successful management. It's rare for just one person to be responsible, because in practical terms alone it's hard to oversee 30 professionals at once. Brian Clough needed Peter Taylor. Alex Ferguson has been at

Manchester United for so long that it's regarded as his success, but there will have been periods when his coaches have played their part. Theo's involvement allowed Eddie to stay a little more aloof than he otherwise could have been.

Eddie wanted things done the right way. He was someone who did things by the book, looked after his body well, and expected his players to do the same. He required them to be well turned out, to prepare properly for a game and not to drink to excess. In retrospect, he carried this too far in the end. I think if you are imposing discipline in any environment, you must always think whether you are being realistic and how you will deal with the repercussions if you don't succeed.

At one point he imposed a ban on swearing and went public on it. It was a good idea in principle, but it was very hard on someone like Charlie Wright, who wasn't used to putting a sentence together without throwing in the odd expletive. He didn't mean anything by it. It was just his way of speaking. The ban also opened the door for other teams to taunt us. There was one match at Bristol City when Harry Gregory was kicked up in the air, after which the home player wagged his finger and said: "Now, now, don't swear or you'll be in trouble." Inevitably, Harry reacted and he was almost sent off.

Contrary to Eddie's views on drinking, it was still usual for players to have a pint of beer or two after the game on a Saturday night and probably more at a get-together during the week. This was alien to him because of his Italian experience, as it would be to managers today, but it wasn't that outrageous in itself.

Dennis Booth reminds me to this day about Theo Foley laying into various members of the squad after a particular defeat about the fact that we had been out drinking the previous midweek. I did diffuse the situation when I pointed out that Ray Treacy and I had been rubbish in the game and we'd been on Coca-Cola.

Normally, I'd have the odd pint but Ray would only ever have a Coke, while the likes of Graham Moore, Alan Campbell, Bob Curtis and Matt Tees would often be found in the local pub playing darts and enjoying a couple of beers. It shows how in that era the players were still happy to mix with the mass of working-class people. There were also players who would smoke on a Saturday night and, if we'd won, might have a cigar. It wasn't thought unreasonable at the time. The prizes weren't as great then, whereas now you are looking for every edge. To that extent, Eddie was ahead of his time, and not old-fashioned as some players thought then.

In many respects 1968/69 was a great season, but it was also a frustrating one for me personally. I was doing well and knew that I was playing a major role, with the full confidence of the management. We faced Millwall on the opening day in front of a big Valley crowd and I scored after two minutes. Our matches were usually very tight and, early as it was, I had the feeling that I might have scored the winner. But we were 4-1 down by the early stages of the second half. Even though we pulled back to 4-3, we couldn't get the equaliser. It was hardly a flying start, but at least we bounced straight back by winning in midweek at Cardiff.

Thereafter, I picked up a series of injuries. The first one came against Norwich City at the end of August. I had tormented Dave Stringer, the right-back, who just stared at me with his icy blue eyes and kicked me from pillar to post all afternoon. But I had the last laugh, when I made the second goal, which proved to be the winner. It was only when I was sitting at home resting after the game that my knee swelled up, which kept me out of the next two matches and proved to be the start of my trouble.

Soon afterwards I was playing in a five-a-side during training and Jimmy Mullen, my understudy at the time, was niggling away at me. Suddenly, I lost my temper and crashed into a tackle with him. The ball popped out and I went to hit it again, but Moore put his foot out and I kicked that instead. My trainer just split and I had shattered the joint of my second toe on the right foot, so for the next few months I had to play with this injury.

Even though the joint was taped up to protect it, I could hardly train all week and after a while I had to be injected in order to be able to play because of the severity of the pain. The specialist assured me that I wasn't doing any further damage by carrying on, so I could leave it until the summer to sort out. Eddie didn't want me out of the side, but this wasn't sustainable. I was seeing more of physio Charlie Hall than I was of my family. Inevitably, I lost my sharpness and that started to affect my game. I knew that I couldn't continue.

The surgeon said that I'd be out for two or three weeks after the operation and then hopefully all would be well. It was arranged for me to have the surgery in January, just after we had faced Crystal Palace at The Valley in the third round of the FA Cup. I was up against my former Charlton teammate Johnny Sewell and we drew 0-0 in front of 30,000 fans. I was booked in to the hospital for the Thursday – the day after the replay.

There were almost 40,000 at Selhurst Park and the atmosphere was incredible. Palace were neck and neck with us at the top of the Second Division, so the game had an extra edge to it, and they must have thought they had done their job by getting us back for a replay. The odds were now against us, but a large number of Charlton fans made the trip. Unfortunately, this meant that the club surgeon, Mr Buck, got held up in the traffic, which left me waiting to have my injection.

We had to ask the Palace doctor to do it, and it took about three or four attempts to push the needle in. Even then I remember him warning me that it might not be successful, which may have been a bit of kidology. It did seem to freeze the joint, but my foot felt like a pin cushion. Still, it got me out there on the pitch for what turned out to be a famous victory, Treacy scoring both goals in a 2-0 win.

It was a euphoric moment and we now knew that we would be playing Arsenal at Highbury in the fourth round. It was a dream tie for us, but I had to go and have my operation. I had 16 days to recover and I hoped against hope I could make the game, but realistically it was never going to be and I missed my only opportunity to play against the Gunners. Arsenal, sadly, beat us 2-0.

I also missed one of the most important League matches of the season, a memorable 2-0 home win over Brian Clough's Derby County, who finished champions that year, on the Saturday before the game at Highbury.

What compounded my frustration when I did return, in the middle of February, was that it transpired the problem hadn't been solved. The surgeon had taken out the loose bits of bone but left a jagged edge, so I only played another four games before I had to have a further operation that kept me out for the rest of the season. I'd been in pain for about five months by then and was at the end of my tether. It was about the only time that Eddie and I were ever at loggerheads. He didn't want to lose me but I just couldn't go on. To this day Eddie tells me that if I had stayed fit then we would have got promotion that year. I suppose that this might just be him being generous towards me, but I do think that with the way I was playing and feeling that year, it's possible that I could have made a significant difference to that side.

The crucial game was the home League fixture against Palace on March 22nd. If we had beaten them then it would have put us level on points and been a major psychological boost, even though we had played 34 matches to their 33 at the time. Instead, they held out for a 1-1 draw and we could never make up the gap, even though we both climbed back above Millwall, Middlesbrough and Cardiff City in the remaining weeks. They eventually went up in second place, with us six points behind in third, which in those days wasn't good enough.

I was very fortunate with injuries during my career, but that season my luck ran out and it's always been a case of looking back and wondering what might have been. It became even harder to bear the following year, because the assumption over the summer months had been that we would be going for promotion again, but instead we reverted to the familiar story of struggle. This was a massive disappointment.

Things began to go wrong in pre-season. There were one or two contract disputes, which was pretty unusual at the time. Matt Tees was one of those involved and a little ill-feeling was creeping in among the senior players. At the root of the problem was the signing of Ray Crawford in March.

Crawford had been a prolific scorer for Portsmouth, Ipswich Town, Wolves and West Bromwich Albion, but he was nearly 33 by this stage and his legs couldn't get him about as much as they had. He had scored three goals in nine games at the end of the 1968/69 campaign, which was a respectable return, but Tees had finished on 15 and had grounds to be unhappy that Crawford was on substantially more money than him.

If a player comes in and is very successful then the other members of the squad are likely to recognise the contribution he is making and accept that he has earned his money, but in Crawford's case that hadn't quite happened.

Then we went on tour to Holland. Eddie banned all drinking of any description, including soft drinks at one stage, which just wasn't tenable and ended up with people sneaking all kinds of drinks back to their rooms. The seeds were being sown for a disastrous season.

In spite of all that we made a good start, with three wins and two draws in the first six games, but then Tees was sold to Luton and we lost the next match, at Swindon, 5-0. This was the one and only time I can remember Michael Gliksten coming into the dressing room straight after a game. As we sat in the communal bath, he stormed in and shouted: "You are all a disgrace and that is unacceptable!" With that he wheeled round and stormed back out.

Tees was very popular, both within the club and among the fans, so his departure had an adverse effect on the players, particularly his great mates Graham Moore and Alan Campbell.

As Firmani's relationship with some of the players deteriorated, simple bad luck also intervened. Just a week after our hammering at the County Ground, Paul Went injured his cruciate ligaments in a match against Cardiff City at The Valley when John Toshack landed on his leg. Paul had been only 17 when he signed for us from Orient in the summer of 1967, but he was already fully mature. He became an immediate fixture in the side and a tremendous influence. He was still a month short of his 20th birthday at the time, but he had the biggest legs I'd ever seen and would exercise them using 100-pound weights after he damaged his knee.

I went to visit Paul in hospital. For most players it was an injury that would have finished their career. He had other ideas and returned to action later that same season, but all was not well and he had to nurse that knee for the rest of his playing days. In later years, it seemed he became like Red Adair, going from club to club to save them from relegation from the Second Division. After he left Charlton he played for Fulham, Portsmouth, Cardiff City and Orient again. It almost seemed that he was destined for this role.

Firmani had also fallen out with Crawford, whose contract was cancelled in October after he failed to turn up for special training at Bisham Abbey. He was replaced by Gordon Riddick, from Gillingham, who also failed to make any great mark, so overall the manager wasn't having much success in the transfer market

One of his last signings was Maurice Setters, who arrived at the end of February, but I believe he was more the chairman's choice than the manager's. Maurice had been a great player during the late 1950s and early 60s, but his knees had gone and he was very bow-legged – the bandiest player I've ever seen. He was a ferocious tackler if he could get near an opponent, but at 33 he was finding it hard to get there. As much as he wanted to do it for Charlton, he just couldn't find it in him.

Setters had played for Coventry City the previous season as a sweeper away from home, which meant that he didn't have to do too much running. They didn't play him at home, where he would have been more vulnerable to breaking forwards. When he came to us, he was put in an ordinary back four, where he was more exposed.

Towards the end of your career, it's very important that the team is doing well, so that they can play to your strengths. When a side is struggling, as in our case, you have to battle alongside everyone else. It becomes every man for himself.

The last of Setters' eight games for Charlton was also Firmani's final match in charge, the Easter Saturday visit of Leicester City. Concerned about the pace of the visitors' wide men, John Farrington and our own former left-winger Glover, he decided to put Mike Kenning – who had returned to the club a year earlier – at left-back. The decision was disastrous.

Lesley and I had just moved into a new house in Okehampton Crescent, Welling, and as was common at that time we had arranged a party there for the evening with the other players. We lost the match 5-0, which was bad enough in itself. I remember thinking that no one would turn up for the party after that, but they did and we all drowned our sorrows together.

By Monday, Eddie had been sacked. Reportedly, Michael Gliksten was terribly upset at having to dismiss the man who had been his hero as a player and who he'd expected to take the club back to the First Division. It was a sad end to Eddie's long involvement with Charlton. He'd been too inflexible over certain issues. The players got the vibes that they weren't coming up to his standards and this ultimately affected their performances. But his single biggest mistake was the sale of Matt Tees.

Theo took over as acting manager for the last four games and we managed to stay up by beating Bristol City 2-1 in the final game at The Valley. It was the Tuesday night after the closing weekend and we appeared to have the game won when we went 2-0 up just after half-time. The season had two final twists in store, however, in my case to my ankle, which meant I had to give way to Harry Gregory with about 20 minutes left. Then Chris Garland pulled a goal back two minutes from time and suddenly we were at panic stations, but with virtually everyone in the ground whistling for time we somehow scrambled through the remaining seconds and were safe.

Theo was appointed manager on a permanent basis a month after the season ended. It was a decision that could only be good news for my personal fortunes and in time it would prove a highly beneficial one for the club as a whole, but his years in charge were not to be successful ones.

The exodus from The Valley continued when Alan Campbell went to Birmingham City and Harry Gregory to Aston Villa in October 1970. Foley in turn went into the transfer market that season to secure three new forwards – Dickie Plumb, Barry Endean and Bobby Hunt. They were wholehearted players, but lacked the quality to take us into the promotion places.

Plumb was a good goalscorer but he had come from non-League Yeovil and was probably more suited to the lower divisions. Endean had done well at Watford, but he endured a torrid time at The Valley and seemed fated never to find the net, to the extent that I can still remember the big cheer when he finally did score the following season. He arrived in February and left in October the same year with just two goals to his name. Hunt did quite well but was plagued by knee trouble. He was a great character, who would have us in fits of laughter.

Possibly it was the available budget rather than Theo's judgement that was at fault. In Cyril Davies, whom he also picked up from Yeovil, he unearthed a very useful midfielder who went on to play for Wales, only to pick up a bad injury after a couple of years and be forced to retire.

I was mainly on the left in those years, but during Theo's reign I had licence to switch flanks and attack the opposite full-back if I wasn't getting any joy on that side. We would play a 4-3-3 formation, with me making up the extra man in midfield. It's an occupational hazard of being a winger, however, that you can play as well as ever and be doing exactly the same things that have brought you success before, but if there is no end-product you may get the blame.

In 1970/71, we came third from bottom for a second consecutive season, albeit with the minor satisfaction of this time securing safety in the penultimate match. A 4-1 thrashing of Bolton Wanderers at The Valley ten days earlier had already sent the Trotters down to the Third Division for the first time in their history. We scored only 13 goals away from home that year and four of them came in one match at QPR, so the other 20 matches yielded just nine in total. Even that was an improvement on the previous year, when we'd netted just 12 goals on our travels. Indeed, the remarkable win at Loftus Road, at the end of November 1970, was the only away victory the first team had recorded in two seasons.

The Charlton substitute in that Rangers game was Alan Ellis, a 19-year-old midfielder who started nine games that season. His career at The Valley turned out to be brief, but he is remembered due to his performance in a charity athletics tournament at White City involving teams from the capital's professional clubs.

I'd love to see such an occasion today. It would attract enormous media attention if it was possible, but sadly the risk of top players picking up injuries while competing in activities like the high jump and long jump make that impossible.

My own event was the 400m, which was run without lanes. Going into the final bend I was in second place and confident of overtaking the leader, but as I attempted to do so an elbow came out and smashed me in the face. It belonged to West Ham's Harry Redknapp, who ran on to win the race. Many years later, when we had both moved into management, I got to know Harry better. He puts the incident down to the fact that he needed the £100 prize money more than I did!

Bobby Moore also made a big impression. His event was last on the schedule and involved chipping footballs into paddling pools set at intervals of ten yards. After each activity was finished the competitors were able to retire to the refreshment tent. The West Ham and England captain had gone there first and undoubtedly enjoyed a few drinks before he was called into action, but he was still able to chip the ball into position with his customary elegance and accuracy. I know I'd have had trouble focusing on the target in that situation, never mind hitting it. Bobby was in a class of his own.

Thanks to Ellis, however, the Hammers didn't have it all their own way. As a middle-distance runner Billy Bonds had no match and it was inconceivable that he could be beaten in the mile. He hadn't even heard of Alan as a footballer, so he certainly wasn't aware of his prowess on the track. Ellis was slightly built and not that fast, but he could run forever. The youngster stormed away with the race and left Bill fuming that we had pulled a stroke by entering someone who wasn't eligible, but that was never the case. Bill's defeat was the sensation of the day.

The 1971/72 campaign was my tenth in Charlton colours and it became a very special year because my service was acknowledged by the club, which duly granted me a testimonial season. I learned a lot from my experiences that year, although the gesture put me in a very difficult position the following summer.

Having a testimonial enables a player to get to know and understand the fans. What I really learned that year was how intense the experience of supporting your team can be. As a professional, you have to harden yourself to get over bad results. If you've played well despite losing, you will still have an inner glow regardless. Conversely, if you play badly and the team lose too, you must have the resilience to bounce back. Otherwise it's quite likely the manager will detect a loss of confidence and you'll be out of the side.

With the fans, the hangover lasts longer. They can't get it out of their systems until the next game and have to carry it until then. When we were doing well, by contrast, the effect it had on people's lives would be positive and could well change a family's whole week. Thanks to my testimonial season, I realised from an early age how the team's fortunes can affect the community.

We played Chelsea in my testimonial match and the official attendance was nearly 17,000. Chelsea had won the European Cup Winners' Cup the previous season and were a big draw. There was a warm-up match before kick-off and so many people turned up and were frustrated by the fact that they were missing out that the crowd burst through the main entrance.

I remember speaking to Sam Bartram, who was there to take part in a penalty competition. He had become quite adept at estimating the crowd in his playing days, having more time than most of his teammates to weigh it up. He reckoned that he could guess the crowd to within a thousand and thought there were close to 25,000 in the ground. It was an unforgettable night and personally I was having a good season. I was in the prime of my career and we seemed to have picked up from the last two years. Then it all fell apart.

Unfortunately, one of the players missing from my testimonial season was Charlie Wright, who left the club for relegated Bolton in the summer of 1971. I had worked closely with Charlie. We would both coach the young boys at The Valley on a Monday evening. He was still regarded as the number-one goalkeeper and I was quite astounded when he told me the news, as indeed everyone was. Charlie didn't want to go and it was one decision of Theo's that I never quite understood. I don't think Charlie did either.

I will always be indebted to him and his wife Helen for the help they gave Lesley when I was away on the club's end-of-season tour to Spain that year. Our 11-month-old daughter Lauren had gastroenteritis and was dehydrating at an alarming rate. Our doctor at the time thought Lesley was just another neurotic mother. He told her not to panic and that he would try to come round that evening.

Lauren's condition was deteriorating by the hour. A frantic Lesley rang Charlie and between them he and Helen convinced her to rush Lauren to hospital immediately. It was in the nick of time. Lauren was put on a drip and admitted to intensive care straight away. The registrar informed Lesley that waiting a few more hours could have proved fatal. The ward sister was adamant that I should come home without delay, as it would be touch and go for the next 48 hours. Charlie took over and contacted general manager Rodney Stone, who arranged my immediate return flight to London.

Lesley and I will never forget the part that Charlie and Helen played that day. I had said to Charlie many times that he had saved Charlton by his performances, but on this occasion he had helped to save the life of my little daughter.

The big characters at a club can have a large sway in the dressing room, so when they leave it can have an adverse effect. There had now been a considerable turnover of the old guard and with hindsight what happened in 1971/72 was almost inevitable, although the way it came about took us by surprise.

In relative terms we'd been enjoying quite a successful season and didn't look likely to be in any trouble, but everything turned on the match at Middlesbrough on March 25th. We were leading 2-1 with a minute to go when Cyril Davies gave away an unnecessary corner and they equalised. At the time, a draw still seemed like a good result. Boro were always difficult to beat at Ayresome Park – they only lost one home game all season – and if we had won that match we would have been in a comfortable mid-table position with nine games to go. That extra point alone would have kept us up.

In the very next match, on Good Friday, Dave Shipperley first conceded a penalty and then scored a spectacular own goal, attempting to pass back to keeper John Dunn but instead sending the ball sailing over his head and in off the post. I pulled one back late on, but we lost 2-1. Twenty-four hours later we played Norwich, the eventual champions, at home and lost again. On the Tuesday, we went down 3-1 at Burnley.

A major factor in our vulnerability was probably the fact that we had lost Peter Reeves to injury in December. He was a lovely lad, certainly the best tackler the club had seen since Mike Bailey's departure. He played in a testimonial match for me, which was a Teachers XI against my All-Star XI at Erith. My old sports teacher was playing and they were all a bit useful. Reeves would always play at the back throughout his career, even in five-a-sides, but on this one occasion he came to me and asked to play up front. He got tripped and a lump came up on his knee, which he showed me afterwards in the dressing room. I don't know if it was something that had happened before and he had aggravated it or if this was the start, but it was the beginning of the end for him. He was some defender and a ferocious man-marker. If we played QPR, we would rely on him to force Rodney Marsh out of the game.

The following week we lost another classy defender, Bob Curtis, with a ruptured Achilles' tendon that was to keep him out for eight months.

With Watford adrift at the bottom of the table, only one relegation place was left open in the closing weeks of the season and we could have done ourselves a power of good by beating Fulham at The Valley. They were prime candidates for the drop themselves. Again we led 2-1 into the closing stages, only to concede an 88th-minute equaliser to Fred Callaghan, a left-back who rarely scored.

Now we'd taken one point from four games, three of them at home. Nerves were starting to jangle. Even though we'd improved our form on our travels that year, recording wins at Luton, Hull and Watford, we had still lost too many away matches that we should have drawn. The next two games were away to Sheffield Wednesday and Queens Park Rangers, a side themselves involved in the promotion race, and it was no surprise that we lost both matches. By the time Portsmouth arrived at The Valley, the smell of relegation was about. Everyone was very jittery, which was evident in the way we were playing. We were losing 1-0 with six minutes left, but I managed to grab an equaliser. It just about kept us alive.

The last home game was against Millwall, who as luck would have it were enjoying what was then their best-ever season and looked poised to win promotion. They were the last team we would have wanted to play in these circumstances. In goal they had Bryan King, who had recently dislocated his shoulder and could barely move one of his arms, but we didn't have a worthwhile shot. They scored twice in the last 15 minutes and at the end their jubilant fans poured on to the pitch to celebrate what they thought was promotion, although their hopes would be cruelly dashed.

It was bad enough that we had plummeted into trouble, but to lose to Millwall in these circumstances was disastrous. Mentally the players were at a really low ebb after that game. Fate had also dealt us another dreadful card on the last day of the season, with a long trip north to Blackpool, who had been relegated from the top flight only 12 months earlier and had one of the better home records in the division. Worse than that, they were managed by Bob Stokoe.

Bob clearly felt hard done by over his departure from The Valley. He was a man who if he got kicked in a match made sure that he got one back in return. So there we were walking down the tunnel at Bloomfield Road and there was Bob to greet us, snarling:

"You lot are going down. You're going down today."

Blackpool beat us 5-0 and Bob was on his feet to celebrate every goal. He had taken his revenge in the best possible way, although to be fair I think he would really have liked his team to have beaten us 10-0. To leave us in no possible doubt, he then put his head in the dressing room afterwards and said: "I know some of you weren't even at the club when I was there, but I want you to know that I'm bloody glad that Charlton have gone down."

I can't blame him, he was a committed man. Most people would probably have felt the same, although they wouldn't necessarily have been so animated about it.

I was totally devastated by the fact that we had been relegated. It has an effect on you as part of the team and for the future of the club, but as a player you also have to consider what it means for you personally in terms of your career. I was probably more of a team player than most, but we were going into a division I knew nothing about. I later spent some enjoyable times managing teams at the lower level, but then these were strange places and unfamiliar clubs. For the first time, I seriously considered whether I had played my last game for Charlton Athletic.

Chapter Six
MIDFIELD GENERAL

I like to think that I always had a good rapport with the fans, but the relationships that were forged in my testimonial year provided me with a real problem once we were relegated. I didn't want to play in the lower division. I had always been an optimist and I felt I'd done well the previous year, but I knew enough about the Third Division to realise that my qualities as a player wouldn't enable me to prosper there. I was still hoping to play in the First Division, rather than drop down another level.

Ray Treacy and Paul Went left, and as well as being two of our best players, they were also very good friends of mine. Bob Curtis and Peter Reeves, who had both suffered serious injuries, were now the only other men remaining from the side that had finished third in 1968/69. But the fact that I had just had my testimonial prevented me joining the exodus. I didn't feel I could walk away from the people I had got to know so well in the previous year and who had shown me such support and friendship. I spoke at length to Theo, who assured me that we would bounce back. But at the time I was disconsolate.

If I had decided to move I'd have been fairly confident someone would come in for me. I'd managed to score 13 goals from open play as a winger in a relegated team. This would turn out to be my highest tally in a season throughout my career and that record alone should have made me attractive to someone.

The process of being transferred was more straightforward than it is now. If another manager made an enquiry about you and it was rejected then 90 per cent of the time you would never even know about it. There wasn't the media speculation that exists today. The other way out was to go on the transfer list and for the first time I was really close to doing that. If ever I was going to move to another club that would have been the time. But Theo had been exceptionally good to me as manager and I had a lot of reasons to be grateful to him. So that was another factor in my decision to stay.

Charlton had treated me well. Now I wanted to show loyalty to the club and help it get promoted back to the Second Division. I steeled myself for what I feared would be a rough ride ahead.

Whatever fate has befallen a team, the arrival of a new season is usually greeted with optimism. However, any complacency in the Charlton camp as the club prepared for Third Division football for the first time since 1935 quickly disappeared when we lost our opening two games, first at Walsall and then at home to Shrewsbury Town.

It was a whole different game in that division. Sometimes things were easier, but at others they could be much tougher. I found it very difficult playing against certain full-backs, who showed no respect for particular types of skill. In the Second Division, you were expected to have the ability to kill a ball when it came to you, so most defenders would stand off you and wait to see what you did next. In the Third, there were defenders who would just charge straight into you, anticipating a poorer touch, taking you and the ball at the same time. Referees weren't as hot then either, which didn't help. There is far more protection today.

A new set of players joined the club as we shaped up to the challenge. Arthur Horsfield was a great buy, a prolific goalscorer who I'm sure would have been good enough to play at a higher level with the right man alongside him. Peter Hunt came from Southend and Richie Bowman broke through from the youth set-up, so there was some quality around. Most significant was the arrival of Colin Powell, from Barnet.

By this stage, Theo was showing his eye for a player. Powell – known as "Paddy" – was elegant on the ball, with a long stride, and very quiet in the dressing room, presumably because he'd come from the non-League environment. I could see that he was an excellent crosser of the ball. I wondered if he was used to having to work hard covering back, but the potential was there all right.

At one point we went to Guernsey for a couple of days and were practising crosses from the right-hand side. The pitch was ankle-deep in mud, so it was difficult anyway, but then Theo started to give Powell some advice on how to do it. After about ten or 15 minutes of this, Paddy couldn't even raise the ball off the ground. It must have been the first time in his life that he'd given his technique any thought. He just did what he did instinctively. It brought home to me that when you buy a player because he's good at a particular thing then the best coaching is to leave him alone. If he's got the end-product right, he should be allowed to carry on in his own way. You might be able to change the way he plays positionally, but not technically once he is in his 20s.

When someone has come up through an unconventional route you can usually say that he would have been a better player if he'd come through the professional structure. However, it isn't always true and I don't know if it would have been the case with Paddy. Some players need to develop their own style and play against lesser opposition so that they can build up a belief in themselves.

Paddy was one of those who came in that bit later, but he went on to give great service to Charlton and was always very exciting to watch. His arrival also meant that as the decade went on I played more of a tucked-in midfield role on the left side. He was an out-and-out right winger, although ironically his most famous moment was probably a cross from the left that led to Derek Hales scoring the ITV goal of the season in 1976.

Mike Flanagan had arrived a year earlier, full of enthusiasm. He had a kind of naivety about him as a youngster and he would bounce along in training scoring imaginary goals. He came as a left-winger but got thrown up front, and he developed into a very prolific striker. One of his first opportunities to shine came after I injured my hamstring in a game against York City.

We'd found our feet in the Third Division by then, with three consecutive wins after that difficult start, including a 6-0 hammering of Swansea City. After York, I missed the game at Rotherham and came back in for a home win over Scunthorpe United, but things weren't right with the hamstring so Flanagan switched to the wing for the home match with Notts County. Incredibly, he scored four times and played a part in two more of the goals as we won 6-1. It was a fantastic performance.

Technically, Flan was sound. He'd had a good upbringing at Tottenham. Now he had the stage on which to develop, but for me he didn't have the guile that you needed to be effective out wide.

Injuries made it a frustrating season for me. No sooner would I get into a rhythm than I would have hamstring trouble. Most people still remembered Charlton as having been a First Division club for many years, so along with Blackburn and Bolton, who won the division with Charlie Wright in goal, we were still a big name to be playing the likes of Bournemouth, Chesterfield and Wrexham.

I remember a match the following season against Halifax Town, which we won 5-2. I felt that I had played tremendously well, but of course my performance received little recognition as it was such a low-profile fixture.

There was a further decline in crowds, with the average at The Valley falling to a post-war low of 5,658. I was used to a livelier atmosphere. It did become harder to get motivated and I know I wasn't the only one affected.

The highlight of the 1972/73 season was a twice replayed League Cup third-round tie with Sheffield United, who were in the First Division at the time. We eventually lost to a hotly disputed goal in the last minute of extra-time at Bramall Lane. I'd missed the first two matches with my hamstring trouble. The second replay was a mammoth game and very draining, although it was a relief to be playing in that kind of company again. Dave Shipperley was doing exceptionally well at centre-half. If Billy Dearden's late goal had been ruled offside we would have had to meet United for a fourth time. There was no provision for penalty shoot-outs to decide cup ties, but at that stage of my career the extra games wouldn't have been a problem for me. What made defeat worse was that once again the prize for the winners was a meeting with Arsenal, so I missed out on that for a second time.

Like many footballers I am prone to the odd superstition and one I developed in this period became a personal trademark. I used to juggle the ball on to the pitch and then volley it into the net. I did it before one particular game and the crowd loved it. I then did well in the match and we won. I gave a repeat performance the following week and again found that I played well, after which we went on a bit of a run, so it became part of my warm-up routine.

I did run into a bit of difficulty before one game at Notts County, however. There was a really strong wind at Meadow Lane on this particular day, so when I came out and did my routine I found myself blown badly off course. I must have cut a ridiculous figure, desperately trying to keep the ball aloft over by the corner flag, with only the handful of Charlton fans in the ground able to understand what the hell I was doing. Eventually, I lost my battle with the elements and the ball fell to the ground. Twenty minutes into the game I pulled a hamstring and we went on to lose 3-1.

My pre-match failure seemed to have foreshadowed an unsuccessful game, but this only reinforced my determination to keep up the ritual. It was something I continued to do for the rest of my playing career. The fans evidently enjoyed it, to the extent that I revived it for a while when I returned to Charlton as a coach, albeit from a less demanding distance, and only stopped altogether a few years ago. When I did, it was much to the disappointment of my good friend and long-time Charlton supporter John Hayes.

At the end of 1972/73 we were 11th and next season things deteriorated further, as we slipped to 14th. That resulted in Theo Foley's sacking, although at the time it was something of a surprise to me. The consensus was that we were too good to be finishing halfway down the Third Division, especially as we now had players in the side like Flanagan, Hales, Powell, Horsfield and myself, who were all capable of playing at the higher level. We scored 66 goals in that 1973/74 season, but conceded 73, which was the root of our problem. Reeves played 30 games but it proved to be his last season due to his knee injury. That definitely didn't help our cause.

Theo had managed the club for four seasons, during which time we'd narrowly survived in the Second Division, then been relegated and twice failed to look like coming back up, so I think the chairman just ran out of patience. What has always puzzled me was the timing of his sacking – with three games left. We couldn't go up or down, so it would have seemed kinder and more logical to leave him in place until the end of the season. I was truly disappointed that he had gone. He had been a good manager for me. He was always approachable, would spend hours with you on the training field to help improve your game and he worked extremely hard.

Les Gore, the chief scout, took temporary charge, but no doubt it was already arranged that Andy Nelson would take over.

Theo had brought in the key players who would now go on to revive the club's fortunes, as well as bringing on others, like Phil Warman, who played an important role. For whatever reason, however, he couldn't quite turn them into a winning combination. Nelson wouldn't have the same talent for pulling diamonds out of the rough, but he did have certain knowledge of the game that cut through the coaching manual. It could be argued that his success was about timing, because many of these lads were still developing, but the truth is that Nelson brought something completely different to the club.

He ruled with an iron fist. Whereas you could converse with Theo and air your point of view, Nelson didn't encourage any form of discussion or even explanation. He didn't allow his players any imagination or innovation and he intimidated the younger ones.

When Colin Powell cut in from the wing at Crystal Palace and scored with a rasping drive into the top corner, Nelson had no praise for him. It wasn't what he'd been asked to do. "You don't shoot from there, sir. If you do it again, you'll be off", was the extent of his comment.

Most managers are strong characters, but Nelson's approach was unique and his arrival had a dramatic effect. He was completely unbending and there were no grey areas or room for discretion. Another manager would have expected his players to use their initiative in a given situation. With Nelson there was a right thing to do and a wrong thing to do – whatever the outcome might be from doing the wrong thing. To satisfy him you had to play like a robot and forget about your instincts.

It was a huge culture shock. He was so totally different from all the other managers I'd encountered at Charlton. His ideas were cast in stone. He saw Hales and Flanagan as essential ingredients to gain promotion, so long as we adhered to a rigid system of play.

He'd been successful with Gillingham the season before and had seen how he could get goals with Brian Yeo, who was a similar type of player to Hales. The system was simply that we used the 4-4-2 formation, got out wide and put low balls into an area between the middle of the goal and the near post. We never hung a ball up to the far post.

I'm sure he'd drawn this from his own experience as a big centre-half. Andy could play a bit, but he'd struggled with the smaller, more mobile players in the box. All the centre-halves in the lower division were of a similar physique and we had the sharpest of all strikers in Hales. Under Theo, I'd be passing the ball to Hales and looking for a quick one-two, but this would often break down because I was obviously not playing to Derek's strengths. Now we passed to an area where all he had to do was arrive in the box at the right time to get the goal. You needed to be a good finisher, but he was the best.

If I hit a high ball to the far post now I knew that I would be in trouble with the manager. Even if it resulted in a goal, he wouldn't be happy, as Paddy had soon found out. But that was the system we played in 1974/75 and it was the making of Hales. With the goals came confidence and with the confidence came a bit more bread-and-butter play too. Theo might have brought Hales in, but Nelson played to his strengths.

The same applied to Flanagan, although he probably felt that

Mike had more to offer in general play. The great thing about converting a winger into a striker is that they can still move out wide and feel comfortable in that territory. Flanagan's change of position was an inspired move by Andy and led to Mike having an outstanding career.

It was a difficult situation for me. I was coming up to 30 and could no longer whiz down the line and cross balls as in years gone by. I knew that I wasn't going to be Nelson's kind of wide man. I needed to tuck in and play more of a midfield role. There was also no kind of relationship with the manager in which I could discuss my problems. He simply didn't allow that. As a result I went on the transfer list just before Christmas, along with Peter Hunt and Phil Warman. In one game Phil and I tore the right side of the opposition's defence to pieces and afterwards Nelson came into the dressing room and admitted how well the two of us had done to save the side from defeat. Then he added: "Don't do it again. Just do what I tell you!"

We couldn't understand what he was talking about. The truth is that he was right. He had a system to get out of the division and it worked. We travelled to Grimsby just before Christmas and drew 1-1. I came on at half-time. We'd beaten Blackburn in the previous game. Then we went to Wrexham and he changed the team to put the three of us back into the side, leaving out Flanagan, who had been playing well. Mike had taken his coat off and hung it on a peg in the dressing room, evidently assuming that he was playing, even though the team had not yet been announced. Andy looked at him and I'm sure changed the side at that moment. But we went out and won 3-0. In the next match we beat Colchester 4-1. He had shaken things up, which was unusual. Most managers hesitate to change a winning side, but for Andy it worked.

Up to that point there had been an obvious doubt among the squad about the way we were playing. It was not enjoyable for a number of us, including Warman, Powell, to a degree, and myself. It stifled our natural game. There were questions to be asked, but we complied, knowing that otherwise we wouldn't be selected. Once we got to February, it was clear that for the first time there was a chance of success. It's important to remember that the club hadn't experienced promotion since before the war, so there was a gathering sense of expectancy around the place. As far as the players were concerned, though, it had taken half the season for confidence in what we were doing to take root.

I wanted to come off the list and said to the manager that it was best if we all showed a united front in our attempt to go for promotion. "OK, fine!" said Andy. It was a big decision for me, but he made it seem of little consequence to him.

Just as in 1968/69, there was a high-profile rivalry for promotion with Crystal Palace. They were managed by Malcolm Allison, a flamboyant former Charlton player whose trademark was his lucky fedora hat. He repeatedly told the press that they would beat us for promotion, so it was sweet to edge them out, although our main focus was on ourselves. I so wanted to enjoy one season of promotion in my career and had reached the point where I was desperately hungry to win something after so many years of struggle. I'd had some great times, but we'd never achieved anything more than survival.

I remember having a drink with Peter Hunt and Richie Bowman the week before the end of the season and telling them that I'd be happy to hang up my boots if I could win promotion just once. We had won the national five-a-sides and I had enjoyed every moment of that, but Charlton had been in the doldrums for most of my career. I never dreamed that Andy Nelson was about to deprive me of what would have been the high point of my playing career and instead give me what became one of my worst football memories.

We'd been beaten 2-0 at Chesterfield on the final Saturday and needed to win against Preston on the Tuesday to be sure of going up in third place. We'd lost our previous two home matches in a bad attack of the jitters, but on the plus side we hadn't been defeated in a midweek League match under the Valley floodlights throughout the whole of our time in the Third Division.

If Nelson had told me of his intention to drop me on the Monday or even called me in a couple of hours early and spoken to me personally, I'd have been better equipped to deal with the situation mentally and emotionally. It would still have been a hammer blow, but he could have made me feel that I'd played my part in getting us that far. Then I could have enjoyed the evening.

But he didn't do that. He left us waiting in the dressing room until gone seven o'clock. Then, instead of announcing the side himself, as was usual, he gave the job to his assistant, Peter Shearing.

It was a bolt out of the blue and left me reeling. I'd started every game since that win at Wrexham, a run of 23 matches, so why should I suppose my place was in jeopardy? It was as much as I could do to wish the chosen 12 good luck before leaving the dressing room. Together with Eamonn Dunphy, who had also been left out, I stood in the car park shaking my head. Eamonn was terrific and said all the right things in an effort to console me.

We watched the match, in which we came from behind to win 3-1 with two goals from Hales. My good mate Peter Hunt had been relegated to the bench and it was when he came on to replace the injured Harry Cripps that the game suddenly changed. His introduction was the defining moment in us winning promotion that night. Afterwards I went down to the dressing room to congratulate the lads, but the champagne never passed my lips. After a respectable period of time, I just went home. In my career I've turned up to all sorts of events win, lose or draw, but on that evening it was impossible for me to go across to the Valley Club for the promotion party.

The following night we were involved in the London five-a-side championships at Wembley, where I was captaining the side. Nelson was there but I was in charge and I must admit that I didn't even look at him when he came into the dressing room. We won the tournament, so that did a lot to lighten my mood. At least I was able to walk down Wembley Way holding the trophy with my wife and kids, hoping that one day my son would perhaps play in the great stadium itself!

There was no way that I could question the decision to leave me out against Preston because on that night winning was everything. Relegation in 1972 had been so disappointing and was the most traumatic time for the club, but from the point of view of being hurt personally this was even worse.

Now I had the summer to recharge my batteries and prepare for the prospect of playing at the higher level again. I was Charlton through and through and had put in so much to get promotion that I was, of course, delighted that the club had made progress. The Second Division years that followed were so much more fruitful for me.

The experience hardened my attitude. I had another year left on my contract and by the time I came back for pre-season I had made up my mind that I was going to play in the way that was best for me, regardless of what Andy thought. If he didn't play me then so be it. I wasn't going to compromise my game for anyone, not least because I knew that Nelson wanted to continue with the same system and I couldn't be one of two wide men at this stage in my career.

I also knew that in the higher division we would need the extra man in midfield that I could provide, so I threw caution to the wind and took it upon myself to play there. Nothing was said. Things just evolved, and after a few games of the new season I found him putting increasing responsibility on my shoulders. I'd be the only person in charge of set-plays, no matter where they were on the field. We had certain free-kicks where we would play two against one or three against two and I would organise these to make sure that we attacked very quickly.

All this meant that I had to get involved in discussions with him. Then one day he suddenly said to me: "I think you need to train less, sir." Every manager has some little idiosyncrasy. One of Andy's was to end every statement in "sir".

He put forward an idea that I think extended my career. I know something similar had happened with Alan Ball. Lawrie McMenemy had told him that he didn't want him to train as hard, so that he could conserve his strength for the matches. It went against the grain for me to take it easy in any session, but Andy suggested that I should rest on Fridays. He felt I was using up too much energy. There is no doubt in my mind that this tactic was beneficial to me. After that I always felt good in the games. It's a lesson that I carried over into my own managerial career with great success.

I became, to a degree, Nelson's general on the field. We needed that different shape in the Second Division, with only one wide man at times, and he was clever enough to adopt that system without spending hours talking about it. When David Young left at the start of the 1976/77 season, I took over as captain. A professional relationship was now developing between Andy and I.

Becoming skipper wasn't the first time I had taken on additional responsibility within the team. After Charlie Wright left in 1971, I'd assumed his former role as the players' union representative. I had to liaise with head office in Manchester, pass on information and organise the payment of subs.

I'd met Jimmy Hill, then chairman of the PFA, as early as 1961, on a school trip to Roehampton. He had told us he was waiting for a phone call that would change the life of professional footballers. It was to do with the abolition of the maximum wage. The way he talked that day made an impression on me and I admired what he had done for the players. It was the first major shift in the balance of power away from the clubs, but there was still more to do and I was interested in being part of that movement.

In the mid-70s I was voted on to the PFA management committee, beating Trevor Brooking in the process. The Wolves striker Derek Dougan was the chairman at the time, with Cliff Lloyd as secretary. Gordon Taylor became chairman as I left. We eventually got the Football League to agree that players could no longer be retained against their wishes at the end of their contract. They would be free to move to other clubs, with the transfer fee decided by arbitration. Even at that time there were some on the committee who argued no fee should be payable. Cliff and Gordon felt that we needed to move towards that objective more gradually.

It happened in the end with the Bosman judgement and I believe that the current position is right, even though the financial power it has given the players makes the job of managing them much tougher. Each step of the way towards freedom of contract was predicted to be disastrous, but every time the game has adapted and moved on. Very few clubs have ever gone to the wall, although there is no doubt the fear of failure is greater than it was in the past. Some clubs who have overcommitted on wages in an effort to win or retain Premiership status have gone into a spiral of decline as a consequence.

We played more football in the Second Division and had more possession in midfield, but our game was still based around the same principles of getting the ball in low and fast to the near post. It wasn't quite as devastatingly direct as in the lower division, and the fact that there was quality in the side was demonstrated when we didn't struggle among the higher company. The point was underlined just after Christmas when we went to play Chelsea at Stamford Bridge. Hales scored twice in a 3-2 win and gave big Micky Droy a torrid time. Although Micky wasn't the quickest defender, Derek was electrifying that day.

This was Hales' year. He went on to score 31 in the season and just his name appearing on the teamsheet was striking fear into the hearts of defenders. For the first time since Tees and Treacy, we had someone up front who was going to score an abundance of goals in this division. Whereas both Tees and Treacy had been a threat in the air, Hales' strength was on the ground, where he could be lethal. He was the closest thing I'd seen on the deck to Eddie Firmani. He was quicker than Firmani, especially in the latter's second spell, and like Eddie he could hit balls hard and low.

The first time I saw him in training he had a flowing mane of hair and looked like a wild man. There was something menacing about him that made people keep out of his way, but we had a mutual respect and complemented each other's style of play.

I also gave him his famous nickname. It came about during a pre-season cross-country run, when I was jokingly offering odds on the other players and naming them as if they were racehorses to add to the comic effect. I called him "Killer" because of the icy stare that he would give anyone who upset him, even in training, but it also summed up his killer instinct in front of goal. The fans picked up on the tag, adopted it as a chant and it stayed with him throughout his career.

Hales enjoyed his "bandito" image and played up to it. He could do a smash and grab on opponents because he was so quick, the fastest I'd seen. It was his ability to accelerate from a standing position that set him apart and we worked on that over and over again. You'd play the ball in and suddenly he'd be there. He left defenders for dead.

Centre-halves would kick him if they could, but a lot of the time they couldn't catch him. Getting that many goals from 12 yards or less required tremendous courage. He was dealing with defenders who might not have been the most skilful players but they were definitely hard men. Like Alan Shearer, Hales was brave enough to keep going in there and risk getting hurt. The big advantage he did have was the ability to get in and out again without being hit.

The flip side to Derek was that he had a short fuse, which got him sent off several times. He also dealt with a few things on the field in the old-fashioned way and that was part of his make-up. He was the sort of player who would exact his own instant justice and accept the consequences.

It's necessary to have players with a degree of power and aggression, to enable those who are less physical but have greater finesse and more delicate skills to shine. This hasn't changed over the years. It was the case with Nobby Stiles and Bobby Charlton at Manchester United, and with Dave Mackay and Danny Blanchflower at Tottenham. Hales and Flanagan provided that combination. Hales had the pace and aggression, but he was solely focused on finishing. Flanagan was the more rounded footballer. He could hold the ball up and bring others into the game and he could also cross the ball accurately. Each benefited from the other in that mid-70s team.

Oddly enough, Derek would often play in goal during the five-a-sides in training. I would always pick him for my team and at one point we had a three-month spell of being undefeated. He had a way of stopping shots, but he was more comfortable in the smaller goals we used than he would have been on a full-size pitch.

As it happened, Hales did get one opportunity to put his goalkeeping skills to the test, which gave a comic twist to one of the most depressing and tragic events that I witnessed as a professional footballer. It happened against Sunderland, at Roker Park in February 1976. I was chasing a ball back along with the home side's Tom Finney. Keeper Graham Tutt went down at his feet to smother the ball and Finney kicked out but made contact with the 19-year-old's head. Almost instantly, Tutt's eye swelled up.

It was a terrible moment and I don't think that any Charlton player on that pitch will ever forget it. The referee deemed the collision an accident and the Sunderland man wasn't booked. It's in the nature of professional footballers to be fleet of foot and when the goalkeeper goes down for the ball in that way to attempt to avoid kicking him. Nothing special had gone on in the game before the incident.

Hales took over from Tutt in goal and made an unusual sight, with his beard spilling over the goalkeeper's jersey. We lost 4-1. He had no chance with the goals, but he wasn't someone like John Hewie or Steve Brown, an outfield player who could do a job at that level. He wasn't tall enough in a full-size goal, he just liked to play there in five-a-sides.

When such an injury happens in a game it is bound to have an effect on the team. You have to carry on, but it's gut-wrenching to see one of your own teammates, especially someone as young as Graham, hurt so badly. We didn't know straight away that it would be his last game for the club, but we knew it was serious and that his eyesight could be in danger. I was one of the last people to leave the pitch that day and as I walked off Bob Stokoe – now the Sunderland manager – was still in his dugout. I never got a chance to ask him about what happened.

Finney joined Cambridge United in August that year and I remember him playing in a reserve game against us. Our centre-half Jimmy Giles ran all over the pitch kicking him, to the extent that Finney never returned for the second half.

Nobody will ever know how good a goalkeeper Graham Tutt could have become. His skills obviously needed refining, but with his size and what he achieved later when playing in America, he must have had prospects. He went on to become a successful coach in Atlanta.

Jeff Wood took over the goalkeeping for the remainder of the 1975/76 season. We finished in ninth position, a strong performance for our first campaign back in the Second Division.

Towards the end of the season I reached 400 League appearances and was presented with a silver salver to mark the occasion by chairman Michael Gliksten, while another landmark arrived in November 1977 when I reached 418 senior outings. Only John Hewie and Sam Bartram had now played more games for Charlton. I was settled to see out my playing career at The Valley. I was 31 and had reached a point where I was now central to the manager's plans. My role on the field was a less spectacular one from the fans' point of view. Obviously, they were concentrating on Hales, Flanagan and Powell. But I was an integral part of what was going on in terms of organisation on the field and these were a very enjoyable few years.

Due to my experience, the game seemed much slower to me now. I was seeing situations that I had been in so many times before and had learned exactly how to react to them. Playing from a slightly deeper position, with more of the game in front of me, I could also be reasonably confident that I was going to play well in most matches.

My own goalscoring suffered now I was playing in this deeper role. I couldn't get into the box as before and I was behind the ball at set-pieces, which are usually responsible for 40 per cent of all goals. But with first Hales and then Flanagan banging them in, it hardly seemed to matter.

I still thought that we had the potential to go on and win promotion to the top division, but we were conceding too many goals. In fairness, we were such an attack-minded team that we may have left a few holes at the back. That isn't to say that we didn't have talented defenders. Right-back Bob Curtis clearly had the natural ability to play at a very high level, but was a bit too laid-back in his approach. Phil Warman was a very good player, a winger converted to full-back, and a great character to have in the side. He was tough and aggressive. He also kept the dressing room in fits of laughter. I would often room with him and he'd make away trips go much quicker, with a string of jokes, sometimes at the manager's expense.

I cite what happened to Phil as an example to our youngsters even now. He was given a free transfer by Foley in March one year and seemed set to leave. Instead he got a break in the side and did really well, secured another contract and was around for a further ten years. This turn of events was lucky for Charlton. Once Phil got his confidence together he became an excellent full-back and always a pleasure to play alongside.

In the 1976/77 season, we scored 52 goals at home and it would possibly have been more if we'd been able to hold on to Hales beyond December. He was simply unstoppable at the start of the season, to the extent that he netted 16 times in the space of 12 Second Division matches, including two hat-tricks and goals in seven consecutive games.

Such prolific scoring was bound to attract the attention of First Division clubs and it was no surprise when Brian Clough's Derby County came in for him, although the move did not work out for either player or club. For all his finishing ability, Derek still had a few rough edges in his game that made it hard for him to prosper in a side which didn't play to his strengths. He did better when he moved on to West Ham, even though they were in a relegation struggle at the time.

One of the more extraordinary features of Hales' departure was that despite all the understandable howls of anguish from the fans, the team didn't suffer to any great extent. It wouldn't be true to say that he wasn't missed, but Flanagan stepped in to fill the breach and we didn't even sign a replacement striker.

We had a great Easter that year, which helped pull us up the table, starting with a rare win over Millwall at The Valley, notable for me because I scored from the penalty spot, regular taker Curtis having been relegated to the substitute's bench.

I believe that if you win the first game over that holiday weekend you don't feel tired in the matches that follow. After a goalless draw at Orient the following day, we certainly didn't show any evidence of heavy legs in beating promotion-chasing Chelsea 4-0, courtesy of a Flanagan hat-trick.

We finished seventh, only four points behind promoted Nottingham Forest. It was the narrowest margin since that big disappointment in 1958. Flanagan ended up with 23 goals to his name, but you still had to wonder what would have happened if we had been able to hold on to Hales until the end of that season and perhaps invested in a defender. Unfortunately, we never seemed to have the money at the crucial stage. All the same, it was an exciting Charlton team and there was a lot of entertaining football played. The question now was whether Nelson could translate this into meaningful success or if the club's financial weakness would keep top-flight football beyond our grasp forever.

Chapter Seven
CAPTAIN OF A SINKING SHIP

After three successful seasons, there was every cause for optimism at the start of 1977/78. Unhappily, I suffered an early setback when my ankle locked in the first week of training. I had to undergo surgery and miss the whole of pre-season. Soon after the operation I was lying on the settee in my front room when there was a knock on the door. Andy Nelson and the chief scout Les Gore had come to see how I was. Their visit was a complete surprise.

Andy took the opportunity to tell me with great enthusiasm about a new striker who he felt would have a great future at Charlton. He wasn't wrong. The summer signing did indeed enjoy an outstanding career at The Valley, but not in the role the manager anticipated. His name was Steve Gritt.

Nelson illustrated the faith he had in me by throwing me straight back into the line-up for the second match of the season. I hadn't played in even a practice match for three and a half months. We were facing Blackpool on a very wet afternoon at The Valley and won 3-1, although I picked up a rare booking for handball. It was one of only six cautions I received in my entire career. The day was otherwise notable for the debut, as a second-half substitute, of the young Gritt.

The next match, against Luton Town at Kenilworth Road, was one of the most embarrassing days of my career. September 3rd was a red-hot day in Bedfordshire and we lost 7-1. Worse still, we were 7-0 down with ten minutes to go, before we managed to make a minor dent in the arrears from the penalty spot. We were wearing yellow on that afternoon. "The only thing you've got right today is the colour of your shirts," growled Nelson as we were slumped in the dressing room afterwards.

Luton had some decent players, but it's hard to say what went wrong that day. Nelson blamed Curtis, who was substituted, in particular, although everyone got it in the neck. Everything the home side tried appeared to end up flying into the back of our net and the already scorching sun seemed to get hotter with every goal that we conceded.

Sometimes a defeat of those proportions can spur a team on to a successful run and that was exactly the case with us. We were unbeaten in our next five games. The last of these was a 4-3 home win over Brighton on a Tuesday night, a real ding-dong affair and a terrific match.

Eleven days later we were due to face Tottenham Hotspur at The Valley for the first time since we'd been relegated from the top division 20 years before. It was a huge game. I used to go to bed about midnight before a Saturday home match and then have a lie-in until about ten the following morning. At the time we had a boxer dog and that weekend I was looking after my mother and father-in-law's boxer too. On Friday evening I took them over the park, as I usually did, and to my horror my mother-in-law's dog bolted and was hit by a car. It was awful, not least because it had happened to someone else's pet for which I'd taken responsibility. She didn't survive, and I was up until the early hours of the morning at the emergency vets. I'd had an extremely traumatic night with very little sleep, so I went out to face Spurs with some trepidation.

Fortunately, I played well and the game turned out to be a really memorable one, although it was marred by our promising young full-back Mark Penfold breaking his leg. We won 4-1, with Flanagan getting a hat-trick, but true to form Nelson gave him a rollicking afterwards. I can still hear him clear as day having a go at Flan, who was sitting in the dressing room clutching the match ball: "You won't score goals if you carry on like that, sir. You were shooting when you should have passed."

Flanagan had just scored three times against the club that had let him go as a youngster. He felt that he'd arrived. It was flabbergasting that Nelson could respond in the way he did, but on this occasion not even he could stop Flan enjoying the moment.

We were going quite well up to Christmas 1977, but then lost 4-0 at Stoke on Boxing Day and it proved to be a turning point. After the game Nelson came into the dressing room to a deathly hush and sarcastically asked Paddy: "What did he have for Christmas dinner then?"

"What do you mean, boss?" replied a puzzled Paddy.

"Alec Lindsay. You spent long enough standing by him

having a chat out there. You must have asked him something."

Phil Warman got tremendous mileage out of that one on the journey back. It was Nelson's way of making sure everyone knew that Powell hadn't done his job. The manager felt that Paddy could be a bit erratic away from home and it showed in his team selections and substitutions. Paddy would no doubt admit that he had his better games at The Valley, but you would expect a winger to have more of the play at home. If you are restricted to an area of the field then you're reliant on service and he was definitely in that category. He wasn't a ball winner, he was dangerous going forward, so he would need the ball given to him. In the modern game, with five substitutes, it's more acceptable to play with four midfielders and then bring the winger on later, but that wasn't an option in 1978. I rate Colin Powell the best crosser of the ball the club has ever had.

We didn't win a single game from Christmas to Easter, but then picked up after a 1-0 victory at The Valley over Palace, which got us going again. The revival also provided the green light for what must remain one of the most foolhardy ventures in which the club has ever engaged. It was decided to let three of our players go on loan to an American club, the New England Tea Men, before our own domestic fortunes were entirely secure.

Striker Lawrie Abrahams, who went first, wasn't a great player, but he might have nicked us the odd goal and in the context of what followed we would have been pleased to have had him around. More significantly, with six games still to play the club allowed first Powell and then 16-goal Flanagan to fly off to join him. It was incredible.

I was livid, because earlier in the season I'd been promised that I could go across to play for California Surf, largely on the basis that Dick Tydeman could take over my role. In the 1970s, few of my contemporaries had been to America, so it was seen as a great opportunity to take the whole family over there for a totally new experience. But Nelson changed his mind. As usual, I would have accepted his decision if he had said no at the outset. However, he went back on his word and I didn't take it well. I felt badly let down, but I carried on. Then, lo and behold, he released Flanagan and Powell to go. Nelson's point was that the club could make money from loaning those two out, but had I gone it would not have been until the end of the season.

On top of that we weren't safe. We were in a pretty decent position, but not yet out of the woods, especially as four of our last five matches were away from home. Powell's last game was a goalless draw at home to Cardiff City. In Flanagan's, we were beaten at home by Hull. Then we went to Sheffield United and were beaten again. The next match was at home to Burnley and we won it 3-2, but after that we had to go to Brighton, who were battling for promotion, where we lost 1-0.

We were really struggling for experienced forwards and had now failed to score in four of the previous five games. This should not have surprised Nelson. Martin Robinson was a regular at 20 but he had only joined the club in February from Spurs, where he had failed to make the grade. Another striker, Tony Burman, was only 19, and had failed to establish himself since being pressed into service when Hales left. The manager had been using the 20-year-old Gritt as a forward, but he didn't have much experience either, so for the trip to Sunderland he asked me to play up front. It was true that I'd recently topped a century of goals, but at this stage of my career I wasn't going to be much use as an out-and-out striker. Everything about that game at Roker Park smelt wrong and it was no shock when we lost 3-0.

I felt that the club had betrayed both the players and the fans. They'd sold Hales and let Flanagan, Powell and even Abrahams go before the end of the season, without securing our place in the division. We were going into the final game, away to Orient, needing a draw to stay up. But we had no strength or experience up front and unless something exceptional happened we were never going to score, especially away from home.

The fixture had already been abandoned at half-time earlier in the season due to a waterlogged pitch. It was scheduled for the Tuesday, but the heavens opened again and it was postponed for a further 24 hours. Orient were also in relegation trouble, but this last-game survival battle was one I'd endured all too often and I was deeply frustrated to find myself taking part in it again.

I remember one incident, involving Bill Roffey, a strong, ginger-haired attacking full-back. We played an offside late in the game, our back four had pushed up and Roffey made a run across our midfield, which I had the chance to pick up. In that split second I had to decide whether to try to track him or let him go offside and hope that the flag went up. If it didn't, he would be through on goal. I chose to go with him and just managed to get a touch on the ball as he went to shoot. It went off for a corner and we survived. There were other chances in the game, of course, but for me this one was crucial, because if I hadn't got there we could well have gone down.

Afterwards we cracked open the champagne in the dressing room, but I still felt the whole episode had been wrong. I'd bounced back on many occasions with Charlton, but I don't think I could have faced going down to the Third Division again at the age of 33.

Whatever the financial rewards, it can't have been a sensible decision to risk releasing players, especially when you looked at the final table. Seven clubs were lined up on 38 points above Blackpool, who ended up as the unlucky side in the third relegation place. Every result went against them for that to happen and their players were on holiday when they heard the news. They'd been promotion contenders before Christmas, but going down destroyed the club and they haven't recovered yet. It could so easily have been us. We weren't looking after our own interests. This feeling was reinforced when we finished the following season with a similar crisis, only surviving on the final day due to results elsewhere.

If the decision to let the players go to America had nearly been a disaster for Charlton, it was the making of Flanagan, who was the star of the North American Soccer League that summer. He was voted Most Valuable Player and could probably have enjoyed a very lucrative career had he continued with New England.

Another interesting development that summer was the return of Hales from West Ham. Nelson had always seen Derek as the key man, despite Flanagan having taken over as the number-one goalscorer in his absence. But the prospect of an amicable reunion between the two was removed when Flanagan was quoted in the press criticising the decision. I don't think it was really anything other than a throwaway remark, but it rankled with Hales.

After the newspaper story appeared Nelson did ask me if I thought there would be any problems, but I assumed that when it came to the crunch they would just get on with their jobs. They had never been bosom buddies, but I'd never seen any ill-feeling beyond the normal kind of rivalry you get between goalscorers. Once they were together in training the relationship seemed OK.

The two played together in the first seven matches of the season, then Hales picked up a serious injury and wasn't able to resume until the end of December. By January, when we met non-League Maidstone United in the FA Cup at The Valley, the furthest thing from the other players' minds was the idea that anything was amiss between the two strikers.

In fairness to Flan, he was the only one on the Charlton side that night who looked any kind of a player. Glen Coupland had put the visitors in front early on and we were abysmal. When I came on just after the hour we were still trailing and it wasn't until the 77th minute that Flan put us level. It all went off five minutes from time when Mike went through. I made a run one side, Derek made a run on the other and really Flan should have put one of us in to score. Instead, he used us both as decoys and then tried to slip Derek through, but the latter was now offside.

Words were exchanged between Hales and Flanagan about the fact that he hadn't passed earlier and the two moved towards each other. They went head to head and Hales threw the first punch. He wasn't the kind of guy to wait and see what the other fellow would do. Blows were exchanged. It looked dramatic, with Derek's fiery temperament exploding to the surface, but it isn't unknown for two players on the same team to square up to one another. What did make it unusual was that it happened during a match. These things go on in the dressing room and on the training pitch, but they are quickly forgotten.

Andy very wisely sent Derek to the dressing-room and kept Mike in the dugout. Knowing Derek, I'm sure he would probably have been willing to take his punishment and forget the whole thing. That was the way he was. Flan, on the other hand, appeared indignant. He had been hit first and had come off worse. He had a nasty cut under his eye. Mike felt that he was the innocent party and probably couldn't understand why he was being punished at all.

The situation was further complicated by Hales' reinstatement, after which Flanagan refused to report for training. Mike now felt let down on two counts. He had a three-year agreement to play for New England that was in jeopardy because Charlton wanted more money to reflect his rapidly rising value as a player. He now had perfect justification to look for a move and capitalise on the success that he'd had in the NASL the previous summer.

Initially, Nelson had lost both strikers, but his objective had to be to keep one of them. From a business point of view that was bound to be Hales. Maybe he was the manager's preference anyway. As PFA representative I spoke to them both on the phone. Hales was the more communicative. Flanagan was immovable and determined to go his own way.

None of this helped our plight. Just as in the previous season, we'd lost our senior strikers. Flanagan had 16 goals up to then. The only one scoring now was Martin Robinson, who grabbed the vital brace on the last day of the season against Oldham.

Nelson's credibility with the supporters had taken a battering and it crumbled completely when he accused some of them of being "village idiots" during a television interview. As soon as I saw it, I knew that he had made a noose for his own neck and that the fans wouldn't easily forgive him for the remark. This wasn't an approach you could sensibly use on the paying customers.

The manager's lack of subtlety had recently been demonstrated to me more directly when we played at Wrexham on April 2nd. I was included in the party to travel but then left out of the team. For once there was an explanation, as he called me over before the game and told me: "Your little legs have gone, sir."

This didn't exactly make me feel six-foot tall! He chose not to expand on his point. As far as Andy was concerned, my legs had gone and that was it. We all know that we can't go on forever, but that was a bit drastic for me to say the least. He had already agreed that at the end of this season, I would finally be able to go to the States, so with his consent I was talking to the Tampa Bay Rowdies and the Columbus Magic. The plan was that I would go out after the final game and return just after the start of the following season. This was by way of recognition for my long service.

We had a better understanding by this stage, so I didn't take his comments to heart. After that Wrexham game I received a phone call from Paul Taylor, the new head coach at Columbus. Gordon Jago – whom I'd played alongside in the reserves back in 1961/62 – had wanted me to join him in Tampa as a player, but he hadn't been able to make me a firm offer, so I agreed to go to Columbus as player-coach. They were the lesser team, but Paul was willing to make the commitment and I wasn't prepared to wait any longer.

Despite the apparent doubts about my legs, I returned to the side a fortnight later for a 4-1 home defeat by Stoke and played in a 1-0 defeat at Crystal Palace, before what was to be my final Charlton appearance in the goalless Valley draw against West Ham United. My old teammate Billy Bonds landed on my shoulder and put me out of the final two matches.

Then out of the blue Nelson informed me that as he wouldn't be using me next season he'd be willing to pay up my contract. He'd made an offer I had to take up. I had nothing to lose financially and I didn't want to be hanging around in the reserves. The one personal ambition I had left was to overhaul Sam Bartram's overall appearance record. I'd passed John Hewie the previous season, but at 591 appearances I was still 32 games short of the great goalkeeper, so that didn't look likely now.

We agreed a settlement, but Nelson delayed handing over the cheque. He kept stalling, until eventually I was told I could collect it from the secretary's office after the final game of the season. It was all very strange. Even more bizarre was his insistence that there was to be no publicity surrounding my departure. No farewells – nothing. All became clear as I turned up at The Valley on the last day. Fans were handing out badges reading "Nelson out, Peacock in", as part of the on-going protest about the manager. Now I understood.

It is still one of my deepest regrets that after 17 years I was deprived of the opportunity to say goodbye to the supporters or even to write an article in the local paper. I walked across the pitch and signed a few autographs for the fans, looking around me and knowing that it was for the last time. We won the game, stayed up, and I flew off the following day.

I'd been captain of the side, had just been voted Player of the Year for a second season running and had appeared in nearly 600 games, yet my long and deep association with Charlton had come to an untidy and unsatisfactory end. Or so it seemed.

Chapter Eight
THE AMERICAN DREAM

Columbus, Ohio, was a new franchise, as the Americans termed their clubs, in the 46-year-old American Soccer League, one step down from the top level of the North American Soccer League. Tampa or California would have been more glamorous destinations than the mid-west, but we looked upon it not only as a new experience but also as a great family adventure. Gavin, who was now 11, and Lauren, almost nine, were taken out of school and preparations were soon underway to make the trip, which was expected to last four and half months.

We lived in a three-bedroom house on a neat complex. The climate was considerably warmer than England and the change of surroundings after so long in the routine of the domestic game gave me a renewed spring in my step from the very beginning.

I was the final pre-season signing and became player-assistant coach to Paul Taylor, against whom I'd played when he was with Sheffield Wednesday and York City, but never really got to know. He had retired early from the English game through injury and gone out to California to play and coach, before taking up his new position with the Columbus Magic.

I didn't get off to the best start in the world with my new club, where my arrival had attracted a lot of media interest. The cameras were set up to do interviews for the local television stations on the second day of training, but in the final session I pulled a calf muscle and had to be carried off. It was a light-hearted work-out and because we had a few pranksters in the squad, particularly a six-foot-five Argentinian centre-half, my first thought was that someone had thrown a golf ball at the back of my leg. Happily, I only missed one game in the two and a half weeks I was out with the injury and was still able to coach in that time.

Our home pitch was made from Astroturf, which was still a

novelty back home. This was in the days before Queens Park Rangers experimented with a similar surface in England. But the climate in Ohio was such that you could suddenly have a tremendous downpour an hour before kick-off, which would necessitate the use of machines to clear away the water so that the match could go ahead. In general the facilities were good. The average crowd was about 5,000 and the seating was set further back from the pitch than I was used to in England.

The majority of the team were British players who hadn't made the old First Division, such as Phil Hubbard, Ron Wigg and Mike Barry. Paul had picked up a number of free transfers, who were sold to the public as big stars. Many players came out and settled, never to return. The lifestyle was far more luxurious than they would have had in Britain.

Due to the distances between the clubs we flew everywhere, and we were very well looked after. The players and support staff would arrive kitted out in powder-blue T-shirts and slacks, providing the kind of club identity that has now become more usual here.

In spite of all the new experiences that our stay in America entailed, the main change for me was that of my role. Although I was still playing, I was now on the other side of the fence and working closely with Paul Taylor.

My first game was in Cleveland, Ohio, and billed as a local derby. They also played on Astroturf so I had my ankles well strapped up, but after ten minutes I landed quite awkwardly and I was in a considerable degree of pain. After my injury in training there was no way that I could come off, so I just had to battle on, but Astroturf is that much harder on the joints than a normal pitch and it was tough. To make matters worse, the game went to overtime. We won it in the last few minutes, but I can still remember the awful throbbing in my ankle. We arrived home about 2am and Lesley sat up the whole night with me and an ice bucket.

The standard of play was patchy. The players from continental Europe and South America, in particular, had great ability and were exciting to watch, but there were a number of Americans learning the trade, who were short on know-how. Their presence was important. The whole point of getting these leagues going was to develop local talent and create interest. I found certain things quite easy, but at times it was frustrating to be working with some players who generally were not on my wavelength.

The Magic team was full of characters, but none greater than

Daniel Mamana, the Argentinian centre-half. A striking-looking fellow with long, black hair, it was impossible for him to pass through an airport lounge without being surrounded by a group of women. Off the field, he was a charming personality. During matches, it was a different story. He had great skills, but lacked pace. He would do drag-backs and play one-twos on the edge of his own penalty area that had Paul tearing his hair out.

There was also a sinister side to his game that I have never encountered before or since. He would bring opponents down and then pretend to help them up with one hand while poking them in the eye with the thumb on his other hand. The first time I saw this I thought it was an accident, but of course it was a ploy. The opponent's eye would come up all red and sometimes his vision would be blurred. He would at least be in discomfort and unable to concentrate on his game.

We went to play in New York and Daniel did it again – chopped the fellow down, poked him in the eye and collected a yellow card for his trouble. This time the injured party swung a punch at him, but he merely backed away and the New York striker was sent off for retaliation. Daniel Mamana had won his battle and we went on to win the game 2-1.

Another thing he did on one occasion was to carry a safety pin in his shorts, which he stuck in the backside of one of the opposition strikers at a set play. Once again there was a reaction, but he acted innocent and again an opponent was sent off. I was engrossed in the game and didn't know what had happened until afterwards.

He had tricks I'd never even dreamed existed and these were just a couple of them. After the US season, he would go out to play in China, where he was idolised.

On a more constructive level, we would also do a certain amount of coaching around the local schools. Although that was something that we had done in England during the school term, this was in the holidays with huge numbers of kids in attendance, much as happens now at Charlton with the community scheme. The youngsters would be given T-shirts and posters and we were all involved in that, to the extent of putting together the goodie bags at home. The players had a really superb attitude towards these visits and were more than happy to take part.

About three months into the season, we flew out to play the Las Vegas Seagulls. I found that city fascinating. We stayed in the Riviera Hotel and it was a challenge to keep control over the players with the level of nightlife going on around them. We had a midnight curfew, which Paul enforced strictly. He was sure that he was going to catch Mamana out, but the only ones who were absent were three young American lads, who hadn't previously put a foot wrong all summer. They had travelled everywhere but not really been involved other than sitting on the bench or coming on for the odd five minutes as substitutes. They'd become frustrated and couldn't see why they shouldn't enjoy what Las Vegas had to offer, which they obviously did. Their punishment was a heavy fine, but they said it was worth it!

We won the match. The temperature in the stadium reached 116 degrees fahrenheit, the hottest I'd ever experienced. I was exhausted afterwards, although it didn't stop me going out to see the great Dean Martin. Later than night I was playing blackjack when actor Nick Nolte sat down. We both lost a few dollars in the early hours of the following day. I could tell from his blasé attitude that he didn't realise he was sitting next to the Football League's first-ever substitute.

From Vegas, it was off to Los Angeles to link up with Lesley, Gavin and Lauren for a few weeks' break. Disneyland, Hollywood and Beverly Hills were waiting. Training at Charlton was now a distant memory.

We did well enough to reach the final of the play-offs, but a match in California towards the end of the season gave me food for thought. A ball came out in front of goal, I read the situation and I should have got there to score the winner, but instead I ended up having to go into a full-blooded tackle. People remarked that I'd been unlucky not to score, but I knew that in the past I would have always got there. Maybe it was a sign that now was the time to hang up my boots. It was the first time I'd had any thought of retiring.

Of course, it wasn't unreasonable to be feeling tired. I'd played more or less continuously from the previous summer. But somehow it didn't seem like that, because life out there was exciting and the whole experience was like one long holiday.

We went on to play the Sacramento Gold in the ASL championship game. Their manager was an Englishman called Bill Williams, who was known as a bit of a joker. Before the final there was a dinner attended by both teams at which each of the managers said a few words. Bill presented Paul with a box of Kleenex for our players to wipe away their tears after the game. Unfortunately, the prediction proved right, as we lost 1-0. Bill would come back into my life a few years later, as general manager of Maidstone United, after managing the Kent team himself for some time.

It had been useful experience for me at Columbus. I had formed a good working relationship, as well as a special friendship, with Paul Taylor. He would subsequently be with me for a number of years back in England. It was also my first taste of being more than a member of the playing side. But home and an uncertain future now beckoned.

The school term was about to begin back in Bexley, so Lesley and the children had to leave for England about ten days before the end of the season, which meant they missed the final. Lauren went to Pelham Primary, in Bexleyheath, and Gavin was due to start at Bexley Grammar School, in Welling. I saw them off at the airport, and Lesley joked as we parted: "Now make sure you come back. You won't just stay out here, will you? I don't want to find the next time we speak you're in California or Florida!"

Those last words turned out to be prophetic. Just before the final I again got a call from Gordon Jago, head coach at Tampa Bay. He wanted me to be his assistant with the Rowdies for the following season. The complication was that for the first time they were going to be involved in an indoor championship from November onwards, so I wouldn't have the luxury of being able to spend the winter in England.

I packed my bags and flew down to Tampa, where I was picked up at the airport by Jago himself and put up in the plush Bay Harbor Hotel, which had spectacular views of palm trees, the swimming pool and the beach. These days British people generally have seen more of the world, but this was still my first visit to the States and Florida made quite an impression. No doubt that was Gordon's intention. He didn't want me as a player, but strictly in a coaching role. He liked to keep the two aspects completely separate. He showed me around the 80,000 all-seater stadium, which had dressing rooms big enough to accommodate a small five-a-side game. I was hooked.

The set-up there was similar to that at Charlton now. There was the stadium, where we played our matches and would train very occasionally, the training ground at the South Florida University, and then the offices downtown. It was much like our split between The Valley, Sparrows Lane and Bexleyheath. But back then everything at Charlton was more or less based at The

Valley, so this was a new concept to me.

The prospect was instantly attractive and I was now 95 per cent sure that this was the time to hang up my boots. I could have gone back to England and played, but a few things had happened with Columbus to make me realise that I didn't want to drop into the lower levels of the Football League. It was commonplace then for players to spend a few years moving down the divisions or even as a part-timer at the end of their careers.

I promised Gordon that I would give him a definite answer in a week or ten days. I needed a detailed discussion with Lesley, who by now had received the predicted phone call from Florida.

I flew back to England thinking that maybe this was the right time to finish, but received a message to say that George Petchey wanted to speak to me at Millwall. I went to see him more out of courtesy than anything else. I knew that he'd always liked me as a player and had tried to sign me at Orient. However, I couldn't really see myself fitting in down at The Den, especially as they had just been relegated to the Third Division.

Players did switch between the two clubs, including the likes of Eamonn Dunphy and Harry Cripps, Phil Warman and Lawrie Madden, but after 17 years at Charlton I don't think my heart would really have been in it. With the Tampa offer on the table, it was really going to take something special to keep me in England.

Lesley and I saw the invitation to go to Florida as a real opportunity, but this time it was a two-year contract and that would mean being away from our parents and other relatives for a long time. We consoled ourselves that they could come and stay for a two or three-month period, as indeed Lesley's parents did.

It was a major upheaval, but we made the decision to go ahead and everything was wrapped up in the space of five weeks. We let out the house at Barnehurst, where we now lived, to a Japanese couple with four children. The father worked for the Japanese embassy. We left on November 5th, 1979, after an emotional farewell as friends and family gathered at my sister's house the night before. It is only in recent years that I have appreciated how my parents must have feared deep in their hearts that we would end up settling in Florida. This, of course, was never our intention.

For the first month, the Bay Harbor Hotel was to be our home. One thing that I'd omitted to make clear to Gordon was about our dog, Candy. He had the impression that she was a lapdog of some kind, not an 80-pound boxer. Candy was seven by then, and we didn't feel we could leave her behind for two years. Accordingly, she was crated and put on the plane. When we arrived at the hotel there was a bit of a panic as the manager wasn't comfortable with the idea of a large canine guest. It was eventually agreed that she could stay on condition she didn't bark. This wasn't something that was easy to explain to her. Fortunately, she was a very obedient dog with a wonderful nature and we got away with it. Candy enjoyed life in the hotel. She ate plenty of extra meals that had been left unfinished outside bedroom doors and in the end became quite a celebrity.

A lot of people told me that taking Gavin abroad wasn't a sensible thing to do just as he was making an impact as a young footballer. Most boys of his age were starting to link up with professional clubs and there was fierce competition for places, whereas the standard wasn't as high in the US. That didn't concern me, as I had my own views about the coaching of young boys. Our main worry was about the children's general schooling. However, we decided that this was going to be part of their education and hoped they would adapt.

Children of professional footballers can suffer from the fact that their father has to move around in his career. However, the huge benefit is that you have the opportunity to spend so much time with your children as they are growing up. As a player I'd be home in the afternoons and able to share time with them when they came back from school or during the holidays, which was so important.

We put the kids in a private school where Gavin was able to play soccer, as they call it. One of the oddities was that although both children belonged to the same school, Lauren's junior section and Gavin's high school were about 12 miles apart. It made things a bit hectic in the mornings. There was no public transport, so Lesley would drive them both ways – a 68-mile round trip – each day. Eventually, they began to take the school bus, which took the pressure off.

Gordon was the complete opposite to Andy Nelson in his outlook. Where Andy had deliberately kept everyone down in terms of encouragement, Gordon threw praise around generously. He was totally positive in everything he did. It was a welcome and refreshing change for me.

In Tampa I was an absolute nobody, and I was dealing with some of the top South African players, like Steve Wegerle, Mike Connell and Neil Roberts. Mostly these were men who had reached international squads or had played in B internationals and were now in the last four or five years of their career. It was an immediate challenge for me to try to win their respect, especially as the reputation of English coaches generally was at a low ebb. Our football was known for plenty of running and hard work. I'd never played higher than the English Second Division and had no international background, so I was starting from scratch.

We had a Haitian centre-half, Arsene Auguste, who put leeches on an injury, something which was ridiculed at the time but I believe has now come back into fashion in some quarters. It was also the first time I got to know John Gorman.

Things were more difficult on the home front. Coming up to Christmas we had been away for five or six weeks and Lesley was feeling homesick. By then we had bought a new four-bedroom house and had a pool put in. The children had started school, but whereas Gavin had been flying at Bexley Grammar he now had to start again and would be the last choice when they were picking sides for American football or basketball. He too was feeling the call of home.

Eventually my name became known as assistant manager of the Rowdies and that kind of role carried a higher profile than it would have had back in England at the time. In fact, it was probably beneficial to Gavin in the long term that he wasn't instantly known as a footballer's son. He had to make his own way. My daughter had adapted the best, but inevitably she was influenced by her mother and brother being unhappy, so there were a lot of tears flowing.

I felt terrible pangs of guilt at seeing Lesley and the kids so unhappy, and I was also missing my parents enormously. A Christmas family get-together in Barnehurst seemed very appealing.

At that stage we could either have cut our losses, jumped on a plane and gone back to the environment that we knew or I could insist that I'd signed the contract and was going to see it through. We sat down to discuss the situation and after much soul-searching it was agreed that we'd all knuckle down and see out the contract.

Soon afterwards, Lesley's family came out for a while and we began to make new friends and settle more into the way of life. The kids began to make their mark at school. Gavin became the star player in the soccer team and was doing very well academically. Lauren was extremely popular with everyone at school and became firm friends with a number of girls with whom she is still in contact to this day. On the domestic scene, things were looking up.

We won the NASL's indoor championship that winter and I

learned a lot from Gordon, working with players of such outstanding ability. What was so good about Tampa was that we had a mix of Yugoslavs, British, South African and South Americans, so when we hit it off we were terrific to watch. When it didn't quite go right we had a few misunderstandings. If the South Americans weren't getting the ball to feet there was no way they would make an aerial challenge. Now and again if a British full-back hit a bread-and-butter ball forward it wouldn't be pursued with the required effort. That was the cultural difference, but it made for exciting football.

I also learned a lot about promoting the game. The Rowdies went out of their way to court each and every one of the fans. When you went back to the office in the afternoon they would have a whole organisation devoted just to that. For example, we might have the Tulsa Roughnecks, the New York Cosmos and the California Surf as our next three home games, only one of which would be a major draw. They would box it up as a three-ticket package. There was always something, whether it was free admission for grandmothers, Kids for a Dollar Day, Valentine's Day specials or whatever. They did all they could to get people through the turnstiles.

The media were accommodated to a much greater extent than they are even now in England, where the press are sometimes seen as the enemy. We would do things like set up staged bits of play in training for the benefit of television companies who wanted to focus on a particular player. It was a million miles from the way Charlton had operated. The clubs were very conscious of the need to sell soccer to the public, and the media were viewed as a key way of doing that. What was missing was any football heritage and the opportunity to reminisce about days gone by. That is a strong source of loyalty and appeal in the English game. The other major US sports had this, but soccer didn't.

Masses of money was going into the sport and there were genuine stars in the league. George Best was playing for the San Jose Earthquakes and one incident in which he was involved nearly got out of hand. It was midway through the second half on a really hot day and a few tackles were flying in. We had a Graeme Souness-type midfielder called Jan van de Veen, who was a Dutch B international. The referee, who was from the Irish Republic, was one of those who kept putting his whistle to his lips and then letting the incident go. One tackle led to another and it was one of those situations where you knew that whoever made the next challenge was going to get booked. Of course, it was Best, who had brought down Van de Veen, and he turned round to the referee and yelled: "Yeah, that's the right colour for you – yellow!"

Whether there was a bit of Irish sectarianism going on I don't know, but the referee responded: "Oh, you don't like that colour, George? Well, how's this one, then?" and proceeded to show him the red card. George turned and went to go for the official. Fortunately, Billy Foulkes, the ex-Manchester United star and survivor of the Munich air crash who was their coach, managed to grab him and pull him away.

Best was an immense talent, but the New York Cosmos were the team to beat. They had men like Franz Beckenbauer, Carlos Alberto and Johan Neeskens, who were only just past their best and still fantastic players. We also came up against the Washington Diplomats, and they had Johan Cruyff, who was still like a greyhound. I couldn't believe how quick he was.

The first time I had seen Cruyff had been in the initial pre-season. Teams from elsewhere would come down to Tampa in February to take advantage of the weather. There would still be snow on the ground in many northern states at that time of year. Gordon would send me over to watch these exhibition games, which were played in a college-type set-up. I would sit on the bleachers in 90-degree heat.

One day I was watching a match between the Tulsa Roughnecks and the Washington Diplomats and noticed that one of the Tulsa defenders kept trying to kick Cruyff up in the air, which I thought was outrageous. As the game went on I realised that this defender looked familiar. He was a thickset man, obviously getting on a bit. After a while, Cruyff came off and soon afterwards the other fellow followed suit, so I moved down the bleachers to get a closer look. It was Alan Dugdale, who'd been at Charlton with me for the last couple of seasons.

It had become a bit of a standing joke that Duggy had had to carry his birth certificate around when he was playing youth football. He had a big hairy chest and always looked older than his years. In fact, he was only 27 and had recently been released by Charlton after failing to make a full recovery from a broken leg. So there I was, thousands of miles from The Valley, in a country where few people would know who I was and I ran straight into Duggy, trying to kick the fabled Johan Cruyff.

It was thrilling for me to see the top players first hand and witness their great skills. Teofilio Cubillas and Gerd Muller were at

Fort Lauderdale. Peter Beardsley came out to play for Vancouver Whitecaps. He was an unknown at the time, and you could see that he might be a star in the making, but he didn't wipe us out in the way that the Mexican Hugo Sanchez did. I didn't see Pele while I was in America. He was no longer playing, but Gavin went to a soccer school that he visited, which was a big moment for my son. Pele had a very big hand in establishing the game in the States.

One innovation that the Americans had made was to introduce a 35-yard offside line, which spread the game out and allowed the midfielders room to play. It made for more goals and a much better spectacle. In England at the time the play was getting increasingly condensed. Sometimes you could look out from the stand and virtually all the outfield players would be within 15 yards of the halfway line, but that wasn't possible under this system.

The following year they scrapped the 35-yard line in order to fit in with FIFA regulations and found that around the country the crowds were booing the games, regardless of the result. English offside tactics were creeping in and the play was constantly interrupted. In the end, the Americans had to reintroduce the rule. Their view was that if the fans wanted it then it had to stay. As a football nation they were a law unto themselves, so nobody could stop them. That separation is also what's prevented them achieving much at international level until relatively recently. I don't favour tinkering with the rules very often, but I still think the game would be enhanced with offside limited to that 35-yard zone.

I was fortunate in the timing of my American adventure because optimism and enthusiasm about the game there was still very high. A lot of money had been invested and players were well looked after, but the clubs were making losses.

If basketball, American football and baseball were ever outlawed in the States, the youngsters who are good athletes would suddenly come into football and some amazing players would emerge. The range of different cultural influences would see to that. High degrees of fitness and powerful physique would enable them to compete at the top level. They are so agile and lithe that if they were brought up with the game you would get giant athletes with a real feel for the ball. As it is, youngsters are grabbed by the other major sports as soon as they show any talent.

Once we went to play the New York Cosmos and were drawing 1-1, when our goalkeeper Winston DuBose injured his shoulder badly. We had a rookie called Kevin Clinton on the bench. He was a bundle of nerves and way, way short of what was required. Gordon had to make a decision whether to risk him and he decided to stick with what he had. We lost 4-1 and the kid might have stopped a couple of the goals. Who knows? What it taught me was that whenever you have a fully fit deputy then it's always preferable to use him rather than someone who may be a better player but is only half-fit. I've always followed that rule throughout my coaching career.

That afternoon sticks in my mind. There were 70,000 people present and it was the first time that I saw replays on the big screen during a match, which meant that the crowd would roar for the goal and then cheer again as they saw the replay. Cosmos had a player called Giorgio Chinaglia, who had started in this country at Swansea City. He then went to Italy and on to New York. He was their top goalscorer in the league for years and such an awesome finisher.

Eddie Firmani had been manager there in 1977 and 1978, steering them to consecutive championships, but he was sacked early in 1979 and had eventually taken over at the Philadelphia Fury, who switched their franchise to Montreal. He'd also been in charge of the Rowdies back in 1975, when they won the NASL.

He had a lot of friends down in Florida and we used to go and ski at a lake where we were constantly reminded that Eddie's thumb had been left behind. We would hold on to a rubber ring while being towed along by a speed boat. It was an exhilarating experience. Apparently Eddie had got his thumb caught up in the rope and it had been severed. The lake was in bayou land and there was a standing invitation to the Rowdies to come along and use it. We'd take a few drinks, some people would go fishing all day, others jet-skiing or water-skiing. As you arrived, you'd more often than not see the owner, Frank Marcheseni, tending the barbecue and his wife lying in her hammock. Frank was an avid Rowdies supporter, with a heart of gold. He derived equal enjoyment from watching soccer and entertaining the Rowdies.

After Charlton, being a part of the American game was like going to Hollywood. It was larger than life and studded with big names, albeit in the twilight years of their careers. Everything was first class. Before a game we would congregate at midday for a pre-match meal, which would conclude with a teamtalk and the side being announced. Then everyone would go home and come together again two hours before kick-off. Here you had excellent warm-up facilities and the build-up was more prolonged.

Even though we were experiencing this more glamorous side of the game, there was an extent to which it was a little bit surreal. I was still aware that there is nothing like doing it in your own backyard. I knew deep down inside that where football really counted was back home in England, or maybe in one of the other big European nations.

In June 1980 I was in Houston, Texas, when I got a call from Mike Bailey, who asked me to become his assistant at The Valley. Then Michael Gliksten came on the line: "Come on home," he said. "It's a Mickey Mouse operation out there."

After two years of narrow escapes, Charlton had finally succumbed to relegation that spring, just as they had gone down at the third time of asking in 1972. Bailey had initially been appointed to assist Andy Nelson, but at the end of a turbulent season amid much confusion over who was really in charge, Nelson had finally gone.

I felt a tremendous tug, but the timing was wrong. I was now eight months into my contract at Tampa and the family and I had overcome all the teething problems. I also felt that Gordon had given me my chance. It would have meant abandoning my plan to spend two years out there, which I knew would allow me to accumulate enough knowledge and develop fully as a coach before going back.

I'm sure that Mike and I would have made a very good partnership. Defensively he knew what it was all about, as his record would suggest, whereas I enjoyed finding ways to break down the opposition. The only time we did get together was years later with the veterans, when I was manager and he was skipper. We are also different types of personality, which might have worked well together.

The only thing I didn't like was Gliksten's condescending attitude, which was almost dismissive of what I was doing in America and implied that I was at his beck and call. Apparently, he thought that if he clicked his fingers I would come running back. I decided to stick to the original plan, but it could have been a mistake because I wasn't to know at that time whether I would be offered any job back in England when the American episode was over, never mind a position at The Valley. Little was I to know that the role would be offered to me again two decades later.

My family had now settled into an easy way of life and we

were all enjoying ourselves. The Rowdies had won the NASL six-a-side indoor championship and I'd been heavily involved in that. Indoor football was my game, so I was still dying to get out there and could have done a job. In fact I did play in one game, when we had an injury crisis. We were up against the Atlanta Chiefs, who now had ex-Sacramento Gold boss Bill Williams as their head coach.

At this stage Gavin was acting as what's known as a "runner", both at the main games and at the indoor matches. Runners were a couple of young boys who would do errands for the teams. In this case, he was based in the opposition dressing room. Williams was saying: "Peacock – he's getting on a bit. Just kick him." Gavin made some excuse to get across to our dressing room and warn me. We did get beaten that day, which was the only time I played in the green and gold of Tampa Bay. I also got a few whacks for my trouble. Thanks a lot, Bill!

The Americans had the indoor game well organised and heavily marketed. There was always a great atmosphere. It was non-stop action, fast and skilful, and particularly good for the television, because it was played in four quarters of 15 minutes to accommodate the commercials. It suited some players more than others and a few unusual methods had to be introduced into training to get everyone comfortable with using the boards. Most of the games took part in ice-hockey arenas, which generally held 10-18,000 people. Ours was at the lower end of that scale and it was pretty much at capacity most of the time.

One night I turned on the television to watch a game involving the Tulsa Roughnecks and the announcer was just explaining how the team was a man down. Inevitably it was Dugdale, who'd just been sent to the sin-bin. "Some things never change," I thought, smiling inwardly.

By the spring of 1981 my thoughts were turning towards what my future would hold when my contract at Tampa expired. I felt I was ready to become a manager and as it happened I did have one opportunity to test my prowess in that role. Gordon had an ear infection at the time and I had to take charge for the home game against the San Diego Sockers.

The visitors brought along an extra man. These days we are used to seeing people in all kinds of costumes at matches in England, but then it was unknown. If mascots Harvey and Floyd had walked out with the team in the early 1980s, the Charlton fans wouldn't have known what was going on. But when the Sockers came to town, "The Famous San Diego Chicken" came too. He would go among the crowd and roll around, but before kick-off he would be on the pitch messing about, going up to their star players and bowing at their feet, much to the amusement of the fans. On this occasion, the chicken even pulled off a few flapping saves behind the goal after shots had gone wide. He'd also act upset if his team conceded a goal, banging his beak against the goalpost.

It was very strange to English eyes, but it was all good fun with no harm done. By all accounts he was a very highly paid chicken. He certainly earned more than I did. We won the game 3-2 and within a short space of time all the cameras and reporters came into the dressing room to get their quotes. I said my piece and was then astonished to find that next in line for interview was the chicken. Of course he couldn't speak, so he just made gestures. It rather put in context my first press conference as a manager. At least the Peacock never played second fiddle to the chicken. That would have been fowl play!

My contract was due to expire in September 1981, so at that point I knew I would have to make a decision about my future. In any event it was pre-empted by Ted Buxton, our chief scout, who would work in England all season and then come over to America in the summer. He informed me that Gillingham were looking for a manager and suggested that they would be an excellent club at which to cut my teeth. Ted knew the chairman, Dr Clifford Grossmark, and had been talking to him in the boardroom at the end of the season about the vacancy. He urged me to call the Kent outfit to indicate my interest.

I wasn't very comfortable with this idea. Throughout my career people had come to me to offer contracts and jobs. I'd never had to ask for either. Eventually I phoned Dr Grossmark, who was an old-style chairman, and enquired about the vacancy.

"You're in Tampa, are you?" he said. "What time is out there? Must be tea-time. But I suppose the Americans don't really have tea, do they?! Hold on a minute."

In the background I could hear a cheer. He was evidently watching a cricket match. After more small talk, he wound the conversation up very politely and rang off, having talked about everything but the job. I put the phone down and cringed: "That was the worst thing I've ever done," I said to Lesley. "He's got no interest in having me there judging by that conversation."

I put the incident out of my mind, but a week later I received a phone call from the Gillingham secretary, Richard Dennison, to say that the chairman would like me to come across for an interview. It was a long way to go if I was unsuccessful.

I flew back and the next day was taken by the television commentator and Gillingham board member Brian Moore to see Dr Grossmark. We had a general chat, but of course he already knew about my long service at Charlton. He was a man who admired steadiness and consistency. He gave me a three-year contract and a new era had started.

Chapter Nine
MAN OF KENT

The moment you meet your squad for the first time is when you truly become the manager of a club. The appointment process and the publicity counts for nothing then, because inevitably you will be judged by how the players perform for you on the field. You are suddenly on your own. You know as you stand there before them whether this is the role that you want for yourself. I never had any doubts when I arrived at Gillingham. I had completed two years as an assistant manager, at Columbus and Tampa, and I felt I was ready to take charge myself.

My intention was to manage with a smile on my face, but at the same time I had certain beliefs about the right way to do things and was determined not to be shaken from them. I have always believed in fostering an atmosphere of hard work, but no one can concentrate all the time. I told the players that there would be periods of relaxation in training, but when they were working they would be expected to show their commitment. My office door would always be open, but they could expect me to react if they crossed the line in terms of discipline and punctuality. It was just then that Pat Walker came into the room.

I was simply astounded. Footballers aren't exactly required to start their working day early by most standards. With a new manager due to meet the team for the first time, the last thing I expected was one of the players to arrive late. He did apologise, but I thought to myself that he would have to be an outstanding player to be able to get away with that on my first day.

Everyone's life is organised around time to some extent, but this is particularly true in football because of the team environment. Everything in a footballer's life is geared to being in a certain place at a certain time and if you can't get that right then you are bound to be heading for trouble. I didn't harbour a grudge over the incident and Pat turned out to be a nice enough fellow. He'd reached a reasonable standard in the reserves, but was never going to be quite good enough to establish himself in the first team. Within a few months, he had indeed left the club.

Youth coach Bill Collins was one of the few people remaining from the previous regime, so I asked him to give me a written rundown on the squad. He was particularly enthusiastic about one 20-year-old central defender, who he claimed was magnificent in the air and would tackle anything that moved. In fact, so glowing was the tribute that I wondered what such a player was doing at Gillingham. I hadn't heard the name Steve Bruce before and entered the dressing room for the first time expecting to see a six-foot-three colossus. I was disappointed, but only because he didn't look as special as he indeed turned out to be.

Overall, the step up to management and the step down from the glitz and glamour of Tampa to the more humble surroundings of the English Third Division had been relatively smooth. Gordon Jago was fine about my premature return. He was aware that the investors in the league were starting to draw back and that the situation wasn't as rosy as it had been, so even he was thinking about retiring. The Rowdies gave me a surprise going-away party, presented me with a silver tray and I said my farewells to players and staff who had become such good friends during this marvellous experience.

I took up my new appointment on July 19th, which by coincidence was 19 years to the day I had signed my first contract at Charlton. Once again I had waved Lesley farewell at the airport, but this time it was me who was flying back to Gatwick. She was left to sell the house, all our furniture and the cars, not to mention bring back the two children and the dog safe and sound. I felt at this stage that it was only right and proper to write off the £300 she still owed me for her return voyage from Australia!

We were saying goodbye to a bright land where we'd had a good social and outdoor life, but England was where we had always intended to be in the long term. Fortunately, the rental contract for our house at Barnehurst expired at the end of the month, and after a few days staying with my mum and dad just down the road, I was able to return home. I was soon reunited with the rest of my family, although the unfortunate Candy had to suffer the indignity of spending six months in quarantine.

As it happened, I started at Priestfield just a month after a change of managership at The Valley. Mike Bailey had walked out on Michael Gliksten to succeed Alan Mullery at Brighton and Mullery, in turn, was soon installed at Charlton as Bailey's replacement. This time there was no phone call to me.

Brian Moore had no doubt been instrumental in my appointment at Priestfield, and he was very helpful to me with several words of advice in the early stages. He was a lovely man and a perfect gentleman. I know that Lawrie McMenemy, the Southampton manager, had also spoken to the chairman and given me a glowing reference. I'd been a thorn in his side as a player towards the end of my career and I'm sure that had made an impression on him.

Gillingham had spent a couple of seasons narrowly escaping relegation and there was an atmosphere of doom and gloom around the place. The board had already opened negotiations with Charlton to take Dick Tydeman back to Priestfield. Dick said to me before he signed that there would be no hard feelings if I wanted to back out. I didn't, because I was more than happy to have him in my team. Although a fairly quiet character, he was a presence for the good on the field and in the dressing room.

Dick has a great sense of humour and we would laugh about that fact that despite being six-foot-one he very rarely headed the ball. In fact, Andy Nelson had used him as a decoy at set-pieces, knowing that he had to be picked up at the near post because of his height. In the early days, the opposition didn't realise there was very little chance that he would do anything in the air. He was always a great help to me at Priestfield but was unable to produce the form he would have expected of himself and of course Old Father Time was beginning to catch up with those long legs.

The good thing about the Charlton situation from my point of view was that Mullery was having a clear-out, which gave me the opportunity to get Paddy Powell as well as Dick for a combined fee of £42,000. Paddy was a first-class crosser of the ball. I had players in the side like Steve Bruce and Dean White who were great in the air, but to capitalise on their aerial talents going forward I needed someone who could flight the ball effectively. It's a highly specialised art, which perhaps isn't always appreciated by the layman, but I knew the value of it because it had also been part of my trade.

I recognised that Paddy's mobility was now limited and that he wouldn't be the most effective player going to some of the more difficult away venues, but he could still produce the single cross or free-kick that would win a game. Other players would have to compensate for the things that he could no longer do, and in an unsung way he became very important to us.

I also picked up another of my former Charlton teammates, Richie Bowman, who was now at Reading, for £25,000 via a transfer tribunal. For the short time we had Richie, he was our engine-room. He brought an effervescence to the side and the crowd loved him. He'd had four or five great years at Reading and made Charlton look a bit foolish for having let him go at the age of 22.

Unfortunately, he injured his knee in a Cup game against Barking after going up for a header in extra-time. He leapt so high that he must have been above the bar, which is amazing considering he is only five-foot-six. He connected with the ball, but it went over and he landed badly. It finished his career and in the process we lost someone who was very valuable to us. It was such a tragedy for the dynamic midfielder and it was heartbreaking watching him work so hard in the gym to make a comeback that was doomed to fail.

I had a slight disadvantage in that I was setting out on my first job and had been off the scene for two years. On the other hand, I had that instant advantage common to all newly arrived bosses in that the players are bound to see your appointment as a fresh start for them as well. I joined the club with an open mind. The club's record signing, Trevor Lee, who had come from Colchester United only six months earlier, needed to show me what he could do just as much as the most junior members of the squad.

Another new recruit was John Sitton, who brought us some aggression – and on occasion a bit too much. He was one of those players who would give you absolutely everything. After one home match in which he was sent off, I made a point of showing the squad the video and playing back the offending tackle several times. It was over the top and could have ended the other player's career. I announced there and then that I was fining John for letting the team down. To his credit, he took the punishment on the chin in front of everybody. I've always felt that if you don't make your position regarding reckless challenges absolutely clear then you can have no real complaint if your own star player gets injured in similar circumstances. John was a real professional. If he did do something wrong, he always took the punishment like a man.

During bad weather we would train about 10 miles away, at Hoo, on the Isle of Grain. This was the venue for the best training-ground fight I have seen. We were having a full practice match, in which John Sitton was up against our centre-forward Ken Price. Price wasn't the greatest player, but he was fearless and would put his head in where it hurts. His touch wasn't perfect and at times he was too aggressive for his own good, but what he lacked in ability he made up with sheer endeavour. He was the type who might miss the simplest chance but then score from an impossible angle.

Something went off between Sitton and Price. Normally these things are handbags at ten paces, but this was a serious physical confrontation between two tough guys. It took three or four players to pull them apart. Dick Tydeman quickly provided some humour to relieve the situation, asking: "Could we have a quick fag, boss? That was a little too exciting for Paddy and me!"

Although dying to laugh at the two jokers pretending to be nervous wrecks, I couldn't let it be seen that I had taken no action over the incident. Sooner or later it would have happened again. I summoned the protagonists individually the next day and said: "I understand how these things come about and that tempers have been lost, but you disrupted my session so I'm fining the pair of you."

It was a hefty punishment, probably half their wages for the week, but it needed to hurt if it was to have any impact on their future behaviour. They weren't the sort of guys who would respond to long speeches. Both accepted the decision and moved on. The fine was paid and the matter was closed.

I conducted my disciplinary process in that way so the players knew that if they crossed the line they would always be penalised. The outcome was that I had few problems, despite having some fiery characters in the squad.

There was another incident with Ken Price after we lost 3-0 at Southend, which brought to an end a good run of results. It all went off between him and one of their players, Alan Moody, who ended up with a cut under his eye. Moody claimed that he had been head-butted after the game and took the matter to the FA. I called Ken in and he was adamant: "Boss, I never touched him."

I told him I would defend him as best I could, but that I had to know exactly what had happened. He remained insistent that Moody had made the allegation up. They'd had a few clashes in the game, but nothing untoward had happened afterwards. He looked me straight in the eye as he said it.

Determined to see justice done, I then spent a considerable amount of time preparing his case and gathering witnesses, including Southend's Dave Cusack, who gave evidence on Ken's behalf. I was every bit the lawyer as I went to the FA to present it, tearing holes in the other side's witness reports by working out angles and distances to demonstrate that they could not have seen what they claimed. Ken got off and I was pleased as punch with the case I had made for him. I believed he was innocent and now he had been vindicated. Some time later I was told by other sources at the club that he had been guilty all along. And there I'd been thinking I was the new Perry Mason. Now I wasn't so sure!

Nevertheless, character and reliability were important considerations for me in selecting a side, as they had been even when I was picking a five-a-side team in my latter years at Charlton. There had been a period of three or four months when I was never on the losing side and the lesson had not been lost on me. Such qualities were very much in my mind as I started my managerial career.

In terms of man-management, I wanted to be as approachable as Theo Foley had been. He was someone you could talk to as a coach and about your role in the game as an individual. Of my other managers at Charlton, Frank Hill and Bob Stokoe had been too remote from me in age, while the fact that Eddie Firmani was a local legend had always coloured my dealings with him and maybe does even now.

Andy Nelson had a big effect on me in terms of certain principles he had used to get out of the division that Gillingham were now in. I'd come to respect his knowledge, but Nelson put a barrier between himself and the players. I was fortunate in that I'd then worked under Gordon Jago, who would make a point of lavishing praise on a player and making him feel like a million dollars.

Although in the early days I didn't enjoy playing under Nelson, it was definitely true to say that when you went out on the field you knew exactly what he required. This wasn't the case under the other managers and I was clear that it was necessary. Equally, I wanted to give the players the licence to respond to particular situations and to play with the freedom of spirit and flamboyance that Jago had engendered. Foley, Firmani, Nelson and Jago had all left their mark on me as I started out, but ultimately I had to be true to my own ideas and I had the self-confidence to do that.

Of course, it was crucial to have reliable staff around me to provide advice and support. I appointed Ted Buxton as my chief scout, while in a reversal of what had happened two years earlier, I brought Paul Taylor back from the USA to be my right-hand man. He was a down-to-earth character, a sound coach with a good eye for a player and again was someone I was in a position to know and trust.

It is essential to have the right blend of people on your management team. If you haven't got staff around you who can be relied upon to support you when your back is turned then you are heading for a fall. I had learned at Columbus – and even more so at Tampa – that if you are not a strong character as a coach or assistant then you can be swayed by the attraction of being popular with the players rather than helping your boss. It's all too easy to say everything the players want to hear, perhaps to the detriment of the manager. You have to be willing to give them time and attention, but in the end you must support the manager. It's vital to let the player voice his opinion, and ultimately to know just what to take on board. It's a fine line and you must never betray the player's trust.

Dave Bassett was the first manager I encountered who was able to make things work without establishing that distance. I've seen him arguing with his assistant in front of the players at half-time and talk to the players like mates, which astounded me. That was his style, it worked for him and he became a very successful manager, but it could never be my way. I liked there to be a bit of banter, but it could only go so far.

My Gillingham players undoubtedly had a moan about me from time to time, but I'd like to think that they would say that overall I was honest with them, even if we disagreed on something. I maintained that you could always handle things in a fair way. For example, I would afford the senior players the respect of telling them personally, and in advance, if they were going to be dropped. It wasn't always the same with the youngsters. They could come in to the office and have the conversation about it if they liked, but I felt it was a part of their education to learn that they could be in or out from week to week. They had to earn the right to that extra personal attention.

We trained hard, but I tried to show the players that I wasn't asking anything of them that I wasn't prepared to do myself. Not everyone could head the ball well and not everyone could tackle, but they could all run and I ran with them, especially during the serious fitness work in pre-season. I may have lost my sharpness but not my stamina and I enjoyed playing in our small-sided games, where I could still show them a thing or two. Even so, I was never tempted to make a comeback. I had no inner frustrations and didn't want the complication of competing for a place in my own team.

In those early months I made sufficient impact on a side that had just escaped relegation the previous season to win the divisional manager of the month award in November. Unfortunately, we picked up a lot of injuries and went into a steep decline, dropping as low as 15th before picking up 13 points from the last five games to climb back up to a respectable sixth-place finish.

Even if we hadn't picked up the injuries, I didn't think we were quite good enough up front to win promotion. I had found the man who was to change all that, however. It was Pete Woollard, my brother-in-law, who first alerted me to a 19-year-old called Tony Cascarino. I was sceptical, because he was playing in the Kent League, which was several divisions below the professional game, but I sent Ted Buxton along to Crockenhill to take a look. His report was favourable, so I watched Cascarino myself in a league representative match at Chatham.

He only played half the game, but he glanced a few headers and showed a decent touch. The difficulty was knowing how he would look in more elevated company. Ted saw him again and still thought he was worth pursuing. I then arranged for him to play in a training game at Hoo. He turned up wearing flip-flops, looking as if he'd just come off the beach.

Nothing much was happening in the game until Paddy went down the right and floated in a cross. Steve Bruce shaped to defend against it and keeper Ron Hillyard came out too, but Cascarino went up and smashed everything and everyone into the back of the net. I turned to look at Paul Taylor and said one word: "Enough."

I was aware that one or two other clubs had belatedly started to show an interest in him, so I dashed him back to Priestfield and offered him a deal on £90 a week. I wasn't going to let him out of the office until he signed, but just as he was about to put pen to paper he paused.

"There's just one thing I need to tell you," he said. "I've got a court case coming up at the end of the season for GBH. It happened a couple of years ago, though."

"Who are you supposed to have hit?"

"A copper."

With the opportunity to become a professional footballer on the table, most people would have signed the contract first and revealed the pending court case later, so all credit to Cas. I wasn't a manager who wanted too many unusual characters around the club, but at the same time you also need variety to provide balance to the blend. He told me the story and I gave him the benefit of the doubt, which as it turned out was exactly the right decision. At the end of the season I went to court as a character witness and he was found not guilty.

Cascarino was a raw talent and for a big man he was unusually willing to run. It was remarkable that such a striker could have reached that age without being picked up by a professional club, but I had seen enough to take a chance on him. He made his debut in a 1-0 defeat at Burnley. He didn't have a great game, but there was enough in what he did do to convince me that he would prove a good signing.

Some of the lads took the rise out of him when I first brought him into training, only because his touch wasn't that great by professional standards. Although the banter wasn't meant to be unfriendly, I could see that his lack of natural control affected his confidence. He had a big heart. I had to ask one or two of the senior players to make sure that they encouraged him instead of giving him stick. In time he would have to compete with the big, tough centre halves who were about in that division, in a way that other players couldn't, and he would get the team goals. Unlike a lot of big strikers, he could run into the channels, making him very difficult to play against.

One or two of the directors were also a bit sceptical, even though I'd only paid Crockenhill a set of tracksuits for his services, which is an illustration of how tight money was at the club. I'd lost a big part of my initial budget on Richie Bowman, who was so badly injured in our Cup run. To me the FA Cup was the glamorous part of the season and a run could be a money-spinner for a club like Gillingham. In fact, we did have a good run, eventually going out to a last-minute goal against West Bromwich Albion, who had quite a team at the time.

I remarked to the chairman after the Burnley game that Cascarino would become the best header of the ball the club had ever seen, with the single exception of Steve Bruce, and so it proved. His touch and control were to improve as each season passed.

I tended not to praise my players too highly in public, not wanting to attract the attention of predatory rival managers. If I'd shouted from the rooftops that Bruce was the best centre-half in the lower divisions then I would have increased the chances of someone coming in for him and I was worried how I could replace him if they did. In retrospect, however, I feel that if

I had been more generous it could have been to the benefit of the players. Instead, I always praised them as a team. I very seldom criticised them, except behind closed doors, either in my office or at a team meeting.

In the first year I had a winger called Micky Adams, who many people felt wasn't going to make the grade. He was an honest sort of player, who had pace and a strong left foot, but lacked a trick or natural body swerve. My solution was to move him to left-back and with the play now in front of him he improved dramatically. Week after week he did consistently well in the reserves and Paul Taylor repeatedly told me that he was ready to step up. My problem was that the incumbent left-back, Andy Ford, was my captain. Leaving him out was a big decision and one that I had to get right. I held back a bit as a consequence, although once I made the change Adams was never going to come out of the side.

Micky was outstanding in the first five games that he played, but at the end of the sixth he came in and apologised to me: "I've dropped my standards," he said. "I promise that won't happen again if you keep me in the side."

In fact, we'd drawn 1-1 and he'd done all right. These days many players are loath to be self-critical. Very few will put their hands up and admit that they have had a poor game. It is easier to place the blame elsewhere.

Micky played 29 games in that first season and the following season he was an ever-present at left-back. While the change of position had allowed him to establish himself, it also attracted the attention of Bobby Gould, then manager of First Division Coventry City. He was one manager who had his finger on the pulse of the lower divisions. I was on holiday in Majorca with my family when the chairman phoned to say that they had received a £90,000 bid for Adams from Coventry. It was a huge sum for a full-back and they had to take it. Even so it was tough for me, striving to build a team to challenge for promotion.

I'd made the transition to management successfully in that first season. Dr Grossmark had asked me to get the team up to halfway and avoid a relegation struggle, so by finishing sixth I had exceeded expectations and he was delighted. In my second year we again got off to a reasonable start, but Steve Bruce broke his leg late in the season and after topping the table in October we had a dismal run in which we won only twice in 21 matches.

We ended up using 27 players during the 1982/83 campaign

and finished 13th. We would have been 12th and in the top half, but for the fact that Bradford City edged above us by scoring more goals. That was a particular disappointment. It was the only time in my managerial career that my team ended up in the bottom half of the table.

Cascarino became top goalscorer in his first full season – a terrific achievement – but it wasn't until March that I succeeded in finding a replacement for Richie Bowman. I had coached Dave Mehmet at Charlton when he was a schoolboy, but it was at Millwall that he served his apprenticeship. He came to the attention of Gordon Jago towards the end of the latter's time as manager at The Den. Jago had then taken him to Tampa with Tony Kinsella for a combined fee of £150,000 in March 1981, just a few months before I left for Gillingham. Ted Buxton had been very instrumental in the deal.

At the end of 1981 Mehmet also returned to England, Alan Mullery eventually signing him for Charlton for a fee of £80,000. However, he never settled at The Valley and little more than a year later I was able to pick him up on a free, despite interest from Brentford. I signed him on the Tuesday and he immediately took part in a training session ahead of an away game at Huddersfield. I said nothing to Mehmet, but when I announced the side he was in it. We lost the game, but I knew afterwards what an important player we had gained, and without paying as much as a signing-on fee.

Mehmet could play in midfield or up front, he was technically very sound and he brought quality to the side. He wasn't blessed with pace and he had a fiery streak, which had to be handled correctly. Nonetheless, he was an asset. However, the truth was that we still had some players in the squad that I didn't think were quite good enough if we wanted to progress. We were an average side.

I tried to improve the quality by signing Phil Walker on loan from Charlton, in a deal that taught me a useful lesson. We found it hard to get players from far away to come to Gillingham – the Medway towns were looked upon as a bit of a backwater – so we tended to look to The Valley or The Den for recruits, especially for those who came on short-term deals.

Walker had previously played with Trevor Lee at Millwall and was rated very highly by Ted Buxton, so I spoke at length to the player, but it was clear from the conversation that he felt he was better than Gillingham. I was so keen to have him that I gave him a sales pitch and convinced him to come anyway. I felt pleased with myself for a while, but as soon as I saw him in training I realised that his heart wasn't in the move. I played him once, but I couldn't put him in again. It was an error of judgement on my part and I let him return to Charlton early. After that experience I swore that I would never sign another player who felt that they were doing me a favour by coming. I would only sign people who wanted to be at the club.

My main task was to find someone to play up front with Cascarino, as Trevor Lee and Ken Price both left the club. But the big disappointment for me in the summer of 1982 had been my failure to land Kerry Dixon when he was out of contract at Reading. I had spoken to him and he'd agreed to come. If he had, and I had been able to play him alongside Cascarino, I am convinced we would have won promotion.

Dixon was 21 at the time and starting to score goals regularly in the Third Division, but it was not until the following season that he really became prolific. He was on about £120 a week at Reading and they had offered him around £180. I could go a bit above that. We just had to go to the tribunal to settle the fee. The chairman was more than a little doubtful, but I'd calculated that the tribunal would not have made us pay more than £40,000 and it would have been a great bit of business.

I was confident of my ability to judge players, but my inexperience probably showed in the fact that I didn't press my case strongly enough with the chairman. I was in a solid position on the back of that good first season in charge and that in itself gave me the licence to be more forceful, but I was all too conscious of how precarious Gillingham's finances were. They paid decent wages by the standards of the Third Division, but they had no lump sums to put on the table. Perhaps I was too understanding. Dr Grossmark declined to progress matters and then Reading manager Maurice Evans got Dixon to sign a new deal at Elm Park.

It was a major opportunity missed. Dixon scored 26 League goals that season and Chelsea paid £175,000 to take him to Stamford Bridge the following summer. Later on he gave Gillingham a big reminder of what we had missed out on when he scored four times against us for Chelsea in the League Cup.

I believe that we would have gained promotion with the addition of Dixon. With a really powerful strikeforce, it is possible to cover up deficiencies elsewhere. At the other extreme, you should always overload your squad with centre-halves. Goals are conceded from all over the place, but the majority will eventually come through the central area. This was brought home to me when I lost Steve Bruce to injury that year.

The man I eventually succeeded in signing to run on to Cascarino's flicks was Wimbledon's John Leslie, who had a good goalscoring record. I picked Leslie up for £10,000, but I knew within half an hour of seeing them in action together that it wasn't going to work. I liked Leslie. He had a great leap, scored goals and had a fantastic workrate. However, I ended up putting him on the right wing and using a centre-half, Mark Weatherly, up front, with another former Charlton man, Peter Shaw, at the back.

Weatherly had been a centre forward as a youngster. He was a manager's dream and would play in any position without complaint, but on paper a strike partnership with Cascarino, another big man, looked unlikely to work. It wasn't until I saw the two of them together that I realised Cascarino wasn't the target man that he appeared to be. What he needed was someone to hold up the ball for him, so that he could peal off and run on to the ball. This was proven again later when he went to Millwall to play alongside Teddy Sheringham.

The strategy also had the merit of confusing the opposition, who naturally assigned their bigger centre-half to mark Cascarino, as the taller striker. This defender expected to stay in the middle and compete for headers, but now he found himself being dragged into territory where he wasn't comfortable at all, leaving the smaller centre-half to mark our target man. This new striking balance worked well for us and we now started to get goals, finishing eighth in 1983/84 and scoring 74 times, our biggest tally since I had taken over.

The season was lit up by a fine FA Cup run. After beating Leamington Spa and Chelmsford, we found ourselves 3-1 down at home to Brentford, with only 11 minutes remaining. In one of the most astonishing comebacks I can remember, we then scored four times before the final whistle.

Our reward was a trip to Goodison Park to face a star-studded Everton side, including Neville Southall, Peter Reid, Kevin Sheedy and Andy Gray. We drew the first game 0-0 and our players were magnificent – none more so than Steve Bruce, who dominated the mighty Gray. Steve was the clear victor in a titanic battle. He won every vital header, every last-ditch tackle and blocked shots that would have folded a lesser man, showing calmness and skill on the ball when necessary. It was the complete performance for a centre-half.

We also drew the replay at Priesfield 0-0, with only Southall's legs saving Howard Kendall's team when Cascarino was through on goal in the last minute of extra-time. For me that was a turning point in Howard and Everton's fortunes. They won the second replay 3-0 and never looked back, winning the Cup that year and then taking the Football League championship in 1985 and 1987, as well as finishing runners-up in 1986.

During this period I would walk through the Medway towns glowing with pride at the way my team was performing. But I realised I could no longer keep Brucie, my valiant centre-half. He had asked to wait until the end of the season before discussing his expiring contract. I respected his decision and was to lose him at tribunal for £135,000. Norwich City were the beneficiaries and Steve was to lead them to glories that would previously have been beyond their wildest dreams. Steve Bruce was the best defender that I have ever worked with. His character was second to none.

The relationship between the manager and the chairman is a key one in most football clubs and, despite my disappointment over Kerry Dixon, I always got along with "the Doctor", as the chairman was known to everyone at Priestfield. This was more than an incidental title, since he was also the club doctor and would often be involved in the treatment of injuries, especially as we didn't have a qualified physiotherapist. He would come in each day to see if anyone needed his attention, so he was much more available than a traditional chairman like Michael Gliksten.

He was also able to give an instant diagnosis when I was sitting next to him in the stand during a game and he would then be in the dressing room assessing the injury after the match had finished. For example, he knew from the outset that Richie Bowman's injury was a threat to his career. This combination of roles was probably unique, especially in the modern game. With hindsight he was a terrific chairman for a young manager to work alongside in his first appointment.

As I had discerned from that first phone call, he was very much the gentleman and he ran an old-fashioned and well-respected club. He made sure that things were done in the correct way behind the scenes. In return he was regarded with great affection and was, I'm sure, one of the reasons that Brian Moore kept up his association with Gillingham. They both wanted things to be done professionally.

I would always join the Doctor in the boardroom after a match to discuss what had happened. What I especially liked about him was that if we had lost badly and I was feeling down, he would find something positive to say to give me a lift. It might be about the performance of an individual that I had brought into the side. Conversely, if we had done well and I bounced into the room, he might highlight something that could have gone wrong. It was not what you wanted to hear at the time, but by using this reverse psychology he made sure that you kept things in perspective.

He never really interfered in the way I did my job, but he would often manage to get his views across in a diplomatic way. He had an excellent knowledge of football, so if I was interested in a player he would either know about him already or he would go off and do some research. More often than not he would come up with some piece of quite obscure information gleaned through his involvement at committee level with the FA. He would use this to put a doubt in my mind if he didn't really want me to sign the man concerned for financial reasons. It appeared that he had mortgaged his house on several occasions over the years to keep Gillingham afloat or to buy new players. I respected his views, although perhaps my ambitions ran a little ahead of his.

Sadly, the Doctor died in November 1983, having been taken ill en route to a match at Walsall. His driver Jock turned back, but the chairman passed away on the A2 before they could complete the return journey. I was told just before kick-off by the vice-chairman Charlie Cox and it made the match seem quite insignificant. I told the players afterwards and the result meant nothing to us that day.

Charlie took over as chairman and initially I was uncertain how things would work out. He had been on the fund-raising side and had always been much more forceful in expressing his own views than the Doctor, who had acted as a moderating influence. Together they had been an effective combination. In fact, although Charlie remained his happy-go-lucky self, he proved to be pretty sensible when things weren't going well. Obviously, he had learnt from the way the Doctor had conducted proceedings.

After he had been chairman for about a year, we went to York City and lost 7-1. I'd never thought that a team of mine would lose by that margin. It was a wet afternoon and I remember the rain beating icily into my face as the game developed. We went 2-0 down and had a goal disallowed ourselves. It was an even game – then we simply fell apart. The pitch was ankle-deep in mud, which didn't suit us at all. It seemed that their striker Keith Walwyn scored every time he got possession.

We had travelled up by train, but our former youth coach Bill Collins, now doubling up as physio and kit man, drove us to and from King's Cross. Bill was never the best of drivers and on this occasion he was horrendous. I think he must have had a few extra whiskies on the train. By the time I got out at Barnehurst I was happy just to be alive, never mind what the result had been at York.

Charlie Cox had been lucky enough to miss the game through attending a dinner that evening, but when the phone rang at 11pm I was apprehensive. It was the first time that he had been under any pressure in terms of a bad result and I feared that it might bring out the other side in him. I braced myself for a heated discussion. What he actually wanted to tell me was that his hosts had rewritten the evening's menu to wind him up, including such offerings as Yorkshire Pudding, Seven-Up and Yorkie bars. He was being hammered.

Although he obviously wasn't happy with the result, I appreciated that this was his way of discussing it with me in a fairly light-hearted vein. After that I felt a lot more comfortable about our relationship. The defeat also spurred us on, and we won five of the next six games. I dropped one or two players and gave the team a tongue-lashing on the Monday morning. It evidently had the desired effect. We went to Burnley in midweek and won 1-0.

In general I rarely laid into the players. I was convinced that it had diminishing effect. If I did it only occasionally then it would have more impact. Players are also quick to spot if you go for the younger or weaker members of the team. The right time for a flare-up is when you are taking issue with the senior professionals.

A key altercation took place during my first season in charge. We were 1-0 up at Wimbledon when Steve Bruce got a bit sloppy and almost gave away the equaliser. He was a class above the level we were playing at and would sometimes take unnecessary chances. When they came in at half-time, I launched into Bruce. The teas were all lined up in front of me and as I spoke I smashed my fist down on the tray. The plastic cups jumped about two inches off the table, with tea splashing everywhere. I remember that even as I went on I was astonished that more or less all of them landed upright. The players were taken aback by my outburst. They had never heard me go berserk before, but they were all salt-of-the-earth individuals and took a rollicking on the chin. Bruce was no exception.

I did get it completely wrong on one occasion. The player

involved was Joe Hinnigan, who I picked up from Sunderland on a free transfer. He was as brave as can be, but I had to nurse him along a bit because he had a dodgy knee.

In this particular game, an opponent was put through close to the halfway line and Hinnigan played him offside, but the referee ruled otherwise and let him go on to score, which from my vantage point in the stand I thought had been the right decision. I gave Hinnigan a real earful at half-time: "You know that we never play offside," I yelled. "We always go with the man if there is the slightest doubt."

Joe replied: "I played him offside, boss. He was well off."

I wouldn't have any of it and, like the good professional he was, he let me have it my way. He was totally respectful of my authority. He started to argue and then thought better of it. It was wise of him to do so. I was always concerned that as there was only a brief period at half-time, we couldn't afford to spend any of it arguing. Decisions I made had to be accepted and if there was any discussion to be had then that had to be reserved for Monday morning.

We drew the match 1-1 and that night I picked up my usual takeaway and a couple of drinks and settled down to watch the game on video. I always liked to watch it again as early as possible so I could confirm what I had seen or change my mind about one or two things, but at any rate get it out of my system mentally. By 9.30 or 10pm after a Saturday home game I would more or less have decided what I was going to do in the next match. Usually, a player is physically tired after a game but mentally buzzing, so he often wants to go out and socialise. As a manager, I just wanted to retreat quietly home to my wife and family.

On this particular night I watched the video and discovered that the opposition player had been well offside. Hinnigan had done exactly the right thing, the linesman had been a bit too close to the action to make the correct judgement and the referee had got it completely wrong, as had I. I called Hinnigan over on the Monday and said: "First of all, Joe, you took my criticism on Saturday like the good pro you are, which I admire. Secondly, you did so knowing that you were right all along. I apologise."

It's only right that you hold up your hands and admit when you are wrong, otherwise the players will never respect you. I believed that handing out a rollicking was an important weapon in your armoury as a manager, but everyone is different. I've seen Jim Smith lose his rag quite a few times, chasing players into the

showers and ranting and raving at them. That is his way. He has
been a successful manager, and if it works for him then that's fine.
At the other extreme, England boss Sven-Goran Eriksson hardly
seems to break sweat. I'd had my own grounding in America and
was confident in these confrontational situations. On the whole, I
never had any real problem in the dressing room.

My aspirations to take Gillingham higher had continued to
build, but without much money to spend I had to decide whether it
was time to take a risk and bring in a more talented individual who
might also have a temperamental personality or buy a lesser
player that I could rely on to fit in well. I'd always preferred sound
characters. In 1983 I had the opportunity to sign Terry Cochrane, a
winger given a free transfer by Second Division Middlesbrough
after falling out with manager Malcolm Allison.

I believed he could become the George Best of the Third
Division and resurrect his Northern Ireland international career.
He played with his socks rolled down, and he could be petulant
at times. He would be a free transfer, but expected top wages by
our standards and also a signing-on fee. I gave him a run-out in a
friendly at Tooting & Mitcham.

Paddy Powell had found things tougher in the second season
at Gillingham and although he played 26 times I freed him to join
Dartford. He'd done well in his time at Priestfield, but unless the
side was absolutely flying he was now a luxury that I couldn't
afford. In practice, we were still an average team and I knew that
if things went against us we could have a relegation fight on our
hands. Now I'd lost the quality of Powell, I needed someone
special to replace him.

Cochrane was the man to provide it, but I knew that he would
be a high-maintenance player. He always wanted the ball and
complained when he didn't get it. I knew I could pick up less than
average players who would pull their socks up neatly and not moan
at their teammates, but I was conscious that if I didn't gamble and we
had a run of bad luck I would live to regret it. So I took the risk.

Terry was sensational. He could cross with either foot right on
the button, he could score a goal and he was a home and away
player, which sometimes isn't the case with wingers. He would do
things that were outrageous and quickly became the player that the
crowd came to watch. He also returned to the Northern Ireland side.

As I expected, I did have to spend extra time with him in the
office. He needed to be reassured about how good he was and it

was easy for me to convince him of that as I thought he was a truly outstanding talent. There was no question that the gamble paid off.

My attacking line was now full of goals. On the right was Leslie, who was really a striker. He would still score from the wing and would work like two men. In the middle was Cascarino, magnificent in the air and a prolific finisher. Cochrane, though principally a creator, would also get his share of goals on the left. I needed another striker, however, and thanks to Ted Buxton we were able to bring in another free transfer from Teesside.

Scotsman Dave Shearer was built like Paul Gascoigne, five-foot-nine and stocky with it. We knew he liked a drink, and when he arrived he was a stone and a half overweight. He had also managed to lose his bag en route, so he had nothing to his name. We put him up in a local hotel. He wasn't good in the air and he had no left foot, but he was altogether fearless. And if the ball dropped on his right foot, there was no way he would miss the target. Within the first few moments of seeing him in a five-a-side, Paul Taylor and I exchanged looks and we knew, without saying a word, that this could be the man for whom we had been searching. It was a truncated pitch, but I knew his touch, ability to score and bravery were things that wouldn't change whatever the environment. The question was whether or not we could get him into shape.

Initially I gave him a weekly contract, then a monthly one. He was just getting things together and had broken into the side when I got a phone call. Homesick and consoled by a glass or two of beer, he had borrowed Cochrane's car and turned it over as he used it to head for his home at Fort William in the Scottish Highlands.

I'd invested a lot of time in getting Shearer into shape. He was the nearest thing to Derek Hales that I'd had, so now there was a big decision to make. His problem was that he pushed his body as hard off the field as he did on it.

I'd lost Steve Bruce that summer and Micky Adams the year before and I could see parallels with what had happened at Charlton with Mike Bailey and Billy Bonds. We were selling our good young players and still advancing. If I was to maintain that momentum, I needed men like Shearer to stay. The board was adamant that he should be released. His monthly contract was coming to an end, so it would have been easy to let him go.

Unusually, I sought advice from another more experienced manager, Southampton's Lawrie McMenemy. He was a man who had shown a talent for handling troublesome characters. Lawrie backed up my true feelings and gave me the confidence to support Shearer. I told the board: "Shearer stays! He deserves a second chance." Although I never gave him as much as an inch for the rest of his time at Gillingham, deep down I just loved him to bits.

I also went back to Charlton in the October of that 1984/85 season to sign Martin Robinson for a £15,500 fee. I used him on the left, with Cochrane switching to the right instead of Leslie. Robbo did exceptionally well for us. He wasn't the most aggressive player, but he was quick and honest, and he scored goals from out wide. Things were looking good for us coming into March. Then Shearer picked up an injury.

Hales wasn't in the side at Charlton. He was now 33 and I felt that Shearer, at 26, was the longer-term solution. I spoke to Hales, but we couldn't agree terms, so I thought that was the end of it. Then I got a call from Charlie Cox to say that something had been sorted out. It was the first time that a deal had been done over my head.

I gave Derek a 15-month contract, but strangely enough it never really happened for him. We scored more than 100 goals that year. If Hales had been able to get us half a dozen more on the run-in then that would probably have been enough to get us over the line for automatic promotion and brought Second Division football for the first time in the club's history. Instead, we finished fourth, one place outside the promotion spots. Looking back, I was asking too much of Derek. He had not played a competitive game at Charlton for some time and had a couple of injuries, so he had needed to build up his sharpness at the time when we wanted him to be most effective. He held his end up well enough but sadly was unable to produce those vital extra goals.

Hales did score a few times the following season. Unfortunately, he also picked up more injuries. His game had developed over the years and he could now receive the ball and hold up play, in the style of Gerd Muller, but he wasn't quite able to finish in the same way as in his younger days. The combination of Hales and Cascarino wasn't ideal either. The way Cascarino played meant Hales had to be the target man. He did this well, but as a result he wasn't there to finish chances, which was his real forte.

His relationship with some of the Gillingham supporters also developed in an unexpected way. After one game in his second season at the club, Hales was physically attacked in the car park by a group of fans from the Rainham End. They had been giving him stick for a few weeks and when he came in on the following

Monday morning it was clear that he had been assaulted.

This was something that I had never come across before and I wasn't sure how to deal with it, but Derek just looked at me and assured me that it wouldn't be a problem. I don't know to this day what happened, but he was never barracked again. It says something about the kind of character he is that there was never any suggestion of him not continuing at Gillingham, which might have been the understandable reaction of many players.

He did his bit in the 1985/86 season and this time we came fifth, but with Hales, Shearer and Cochrane at the club one thing was for sure. We didn't have the quietest dressing room in the country.

Chapter Ten
A BLUE CHRISTMAS

By the summer of 1986, I had been at Gillingham for five years and had established my credentials as one of the more successful managers in the lower divisions. Leaving aside the relative disappointment of 1982/3, we had finished sixth, eighth, fourth and fifth, which at the time represented the most consistently successful period in the club's history. Considering that we also had to sell to survive, it was an achievement that we did so well. I could take pride in my financial record, as well as our performances on the field. I was happy at Gillingham and now felt we were increasingly capable of taking the next step, but in the meantime I had received one invitation to go elsewhere.

There had been further managerial changes at Charlton in 1982, with first Ken Craggs succeeding Alan Mullery and then Lennie Lawrence taking over a few months later. Lawrence became a fixture for the next nine years, meaning that as my own reputation rose there was never a vacancy at The Valley. I would probably have been a strong contender for the Charlton job in the late 1980s, but Lennie's success in restoring the club to the top division against all the odds and then keeping them there for four years on limited resources quite rightly ruled out any change.

When an offer did come, in the summer of 1984, it was from Tottenham Hotspur. Peter Shreeves had just taken over at White Hart Lane from Keith Burkinshaw. Peter had been on the coaching staff at Charlton under Theo Foley, so we were no strangers. He called and offered me the chance to go to Spurs as his assistant.

Tottenham had just won the UEFA Cup and had the likes of Glenn Hoddle and Ossie Ardiles playing for them. The prospect of working with that standard of playing squad and getting involved with European football was a big attraction. We met to discuss the offer and I was greatly tempted, even though financially I would have been no better off than I was at Gillingham. I thought about it, and the answer was no.

I think Peter had been sure that I would agree to join him and was surprised when I declined, but I had only ever seen being an assistant as a stepping stone. Once I had become my own man I could never see myself being anything different, despite the way things would turn out in the years to come. In fact, I wouldn't even have considered going back to Charlton as a number two at that stage if the offer had been made. I was intent on forging my own managerial career.

Gillingham weren't even aware that the Spurs offer had taken place. In the light of what happened subsequently at Priestfeld, I think I made the right decision in turning Tottenham down. In the summer of 1986, we were about to embark on the most exciting and rewarding season that I was to enjoy as a manager.

Before the campaign began there were several changes behind the scenes, and again Spurs were involved. Ted Buxton had the chance to go to Tottenham and I decided that instead of replacing him on the scouting side I would take the opportunity to bring in an extra coach. John Gorman was someone I'd played against many times and when I'd met him at Tampa I'd thought he would do well on the coaching side. He was out of the game at the time and had asked me to alert him to anything that came up. In the meantime, he was doing some painting and decorating in Phoenix.

Embarrassingly, as it turned out, the Orient manager Frank Clark had happened to mention to me that he was looking for a youth coach. I told him that he couldn't go wrong in employing John, who would be great with the kids, and Frank agreed to take up my recommendation. No sooner had I done this than Ted had the chance to go to Tottenham as chief scout, which put me in the position of having to go back to Frank and apologise for hijacking my own recommendation. So it was that Gorman came to Priestfield and cut his coaching teeth with me in the old Third Division.

There were also changes in the boardroom that year, with Roy Wood taking over as chairman, having come on to the board as a friend of Charlie Cox. At the same time, Brian Moore left, which with hindsight was an ominous sign. In fairness, the new regime didn't interfere with what I was doing the following season.

Initially, however, I did think that there were going to be difficulties over the signing of central defender Colin Greenall, from Blackpool. I'd originally replaced Steve Bruce with Keith

Oakes, whom I'd picked up from Newport County. He'd done a great job for me, but I knew that I needed to upgrade and fortunately I was able to sell him on to Fulham at a profit. The problem with Greenall was that the fee had to be decided by tribunal and the new board was hesitant.

On this occasion I did make a stand. I knew that if we didn't get another centre-half then we wouldn't be anywhere near the force we had been the previous year. In the end they did back me at the tribunal, where I was up against a lawyer-chairman who had all kinds of arguments as to why Greenall was worth £150-£200,000, when I was coming in with an offer of only £40,000. I was a trifle nervous, since I'd promised the board that the fee wouldn't be any more than that. I was well briefed and I had all the relevant arguments about his deal at Blackpool and what they had offered him. My summation was five minutes and my opponent's seemed to last about three quarters of an hour, but we got Greenall at my price.

Once again I knew within ten minutes of seeing him jump up and head a few balls in his first practice game at Priestfield that I had got myself a player. He wasn't another Steve Bruce, but he was better than I could have hoped or expected. Greenall would eventually be sold just after I left the club for £300,000, so apart from what he achieved on the field in the meantime, it was another financial coup for Gillingham.

For advice on this signing I had turned to ex-England full-back Jimmy Armfield, whose opinions I respected. He strongly recommended Colin. Jim was the best full-back I had ever faced, even though it was towards the end of his career when I came up against him at Blackpool in 1967/68. He did me no favours at Bloomfield Road, almost crushing my confidence as an up-and-coming Charlton winger, but he more than made up for it with this excellent recommendation.

The previous year at Gillingham we had scored in every home game. Now goals were not quite so plentiful, but we tightened up at the back. In my second season in charge there had been games when I'd had to go looking for a draw and set my tactics accordingly by playing an extra centre-half or wing-backs. We ploughed out a few results that way, and I had gone into the dressing room afterwards and congratulated the team, but I'd hated watching us. Those games were poor entertainment and I found no excitement in what we were doing.

I was very much aware of what was needed defensively, but there is no doubt my satisfaction came from forward play. Fortunately, Paul Taylor had been a defender, so he was able to bring particular insight to that area. It was a good combination, in terms of both our different characters and our different strengths.

Approaching Christmas 1986 we had been second in the table since the start of November, but Shearer was out injured and Hales, by now, had retired. I had agreed a £90,000 fee with the QPR manager Jim Smith for their striker Leroy Rosenior, having seen a lot of him in their reserves, where he was playing alongside Gavin. I had no doubt that Rosenior was the man who would get us up.

The worst possible thing happened, in that the board agreed to make the money available and then changed their minds. The problem was that before I could complete the deal we played Bristol Rovers at Priestfield on the Friday before the holiday and beat them 4-1. I had put Martin Robinson up front, which was something that I knew I could do for a game or two, although ultimately he would always have go back out wide. He did really well in the game, scoring one of the goals. Afterwards, the chairman said that he'd had a talk with the other directors and they had decided that the money wasn't there. They had been swayed by the result and Robinson's performance, mistakenly thinking that he could do the job for us instead and save the club a considerable sum of money.

That was the moment when I should have taken a leaf out of Kevin Keegan's book and stood my ground. We were doing well in the table yet again and I should have insisted that they had to come up with money. Instead, I accepted the knock-back and we lost the next home game, against Swindon. After that our results became erratic. There was too much pressure on Tony Cascarino. Shearer staged an abortive comeback, but he wasn't able to resume on a regular basis until March. The combination of the way he played and his lifestyle was beginning to catch up with him, and he was starting to lose his edge as a result.

We missed out on automatic promotion, but on the final day of the season we still had a chance to take the last available place in the play-offs. These had been introduced for the first time, making the last Second Division place the prize to be won in a knock-out competition. The format was crucially different from that which subsequently became familiar, because it also involved one team from the higher division, who would be trying to stave off relegation. This element only survived two years and just one club –

Charlton – were ever successful in defending their status. As the play-offs were eventually to be constituted, with four contenders from the same division, Gillingham would have qualified three times already.

In this case, we had to finish fifth. To do that we needed to get a better result at home to Bolton Wanderers than Bristol City managed at home to Swindon Town. The odds seemed to be against us. Swindon were already in the play-offs and couldn't take an automatic promotion place, so they had little to play for except local pride. Fortunately, that was enough and they came from behind at half-time to earn a draw, while we beat Bolton 1-0. For the first time since they had emerged from the Fourth Division 13 years earlier, Gillingham had something to celebrate and the fans spilled on to the pitch at the final whistle, with the players called out to salute them from the directors' box. It was most fitting that Cas scored the goal to take us into the play-offs.

As we had finished fifth, we had to take on the team from the higher division, which in this case was Sunderland. They were a massive club by our standards. We managed to beat them 3-2 at Priestfield in a real thriller, with Cascarino getting a hat-trick in front of nearly 14,000 people, but in the back of my mind I knew that away goals would count double if the scores were level at the end of the second match.

Just going to Roker Park was a momentous event for Gillingham, even though the odds now had to be stacked against us. Not for the first or last time, Sunderland were about to play a significant role in my career. It was where I had made my debut, in the area from which my family hailed, and now I was taking my own team there to play. To add one more touch of irony to the occasion, Sunderland were managed by my old boss Bob Stokoe, the man who as manager of Blackpool had taken such delight in seeing Charlton relegated from the same division with me in the side in 1972. Could I now turn the tables on him?

We stayed in the Roker Park Hotel and had a relaxed training session on the beach on the morning of the game, the pitch getting shorter and shorter as the tide came in. My dad had come up with Lesley, Gavin, and Lauren, so it was a true family occasion for me in front of a 25,000 crowd. As well as the fans who had made the trip from Kent, Gillingham also had the backing of about 1,000 Newcastle supporters, who were there to cheer for us. They wanted to see their old rivals go down.

The game was the most astonishing that I had yet been involved in. It was such a ding-dong affair that there was a point when we were genuinely struggling to work out the implications of the aggregate score, which was complicated by the away goals rule. We were 2-1 down at half-time and 3-2 down after 90 minutes, eventually losing 4-3 after extra-time. However, that meant the aggregate was 6-6 and because we had now scored more goals at Roker than Sunderland had managed at Priestfield, we had won.

Stokoe had only been appointed in April after the sacking of Lawrie McMenemy, with a brief to save Sunderland from relegation. It looked for a while as if he had succeeded. He jumped off the bench when they went into the lead at one point and gave me one of his mad looks, as if to say they had done it. We replied, but then they got a late equaliser and it looked as if we weren't going to pull it back, so he came bounding across. There was nothing personal in his behaviour, because we always got on fine. He just got carried away by the emotion.

"It's not over yet," I insisted, privately fearing that actually it was. An inspired Cascarino rescued us with an even later goal and Sunderland were faced with the shock of going down to the Third Division for the only time in their history.

It was an unforgettable triumph for Gillingham, for the fans, for the club and for me personally. I even took my dad back out on the field afterwards, although unlike many of the Newcastle fans his pleasure was in our achievement, rather than Sunderland's failure. His pride was in the fact that his son had managed a successful team and here he was standing on the pitch in a stadium that would have been one of the Meccas of his youth. I couldn't even look Lesley in the eye in the boardroom afterwards. I was too emotional and she knew how desperate I was for the Gills to succeed. We hadn't even won promotion, but after that rollercoaster game it seemed for a few hours that we were invincible.

The team we had to beat was Swindon, under Lou Macari, who we'd twice failed to defeat during the normal season, losing at Priestfield and drawing 1-1 at the County Ground in our penultimate game. They were favourites, as they had finished higher in the table by a margin of nine points. In those days the play-off final was over two legs, home and away. This time, however, away goals didn't count double, because there was scope for a replay.

We won the first leg at Priestfield 1-0 with a goal from Dave Smith, a winger I'd signed from Welling United, who smashed a

free-kick into the top corner of the net. When Karl Elsey gave us a
first-half lead at the County Ground, putting us 2-0 up on
aggregate, things looked to be working out in our favour.

Swindon played at 100 miles per hour and had two men up
front who were a real handful. One of them was Steve White, who
had previously been at Charlton. I had another ex-Valley man, Les
Berry, at the back, and he found White difficult to handle. I also
had Greenall, who had been a mainstay that season. He wasn't
quite six-foot tall and he was up against his brother-in-law, a
gangling six-foot-three striker called Dave Bamber. The taller man
was five years older than Greenall and somehow he seemed to
dominate him psychologically.

Swindon pulled a goal back. Just previous to that, however,
Elsey picked up an injury. Dave Smith was on the bench, but in this
situation he was the wrong man for the job. He had lightning pace
and was someone that could open the game up for us, but it was
sometimes risky to play him away from home. In trying to support
him we would become stretched as a team. I needed to tie up the
game by bringing on a midfielder or a defender. By the following
season I would have been allowed two substitutes. Now I had no
choice but to bring on Dave, who could only play one way.
Defending was not his strength.

The game now swung from end to end, and with 11 minutes
to go they got a second goal to level the aggregate score. Until that
injury to Elsey, I had felt that we were going to do it. It was tight,
yet at 2-0 up I believed we would make it. Things changed around
in that instant. Even the rules conspired against us, because we had
an away goal and they didn't. If it had been the semi-final and not
the final, we would have won.

Now there would be a replay at Selhurst Park, by this point
the venue for Charlton's home matches as well as Crystal Palace's,
and I was well aware that they would be fighting for their First
Division lives the same night against Leeds United at St Andrews.
If things had worked out differently, we would have been playing
each other the following season.

Even though success had been snatched away from us at the
County Ground, I was confident that we could win. This was our
63rd match of the season and it took place on a Friday night, May
29th, so it was well and truly an extended season. It was fantastic
to see all the Gillingham supporters in their blue and white in the
Holmesdale Road end at Selhurst. Unfortunately, Swindon got a

goal in each half and we could not find a reply. Their strikeforce had the edge over our central defensive pairing. The replay had proven one hurdle too many for us.

I was an attack-minded manager, but I chose to put Dave Smith on the bench that night, hoping to keep the game tight and bring him on in the second half. I did just that, but it was too late for him to rescue us. Maybe by making him substitute I sent out a signal that I was treating the replay as an away match. I wish I'd started him.

Afterwards the fans were still applauding the players long after they had disappeared down the tunnel, but the tears flowed in the dressing room and defeat was a bitter pill to swallow. We had the normal club function afterwards and overall it had been a brilliant year. Just to have got as far as we had was great for the Gills. Although we were gutted not to have made it in the end, at least we'd had something to cheer in the two-legged victory over Sunderland and then the three nail-biting games against Swindon.

It was June by the time I'd recovered from the play-off final replay and I had set aside a week to sort out loose ends before going on holiday. One rainy afternoon I went out for lunch with Roy Wood to discuss plans for next season. On returning to the ground we were told that there was a message for the chairman to call a Mr Cobbold. I found myself listening to one side of the conversation as the Ipswich Town chairman made a formal approach for permission to speak to me about the vacant manager's job at Portman Road.

Ipswich had become a successful club under the leadership of Bobby Robson from 1969 to 1982, and had spent 18 years in the First Division before dropping down the previous summer. They had just parted company with Robson's successor Bobby Ferguson after failing to regain their top-flight place at the first attempt, losing in the play-offs to Charlton. Roy Wood was realistic enough to understand that other clubs could come in for me, so he granted Ipswich permission to talk. However, the events that followed turned out to be bizarre. With hindsight, the way the Suffolk club conducted proceedings put me in an awkward position.

They shortlisted six people and allowed the details to become public knowledge. Steve Coppell, Lou Macari and John Duncan were among the other candidates. You could more or less pick out the names from the up-and-coming managers from the Second Division downwards. The interview of each prospective manager was being announced on Teletext each day.

Eventually, they phoned me to say that they had reduced the

field to Duncan and myself, but there was one director who hadn't been available the first time around and they wanted him to be present for a second interview. This was David Sheepshanks, who later became the Ipswich chairman.

It was almost as if I was being asked to take part in a second play-off final. I was emotionally and physically drained from the first one and just wanted to go away on holiday. Even so, I knew that in football you had to take your chances when they arose and it would have been foolhardy to let this one slip by.

I felt afterwards that I had been right to speak to them, but I should never have allowed them to use my interest in the job in the public way that they did. The whole episode dragged on too long, but eventually they rang to inform me of their decision to appoint Duncan. It had been very close and I had only narrowly missed out. It was a disappointment, but also a compliment to have been so carefully considered.

I don't know even now what had been going on behind the scenes during this time. Gillingham could have been asking for compensation, as I had two years of my contract to run. Personally, I felt Ipswich had made the wrong choice, but I was hardly an unbiased judge!

Wimbledon had also asked to speak to me and they were in the First Division, so that should have been more attractive still, but I had to be honest and say that I didn't fancy the job. My heart wasn't in going there to discuss it, but I felt that since they had made an approach they deserved that courtesy. Nothing materialised. Probably it was clear from the meeting that I wasn't really interested.

I told Lesley that whoever replaced Dave Bassett as the Dons' manager had no chance of succeeding. He would be unable to maintain the unique spirit and atmosphere that had got them where they were. The job wasn't offered to me and I've never had any regrets about that. They went for Bobby Gould and much to my surprise he did manage to keep the show on the road for several years to come. I doubt that I could have done as well.

I had been put in a tricky position. I didn't really want to leave Priestfield, but I knew that if I hadn't shown some interest in these offers I risked being labelled unambitious. I couldn't possibly have imagined at that juncture that I would be out of a job at Gillingham before the end of the year. Not only were bigger clubs interested in me, but my record to date was sound to say the least. The only cloud on the horizon was the fact that I was about to lose my two key strikers, which did impose a limit on my expectations for the new campaign.

I had kept Cascarino for a long as I could. If we had gone up he would have stayed, but he needed to step up a division. Millwall had already come in for him on the transfer deadline, only to back out after watching him play poorly in one match. They came back at the end of the season, so in the end I lost my top goalscorer.

Shearer was showing signs of being past his best and with this in mind I'd already brought Steve Lovell in from Millwall as his possible replacement.

I signed George Shipley, a hard-working midfielder, from Charlton, although it was a very protracted affair. A routine medical revealed a doubt about his knee. The doctors did all manner of tests on it, despite the fact that George was adamant that it had never been any problem. After a week of torment he was finally cleared to sign. He was a good buy, but eight games into the season he went over on his knee and never played for me again. He made several attempted comebacks, but the injury finished him in the end. The remarkable thing is that it wasn't the same knee that the doctors had been worried about.

Gary West came in at centre-half. However my priority was to replace Cascarino. I was finding it difficult, so I started the season with two smaller men up front, Shearer and Lovell. What I needed was a big man. I was phoning everyone, including Lennie Lawrence, who didn't have anyone available.

My hunt for a striker appeared somewhat unnecessary when we beat Southend 8-1 at Priestfield on the last Saturday of August. Two days later we drew 1-1 at Wigan Athletic. Our visitors the following weekend were Chesterfield and this put me in a quandary. What could I say to a team that had scored eight goals in their previous home game? Although they had struggled the previous season, Chesterfield were unbeaten so far and had taken ten points from their opening four Third Division games. They had yet to concede a goal. After the previous week, I would happily have settled for a 1-0 win.

I would sometimes vary my routine before a game to ensure the players didn't get bored. This particular afternoon I stayed in my office until 2.45pm. Then I strode into the dressing room without saying a word. Some of the players liked a bet, so I decided to set myself up as a bookmaker and wrote up on the tactics board the odds for each player to score, right the way from Shearer and Lovell at 6-1 down to Greenall at 25-1, with the goalkeeper at 6-1 against having a clean sheet. I was happy to pay out a few quid, but each player could only bet on themselves and the limit was a fiver, so I was sure any losses would be manageable. They all lumped on and Bill Collins held their money. There was no teamtalk whatsoever. I just marched out to the dugout, not knowing whether my actions had been bloody stupid or a touch of genius. I was about to find out.

What followed was the most unbelievable game. We won 10-0. The scoreline was phenomenal, because it wasn't as if we were playing a non-League team in the FA Cup. Our opponents were a very efficient professional side. We played some terrific stuff and the players simply rose to the challenge that I'd set them. Karl Elsey came over to the bench to rub it in that he'd won his bet after getting the fifth and as the goals continued to fly in they were all looking across to gauge my reaction.

It was 5-0 at half-time. I warned them not to get complacent. I'd seen that sort of situation before. The foot tends to come off the pedal and you often find that you struggle to win the second half. Either way, there wasn't much need for a teamtalk, so I sat in the dressing room for a while and then left to take my place on the bench, waiting for them to re-emerge.

I thought we'd win about 5-2, but with 21 minutes left we were 9-0 up. Then Greenall, my outsider to score, got the tenth with a header. There was still a fair bit of time left after that. As I was thinking how fantastic it was, I glanced across at their manager Kevin Randall on the opposition bench. It was the first time that I really felt sorry for my opponent. Usually, there's no time for sympathy in the dog-eat-dog world of football.

Lauren had won a mini-break in Bruges by coming first in a beauty contest and the tickets had to be used that weekend. We weren't scheduled to return until Monday evening, so for the first time ever I was due to miss training at the start of the week and I'd been hoping for a respectable result so that I could go with a clear conscience. I certainly got that, although the trip meant that I missed all the publicity that followed.

The chairman and some of the other directors had missed the Chesterfield game, but drawn their own conclusions. They must have thought the result meant we were now too good for the division. The board had only really tasted success since taking over. I knew that what had happened was freakish. I still needed that striker. Soon afterwards, Shipley got injured. Shearer's problems were also beginning to show, and I sold him to Bournemouth. He'd been magnificent for the Gills, the crowd loved him and he was undoubtedly one of the best strikers with whom I had worked. However, at £25,000 the deal was too good to turn down. The timing was right.

I should have replaced him with Archie Stephens, who was a striker with an established record in the lower divisions. The problem was that the directors knew that any sum spent on him would be dead money in two years' time. They preferred to buy 20-year-old Mark Cooper from Spurs for £100,000. He was a bigger gamble, but I knew he would do a certain job for me and that in view of his age I would probably be able to sell him on for three-quarters of the original fee, even if things didn't work out.

I had recently taken Gavin on loan from Queens Park Rangers, and now had the chance to buy him for £40,000. I persuaded the board that between him and Cooper the club would make a profit. I should have sold them on the idea that Gavin was the one for the future and Stephens would provide what we needed now.

I spoke to Lennie again soon after the 10-0 victory and we had a joke about me wanting a striker: "We wouldn't get 18 goals in 18 games," he said. "You haven't got an outstanding goalscorer there, so the statistics say that over the next two or three months you will hardly score at all. Things will even themselves out, because that's what always happens."

He was a great one for statistics. I discounted his comments at the time, but to some extent his prediction came true. We won five more games between then and Christmas. Our League position was sagging, even though we had reached the third round of the FA Cup. We drew 1-1 with Bristol City on Boxing Day, which meant we had won seven, drawn ten and lost six. We went into the next game at Aldershot two days later with a few injuries. I had to change one of the full-backs and we had a torrid time, trailing 5-0 at the break. We eventually lost 6-0.

Aldershot were a small club in that division and wouldn't have been expected to thrash us, so it was a hard result to take, especially as we dropped into the bottom half of the table for the first time that season. Everything that could go wrong that day did, but having had two such big wins earlier in the season it may be that we had been due such a disaster. It wasn't nice, but I hoped it would act as a kickstart for us in the same way that the 7-1 rout at York had in the past.

However, it was the first time that this group of directors had been faced with a defeat of any severity. Afterwards, Roy Wood said that he'd like to see me in the office at nine o'clock the following morning, but nothing more than that.

I told Lesley on the drive home that I had a feeling they were going to sack me. My head was telling me that they couldn't possibly do that. It didn't make any sense. However, that was my gut feeling. It would have been quite reasonable for them to call a council of war, even though we hadn't had a crisis in the six-and-a-half years that I had been in charge. But they had never encountered this kind of setback.

It was clear the minute I walked into the boardroom that my instincts had been right. The board was all present, each of them carefully studying the table and not one of them looked up. The chairman asked me what I had to say about the game, so I explained about the injuries. Without further ado, he announced: "Well, we've decided to call it a day."

I wasn't about to justify myself any further. I was on my way. Nothing has ever changed my opinion that the board acted impetuously. My dismissal was a knee-jerk reaction to one or two bad results, coupled with inexperience and naivety on their behalf, rather than part of any long-term plan. That the move wasn't premeditated was evident from their enthusiasm to sign Gavin only three weeks earlier and also the fact that they hadn't given any thought to the financial implications of my dismissal. I had 18 months of my contract outstanding and it took about a month to reach a settlement. The negotiations didn't drag on, compared with the experiences of some other managers in those days.

The directors came under a lot of pressure from the fans, both at Priestfield and in the local press. Usually when a manager is sacked, he either has lost the confidence of the home crowd or it will have turned on the board for not providing him with enough support. Some directors find that difficult to deal with. They will often have come into football on the back of being successful in walks of life where their mistakes rarely become a matter of public debate. When you have had a career in football you get used to criticism alongside the accolades, so you learn to cope with it much better. It isn't pleasant, but it is character-building.

None of this discontent had happened at Gillingham. We had reached the play-offs earlier that year and even in the current season we'd had those two sensational home wins. Indeed, I received more than a hundred letters from Gills supporters expressing sympathy and disgust at my dismissal, all of which I sincerely appreciated. They helped me through a difficult period and to this day I have retained a soft spot for the club's followers.

I returned to Priestfield to watch Gavin play against Birmingham City in the FA Cup third round. Afterwards in the car park I found myself hoisted up shoulder-high and carried back to the offices. This was an experience that I hadn't come across before in my career and I was both moved and flattered by the supporters' obvious loyalty – but it was as terrifying as it was gratifying. The directors were so shaken by this turn of events that they let it be known that I would be banned from the ground if I turned up again. I'm surprised they didn't accuse me of disturbing the peace.

I was touched by the supporters' reaction and with hindsight it probably unnerved the board rather more than the 6-0 defeat at Aldershot. They hadn't foreseen this unprecedented behaviour and to be honest neither had I. But there was no going back. For the first time since I had reported for duty at The Valley more than a quarter of a century earlier, I was officially out of work.

Chapter Eleven
ROLLING STONES

The first few weeks of 1988 were a time of welcome relaxation after the pressure of the previous six and a half years. As a manager I had found it hard to prevent the day-to-day affairs of the club preying on my mind even when I should have been enjoying my leisure time. Lesley and I are great film-lovers, but unless the movie was particularly gripping I would lose concentration and let my attention drift back to football. Now I was able to focus fully on everyday life, something I had almost forgotten how to do.

Together with the fans' concern, I received many phone calls and letters of sympathy and support from people in football, including George Graham and Jim Smith. But the first person to ring, within hours of the news being announced, was Terry Cochrane. I'll never forget that call. I found it quite overwhelming. People were extremely complimentary about my achievements at Gillingham. It is paramount to gain the respect of your peers whatever line of business you may be in.

Brian Moore rang and said that if the old board had still been in place they would have been looking to extend my contract and plan ahead, rather than asking me to clear my desk. But football isn't always fair or predictable in that way.

It wasn't too long before I got a call from Frank Sibley, who was on the coaching staff at Queens Park Rangers, to let me know that there was an opening at Loftus Road. Bobby Campbell had been taking their reserves, but he had moved to Chelsea, creating a vacancy. I still thought of myself as a manager in my own right and I wasn't under any immediate financial pressure to work, but when Jim Smith offered me the job I wanted to take it. I had been out of the game nearly two months and was beginning to miss the involvement. The decision I had to make was whether to work or wait for a manager's post to come up. I chose to work.

It was comical really. I was now based at QPR and Gavin was at Gillingham. Our employers had been reversed in a matter of weeks. Such is football.

Peter Shreeves was already installed as assistant to Jim, and Frank had done a couple of spells in the hotseat there himself, so with my arrival in March – initially until the end of the season – there were four experienced managers in charge of the playing side. It was an unusual situation to say the least.

Working with Jim was an education in itself. He is a great character, with keen instincts that he would use in remarkable ways. He was ever capable of changing a winning side at the last moment after spotting something in training, such as the way a particular player was moving or the confidence he was showing on the ball. And 90 per cent of the time these decisions paid dividends. Most coaches work within a fairly rigid formula and sometimes lose out as a result, because they won't take risks. He had sufficient faith in his own judgement to make those late calls.

My challenge in those first few weeks was to get accustomed to having less responsibility, and also to cope with being kicked by Mark Dennis. I was still only 43 and reasonably fit, so I quickly found myself joining in five-a-sides, which was also a good way of getting to know the players. Dennis introduced himself with an over-the-top challenge that left marks right down my shin. He saw nothing unusual about doing that to the reserve coach in training. He was an engaging personality and you couldn't help but like him. I also had the considerable consolation of bending a great shot into the top corner past David Seaman, who would go on to play for England for the first time the following year.

The main problem I had to combat in my new job was the tiresome journey from Barnehurst to the other side of London. Most days it took me about an hour and a half. Getting there was like a daily assault course, taking advantage of little bits of local knowledge and tips that Gavin had given me in order to gain no more than a few hundred yards at a time. Such was the frustration that I felt like jumping out of my car and punching the air when I finally arrived each day.

I'd really been very fortunate that this was the first time in my career that I'd had to travel any distance. It was 11 minutes to work at The Valley on a bad day and when I was driving to Gillingham I was always against the traffic, which was ideal. Even when I went scouting in those years, it was always possible to stop off at home to spend a few hours with my family. The travelling made me take a much more serious attitude to the issue of players making long journeys to training. It wasn't quite so bad for me as a coach. If I arrived tired I could cope, but you can't afford travel fatigue as a player or a manager.

My arrival did create one problem for Jim Smith. He had spent the previous year and a half trying not to call Gavin by my first name. No sooner had he mastered this than we had swapped clubs and now he found himself referring to me by my son's name.

For a while there was an enjoyable atmosphere at Loftus Road, but two things happened to change the set-up. The first was the sudden death in September that year of the chairman, David Bulstrode, at the age of 48. His successor, Richard Thompson, was only 24 and became the youngest chairman in the Football League.

Three months later, Jim Smith quite suddenly accepted the opportunity to manage Newcastle United. Given his experience as manager of Spurs, Peter Shreeves was the obvious choice to take over. He invited me to be his assistant.

As luck would have it, our first game was against Charlton, at Selhurst Park. For the first time I got a taste of what the Addicks fans had already had to endure for more than three years, watching their side play its home games on another club's ground. I hadn't come up against my old team at senior level since I had left ten years earlier, even in a friendly, but it didn't seem as if we were playing Charlton at all. There were none of the markers that would have told me I was going back to face the club where I had spent so much of my career.

Lennie Lawrence was still the manager, of course. I had met him for the first time in 1982. He had seemed strikingly self-assured for a man who had just started his first managerial job and I was quite taken aback by his manner, but over time I had realised that this was just how he projected himself. We often spoke on the phone about players and I had always found him upfront and helpful.

Mike Flanagan was on the coaching side, Derek Ufton was now on the board, and Steve Gritt provided one piece of continuity on the pitch by scoring Charlton's goal that day. Otherwise there were few obvious things to link this club with the one I had known. The game ended 1-1, but the result was overshadowed by a serious and extremely unfortunate injury to the young Charlton winger Micky Bennett. It was to hinder him in fulfilling his potential.

As it turned out Peter Shreeves and I were only in charge for two games, even though he had been told the job was his until the end of the campaign.

The previous season we had signed Trevor Francis from Glasgow Rangers. He was nearly 35 by this time. Always a great professional, he was still really sharp over ten to 15 yards and very dangerous in and around the box. It appeared that the young chairman quickly came to the conclusion that Francis was more in tune with his way of thinking than Peter. It soon became evident from the media that changes were afoot behind the scenes. At one point I had to go out and buy *The Sun* each day so that I could find out what was going on, which was a terrible indictment of the way things were being handled.

The situation was worse for Peter than for me, since I had always considered my position temporary, but he figured that until we were told otherwise we had better get on with the job in hand. Eventually, we were left in the invidious position of preparing the team for a game at Wimbledon, with everyone concerned knowing that Trevor was likely to take over afterwards. Nothing was said beforehand, nor could it be. Peter handled this with his customary aplomb, but afterwards when Francis was moaning how poorly the team had performed in the 1-0 win, Peter and I left the dressing room. It was then announced that Trevor would be taking over as manager. In the meantime, Wimbledon coach Don Howe had congratulated Peter on our excellent performance.

Fate had intervened to prevent Peter and I from forming a partnership. I still learned a great deal from him, not only in terms of the inspired variety of coaching sessions he put on, but also from the way he conducted himself in the face of adversity.

Peter reverted to being assistant manager and I resumed charge of the reserves, but it was Trevor's first job and as he had no coaching experience he found it tough. I got on fine with him, but he was surrounded by ex-managers and should perhaps have utilised our experience to help him. Trevor didn't do that and had a bit of a rough ride as a consequence. However, he went on to have great success at Sheffield Wednesday and Birmingham City.

The situation was short-lived for me anyway. At the end of the 1988/89 season I received a phone call from Bill Williams to ask if I wanted to manage Maidstone United in their inaugural season in the Football League. Bill was then the general manager at Maidstone, having previously been in charge of the playing side there. Although they'd only just been promoted to the Fourth

Division, they were very much Gillingham's local rivals and the fact that I had been manager at Priestfield was no doubt a large part of my attraction for Maidstone.

Paul Taylor had kept things on an even keel at Priestfield after my departure, but was then sacked, with Keith Burkinshaw brought in to replace him. Keith was a terrific coach and treated Gavin well, but I feared for him as a manager, knowing that he didn't have much experience of the lower divisions and how difficult it can be to adapt to that level. Gillingham had gone down, so they were now in the same division as Maidstone, although obviously still the much bigger club.

I had been at QPR for 15 months and it had been invaluable, providing my first real exposure to the top division of English football, even though I had already had a taste of the big time in a different context at Tampa. It had also been my first time running a side for which results were not the first priority, something I would be able to draw on again later. I'd had an agreement with Jim Smith that I could leave if and when a manager's job came up and QPR agreed to honour that and released me from my contract.

The only thing that worried me about my new appointment was what had happened to John Still, the manager who had done such a good job to get them into the League. I was told that he had always been part-time and wasn't prepared to give up his main job. I took that at face value and agreed a two-year contract, but I have never really spoken to John to find out the facts. At the time I rated him as the best non-League manager that I had come across, particularly in terms of spotting players who could do well in the lower divisions.

Maidstone were in a similar predicament to Charlton. They had sold their London Road ground for redevelopment and moved in with Dartford at Watling Street, which ultimately had disastrous consequences for both clubs. I kept well away from the politics. I was just pleased to be getting back into management. It seemed to me that the Maidstone fans wanted their team to return to its home town, but they didn't have the same burning resentment as the Charlton supporters. It might have been because they were seeing League football for the first time and accepted exile as the price. Watling Street needed quite a lot of work to bring it up to the required standard for the Fourth Division and it was a last-minute dash to get everything ready. Considerable improvements to the dressing rooms and other facilities did finally take place.

My first major challenge was to get set up in time for the start of the new season. The plan was to assemble a squad of 18 players, about half of whom I kept from the previous year. Some I knew and others I had watched on video, taking advice from Bill Williams. What really staggered me was the appetite shown by some of those in their late 20s who were willing to take the risk of giving up their regular jobs to have the chance of a one-year contract as a professional footballer.

One very familiar face was defender Les Berry, who had played for Maidstone the previous season in the Conference and had been with me at both Charlton and Gillingham. He was 33 and now didn't need to train as much. He was also looking to move into business, so he became part-time and that suited both of us.

I then had to find the other half of my squad, who were mainly free transfers. One was Karl Elsey, whom I'd had at Priestfeld. I also got a tip from John Still about Warren Barton and paid Leytonstone & Ilford £8,000 for him, plus another player who went the other way.

It was a blisteringly hot pre-season that year and I found it so refreshing to see the players' attitudes, especially the ones who were stepping up from part-time. They simply tore into every session, despite the heat.

I'd struggled to find an assistant, but eventually appointed Tommy Taylor, the former West Ham and Orient player, who was very keen to take on the job. I was a little cautious because I didn't really know him, however he proved to be an excellent choice, very hard-working and loyal.

One of our early tasks was to try to introduce the players to more professional habits, which included moderating their drinking. As part-timers they were used to having a good drink after a game, and even after training. My captain Tony Pamphlett had been banned from driving, having been caught behind the wheel when over the legal limit following a drinking session after training. It was not unusual to see his bike in the car park, as by necessity he now cycled to work. It was also foreign to me to have a chairman who liked to socialise with the squad after a game. He would even drop one or two of them off home when they had finished. I found this mind-boggling.

A pre-season tour of the West Country had been arranged before my appointment and we did quite well against minor opposition, so I gave the players an extra hour or so after the usual 11pm curfew and allowed them to go out together as a team. I felt it was important not only to reward them for their efforts so far, but also to give them a chance to bond as a group. It was also a test to see whether or not they would abuse my trust. Three of us were left at the hotel playing snooker, Tommy Taylor, physio Ken Steggles and myself.

The clock ticked round to two minutes before the deadline and I turned to the others and said: "They're not going to do it, are they?" My heart sank. I now had a problem. They hadn't shown me the respect that I needed. Then I looked out of the window again and there they all were, jogging into the grounds in military formation, singing an army marching song and with the skipper leading from the front. I knew then that I had a chance of moulding them into a team.

Our first-ever League game was at Peterborough and we lost 1-0, but we did all right and I had a good feeling about the squad. Maidstone had played with three at the back the previous season and I kept that going in the knowledge that they had been successful with that system and certain players were happy within it. I would start matches in this way and then, if we needed to change, we could. We had the right personnel to make the switch. If we were chasing the game I would move to a 4-4-2, my left-sided centre-back would go to left-back and my left-wingback would become my left-winger. Since then my preference has been to change formation in a simple way like that, rather than have to pull people off the bench to do it.

After ten games, we had won two, drawn one and lost seven, and we were two places off the bottom. The chairman simply wanted me to keep us in the League, but I was convinced I had a side that could do better than that. At one point I went to a reserve game at Millwall and found myself sitting next to Chris Turner. He was manager of Cambridge United, who were one place below us in the Fourth Division. I asked him how he was doing and he replied: "I've got a terrific side, but I can't win a game."

I looked at him in surprise and replied: "Me too!"

Although Chris would no longer be in charge of team affairs at Cambridge by the end of the season, both our instincts would be proven right. I thought that I was one player away from having the team I wanted and I was lucky enough to get him. This was Howard Pritchard, a winger I picked up from Walsall for £12,500. He was the missing ingredient. Now I could play with three at the back, four across the midfield, two up front and Howard as the winger on either side. His ability to switch flanks was most important. Suddenly we kicked on, winning three games in a row, then we had a draw and a defeat, followed by five more straight victories.

Although we were now exciting to watch, I was a bit surprised by the reaction of the Maidstone crowd. There were times when we would produce a great piece of play and I expected to hear applause but none came. This disturbed me a bit. We didn't get very big crowds at Dartford, which was understandable. It seemed that those people who did come preferred the direct approach they had been used to watching outside the League.

Whether the way we played was appreciated or not, we climbed the table and by the time we went to Priestfield on Boxing Day we were halfway, just one place behind our big rivals. They had been expected to win promotion, so relatively speaking our respective positions represented success for us and failure for them.

In those days you had to walk across the pitch to reach the dugouts and as I did so the home crowd gave me a standing ovation. It was a tremendous feeling and even produced goosebumps. It would have been a special occasion for Kent football even without my previous connections and those of one or two players in my team, and as it was Christmas we'd entered into the spirit of the occasion by throwing chocolates to the crowd. However, the personal recognition I received was something I'll never forget.

I didn't have any animosity towards Gillingham, but because of the way that I had left it was a game that I dearly wanted to win. Before the match I deliberately kept out of the dressing room until as late as possible. I wanted their manager Damien Richardson to see me and wonder why I was so relaxed. I knew that Gillingham had to be uptight about the possibility of losing to us and that the importance of the result would be laid on the line to their players, so I made a point of being excessively casual.

We won 2-1 and it was one of the sweetest victories I had ever enjoyed, for all the reasons that had made the game special. Maidstone had lived in Gillingham's shadow for their entire history and now they had gone there and beaten them in the Football League for the first time. Even better, it meant that we overtook them in the table.

As the season wore on we continued to do well, but with the limited budget that I had it was a test of my ingenuity to find things for the players to do as diversions from the normal grind of training. We were now getting close to the play-offs, but I could sense that some of them were becoming a bit tense. I wanted to lighten the mood, so prior to a game against Colchester United we went paint-balling. This was before it had become a fashionable thing to do.

We had to split into two teams and I made Steve Galliers, who was five-foot-five, general of one and Tony Pamphlett, who was six-foot-three, general of the other. The aim is to capture the other team's flag, but it's funny how people show their natural characteristics in this game. Those who are cautious on the pitch will be the ones who stay on their home base defending the flag, while the men who will win matches for you are often the ones diving in and out of the bullets. If you get shot with a paint-ball then you are out of the game, which you obviously try to avoid, but also because it can be quite painful if you get hit on the hands or around the neck.

Naturally, the players all wanted to get me. After all, how often do you get the chance to kill your manager? The best moment came when Tommy Taylor got shot by our only apprentice, who was on his own team. Tom had just killed two of the opposition, which was a breakthrough, but as he stood up the kid shot him in the back. Tommy went berserk. Game or not, the lad was lucky to escape with his life.

The value of the exercise was that going into the following match they were totally relaxed. They were still talking about who had done what to whom and I fanned the flames of this by joining in. I wanted to keep the atmosphere light and their minds off our prospects on the pitch. We beat Colchester 4-1.

We did make the play-offs, finishing fifth. Gillingham beat us on the run-in in the return fixture, but they ended up 16 points behind us in 14th place. This time there was a Wembley final as a prize if you could get through the semi-final stage. It was an incredible incentive for the players.

As fate would have it, we had to play Cambridge. They were now managed by John Beck, who was busy establishing his own peculiar brand of football, which was soon to become notorious. His management technique was an extreme version of the way Andy Nelson had handled things and, although I was never an admirer of Beck or his methods, they did bring him some initial success. He had some good players at the club. Dion Dublin and John Taylor were up front, with Liam Daish and Phil Chapple at the back, along with a former Charlton man, Alan Kimble, and John Vaughan in goal.

They were a better side than us, as had been demonstrated by our League meetings, in which we had only picked up one point. They had enough strength in the centre of their defence to nullify the threat of our forwards, so we really couldn't afford to concede.

We did quite well in the away leg, looking reasonably tight and well organised, but we had gone a goal down and I still wasn't sure how we could score against this team. Two minutes from time, Mark Gall got us an equaliser. It was also an away goal and again they counted double after extra-time in the second leg. This meant that if we could manage to grind out a goalless draw at Dartford we would be through. For the first time I felt that we could do it. We didn't have to score, we just had to stop them from getting a goal.

As expected, it was a tight game, 0-0 at half-time and again after 90 minutes. Now we had to get through the extra period. We didn't have enough going forward, but we were dealing capably with the threat of Dublin and Taylor. It was still 0-0 with 11 minutes to go, then something happened that was beyond my control. We won a corner and they left four players up to counter-attack, but my main centre-half Mark Golley went up for the set-piece.

Mark had been a stone overweight when he'd arrived at the club. After I'd told him that it had been a waste of time signing him, he showed tremendous dedication to get the extra weight off, with some help from Tommy Taylor. He had become my man mountain at the back and he was holding us together.

We had kept four men back to defend the corner, but he was the only one with the strength to knock back Dublin or Taylor when the ball came out. I didn't see that he had gone up until it was too late and as soon as I did I started shouting for him to go back, but to no avail. What followed was like a slow-motion sequence. They cleared the ball as I had feared and before Golley could make up the ground it was in the back of the net. We had given everything, but it wasn't enough. Cambridge now had the psychological advantage and went on to get the second right at the end.

It had been terrific to get as far as we did in our first season in the League, but having been so close to Wembley it was heartbreaking to miss out on such a big occasion, even though we might still have lost out on promotion in the final. Cambridge went on to beat Chesterfield.

What also stuck in my throat a bit was the way Beck was so full of himself after the semi-final. When we had finished the play-off matches with Swindon there had been an exchange of looks between myself and Lou Macari as we shook hands. We didn't need words and they wouldn't have been much use anyway, but we both understood what the other had been through and how we were feeling now. There was none of that with Beck, who made no concession to sportsmanship that night.

The other thing that really made an impression on me after the Maidstone play-off was the effect it had on my daughter Lauren. When I was at Gillingham we had found her a little job to do on matchdays, as she had reached an age when she needed something to keep her occupied on a Saturday while the rest of the family was busy with football. She would help with the teas and I paid her a couple of pounds out of my own pocket, which I kidded her came off the pay-roll. But she also started watching the games and began to look forward to them.

By the time I got to Maidstone, she was in her late teens and football had captured her interest, but it struck a chord when she burst into tears after we had lost to Cambridge. She was so upset for me that I had missed out on success again. When she gave me a kiss and a hug in consolation it gave me a sharp reminder of the way in which my job was affecting my family. Her concern for my disappointment is something that I shall always remember.

I've been so lucky to have had a very close relationship with my daughter. I may not have encouraged her to play football, but strangely enough she has been an integral part of my career virtually all her life. Even now she can usually be seen by her mother's side in the directors' box at The Valley. Seldom does a day go by without us seeing or speaking to one another.

Lauren has a terrific sense of humour and can bring a smile to my face no matter how I feel. However, when pursuing her modelling career at this time she reduced me to a nervous wreck. Seeing Gavin play at Wembley was relaxing compared to watching her compete in various beauty competitions around Kent. Naturally, I was totally biased and the judges were completely wrong if she didn't win. I must have been an absolute embarrassment. Sorry, Lauren, but I was right. You were always the best!

I was happy with what we'd achieved that season, but the set-up was still not entirely satisfactory. Chairman Jim Thompson liked me to have lunch with him on a Friday, which was not at all convenient. It was a busy time for me in preparation for the following day's match. The meal also included a drink, hardly the right thing to set me up for the afternoon. I think he probably found me a bit reserved, but I wasn't comfortable with the type of relationship he wanted with his manager. Maybe I should have been more flexible.

He had also liked to come into the dressing room after games to speak to the players, as he had done when John Still had been there, but I had put a stop to that. Tommy Taylor would guard the door to make sure that no one came in until I was ready. To be fair to Jim, he accepted all the changes I made.

We trained at Corinthian, which was a far better facility than we'd had at Gillingham, with the matches played at Dartford and the offices located in Maidstone. The split was not unlike that at Charlton now. In the offices, however, the chairman was very much the boss. All the staff, including Bill Williams, seemed to be wary of upsetting him. Not being accustomed to this kind of working environment, I didn't defer to him in the same way that others did. I treated everyone alike and spoke to the kit man in the same way that I addressed Jim Thompson. I never had any real altercations with the chairman, but I knew deep down inside that our relationship wasn't entirely secure.

Things should have improved as a result of a deal we did that summer. Just as he had taken Micky Adams from me when I was at Gillingham, so Bobby Gould now came in to take Warren Barton to Wimbledon. He offered £150,000, nearly 20 times what I had paid a year earlier and a huge amount of money for Maidstone. Although they had been regarded as a buying club in non-League football, the fees they had paid had been a fraction of this. Jim would happily have accepted the bid there and then, but I assured him that if he left it to me I could get double what had been offered. He took my advice and we got £300,000, which for a full-back who had only played one season in the Fourth Division was astounding.

Warren Barton went on to justify the fee and more, winning three caps for England and costing Newcastle £4m, but at the time there was no way that Maidstone could have rejected Wimbledon's interest. It was good business for the club, but it also meant that I had lost my best player. I would probably have been entitled to ask the chairman for a better contract at that stage. I only had one year left, but in my heart I was already thinking that this job wasn't forever. How right I was.

I signed midfielder Dave Madden from Charlton, a good player with no pace and an explosive temper, as he soon demonstrated against his former club in a friendly at Watling

Street, when I had to withdraw him before he got sent off. He could be the most amiable character off the field and on it he would show some superb skills and encourage the other players, then someone would upset him and he would just blow.

We were playing up at Whitley Bay in another friendly when he was fouled from behind and he chased the guy half the length of the field before kicking him up in the air. Again I had to get him off the field. Unfortunately, he suffered with knee trouble and we lost him after the opening run of games.

We were doing better than average in my second season, but we lost a couple of games over Christmas and dipped into the bottom half. Then we beat Chesterfield on New Year's Day and were due to play Halifax Town, who were bottom, on the first Saturday in January, but the game was called off.

Tommy and I went into the offices straight after training on the Friday and he got a call from Howard Pritchard, who was no longer at the club. Howard had heard through the grapevine that the chairman was looking for someone else to come in next season and Graham Carr's name had been mentioned. This had the ring of truth because I knew that Graham was out of work and often in touch with the club. He was also more Jim Thompson's idea of a manager, both on the social side and in the volatile way he behaved on the touchline.

Normally I would take a while to gather my thoughts at such a time before I reacted, but on this occasion I was so incensed that I walked straight into the chairman's office. Looking back I put Thompson in an impossible position. I told him that I was a straightforward person and I expected to be treated likewise. I had just heard that he was lining up Graham Carr for my job and I wanted to know if it was true. All I got from Thompson was a mumbled response. I'd caught him off guard and embarrassed him. I don't think he was used to being confronted in that way.

I was probably wrong to act so uncharacteristically and pre-empt the situation. In football things do change around quite dramatically and in provoking the crisis at that stage I hadn't allowed an opportunity for that to happen. This time my departure was down to my own impetuosity. Maybe I allowed my heart to rule my head because I wasn't entirely happy with the set-up at Maidstone.

When I came in on the Monday, Thompson had prepared a cheque for full compensation of my contract and added a bit more in recognition of how well I had done for the club. His only condition was that as far as the public was concerned it was to look as if I had been sacked. That wasn't going to look too good on my record, but he left me no option.

The unhappy postscript for Maidstone fans was that a year and half later the club was forced to resign from the League and ceased to exist at senior level. Watling Street was sold to developers and hosts Dartford began a long exile of their own. Maidstone's League career lasted just three seasons, but at least I could say that I had given them their one and only taste of professional success.

Chapter Twelve
THE FAMILY BUSINESS

It's not unusual for fathers to want to live out their football dreams through their sons. Anyone who has been involved in the junior game will know the extent of the parental enthusiasm it generates. However, when you've been a professional player yourself, things are somewhat different. I never forced football upon Gavin, but I did derive untold satisfaction from the successful career he had in the game. I also take pride in the fact that he went on to greater things than I had as a player.

When Gavin was a toddler, Lesley would sometimes have other young mums round at our house in the afternoons when I came back from training. Most dads would probably have kept their distance, but I used to get the kids together and hold little competitions, such as seeing who could crawl the fastest. Apparently, I had the coaching instinct even then.

I admit that in the early years I did look to see whether Gavin had any feel for the ball. He appeared to like it and I encouraged him to take an interest by making sure there were plenty around, even when he was still using his baby-walker, but no more than that.

One setback came when I bought him his first full kit for his fifth birthday. We were all ready to go to the park when one of his mates appeared at the front door with some thrilling news. The lad's mother had given him some material and he had come to invite Gavin to join him in turning it into scarves. My son was immediately diverted and I was left standing there, wondering where it had all gone wrong! Seriously, though, I was always very much aware that he should be allowed to make his own choices.

By the time he was five or six, I could see that he was going to be better than average at football, the sort who made the school team before most of his age group. Even at six, it is possible to tell whether a lad is developing a football brain.

One thing I could provide was a good example, just as I had learned from my father and from my sports teacher, John Attwood. The importance of being able to kick with both feet was duly passed on to the next generation, too, and with evident success as Gavin went on to score a substantial number of goals with each one.

He was also exposed to the camaraderie surrounding the game from an early age. Once when he was about three he came down in his pyjamas late one Saturday night to find a party in full swing. Many of the Charlton squad were there and it wasn't long before he was kicking a big Jaffa orange at Charlie Wright. When he was a little older he'd be down the tunnel at The Valley knocking a ball about as he waited for me after a game. He got to know Derek Hales and a lot of the other Charlton players quite well. On one occasion he even ran out with the team as mascot.

The first club he joined was Teviot Rangers, when he was seven. We lived in Okehampton Crescent, in Welling, at the time and they were based nearby, over the other side of the Fanny on the Hill open space. At first I just went along to watch him play, but it wasn't a surprise that after a while I was asked to help out with the coaching. Gavin was always one of the more able boys, so there was never any question of favouritism over his selection.

Then we moved to Barnehurst and he transferred from Hillsgrove School to Pelham. By the second year he was involved with the second team and 12 months later he was promoted to the first team, in which he was a year younger than most of his teammates.

It would be hard to exaggerate how much I enjoyed watching him in those days. My training commitments at Charlton would usually allow me to see him play after school and I could also get to the Saturday morning games, unless we happened to have an away fixture. My own career was drawing to a close, but I would get just as much satisfaction from seeing him do well and score as I would from my own game.

I'd concluded by now that he had the potential to have a professional career, but of course nothing was guaranteed. I'd seen boys who were better than him at the same age fade into obscurity once they got to 14 or 15.

I coached football at Crown Woods School, in Eltham, for several years while I was playing. Then, for a decade, I did the same at Alexander McLeod School, in Abbey Wood, under headmaster Roy Porter. At Alex McLeod there was one boy in particular who stood out, a lad called Tony Hazell. I watched him from seven to 11 and I would have put money on him making the grade, but he just didn't progress when he got older.

Character is as important as ability. Even if you teach a boy to behave in the right manner, he needs to have a certain level of determination to overcome the setbacks that inevitably come his way and the single-mindedness to devote his energies to learning his trade. It wasn't hard to nurture those qualities in Gavin. Even at the age of eight or nine he had the required level of self-discipline.

His sister Lauren was different in that respect. She was a very popular girl who did well at school and was generally good at sport, but her nature meant she was happy just to take part in a game or event rather than keen to win. Lauren always liked being with me but this could be a bit trying for her if I happened to be watching Gavin play. I tried to stand back from these junior games, but I would be up and down the touchline with the five-year-old Lauren in tow as I followed play from end to end.

Gavin's involvement in football could easily have meant that he got an unfair share of my time and attention, which could have been a problem. Thankfully, there was never a competitive edge between the two of them. Lauren had other qualities. She was always most concerned about my welfare when I got injured. She was almost the perfect daughter, with a great disposition, and she invariably brought the best out of other people. I confess that I was probably softer on Lauren because she was a girl, and she certainly got her share of privileges.

By the time we left for America in the summer of 1979, the year Gavin was due to start at secondary school, he had passed his 11-plus examination, and was playing for both the district and Kent representative sides. He was a good player at county level, but not outstanding. It's a mark of the extent to which he subsequently advanced that, apart from him, only Neil Ruddock, then a left winger, made the grade from that Kent side.

It was natural that I hoped Gavin would aspire to be a professional footballer. I loved to see his games, but I was equally happy watching either of my children perform, whether in school drama, on sports day or, as in Lauren's case, a hockey match.

The two years we spent in America could have disrupted Gavin's progress, both academically and on the football field, but in fact they gave him a boost, certainly in terms of his sporting prowess. He did so well at Tampa that he won the top prize for Latin in the entire school, which landed us in a tricky situation. The awards ceremony clashed with a semi-final for the junior club he was representing. Gavin was the star of the team and the coach was desperate for him to play, so we planned it that he could appear in the first half and then make a dash for the school presentation.

It turned out to be a really close game. The score was 1-0 at the break, so he went out for the start of the second half. Fortunately, he soon made a second goal and we were able to rush him off the pitch. He changed in the car as we sped off to the school. It was all a bit Keystone Cops.

Tampa provided a great opportunity for him to see some big-name stars up close and he learnt a lot from the experience. I knew as soon as I saw him in the Kent trial after we returned that he had made immense progress. Two years earlier he had looked steady but other boys had been better than him. Now he looked a class apart.

It wasn't all about what he'd seen. His confidence had also benefited from playing in an environment where he was the undisputed top dog. It's important to have competition at times in your life, but equally being the best means that you start to make decisions and take risks without fear of failure. If you are constantly under fierce competition then you begin to play a percentage game and hold back from experimenting.

For a number of months after we returned from America, Gavin's movement was more like that of a South American than an English youngster. He would do outrageous twist and turns, changing direction and playing reverse balls and backheels. A number of professional clubs came to see him in this period and were eager to sign him, but I felt he was getting enough football. Even so, he did go down to sessions at Charlton a couple of times.

During 1982/83 he was recommended for trials for the South of England and went head to head with Paul Ince, from Essex, for a place in the national set-up. It takes a little luck to get that far. It's impossible for anyone to identify the best 11 or 16 boys in the country, simply because of the size of the field. You only have to think how hard it is to agree on the best side for the full England team, drawn from a much smaller number, to realise that. Even so, Gavin was judged to be just ahead of Ince at that stage and got the nod. He made his international debut against Northern Ireland.

The fact that I was in charge of Gillingham made it difficult for me to see his England games, as we were usually in action at the same time. On one occasion we had lost 3-2 at home to Cardiff City and it was like an adrenalin shot when one of the reporters told me afterwards that England Schoolboys had beaten Wales 4-0, with Gavin getting one of the goals. Luckily, Lesley and Lauren had been able to make it to the England match. They certainly hadn't missed much at Priestfield!

During the school holidays I had him down at Gillingham to join in a couple of training sessions with the first team. He showed inexhaustible running power and at 15 he could already compete with the top athletes in my squad on their pre-season runs and the 4x400m relays.

By now it was clear that he could have the career in football he so passionately desired. Even so, he didn't neglect his schoolwork, picking up ten GCE O-levels, a couple of them taken early despite the distraction of playing for England at Wembley around the time he sat them. He was in the top half-dozen pupils at Bexley Grammar, which only admitted children from the brightest 25 per cent of the local population, so was a prime candidate for university. However, that wasn't his preferred route and I was always confident that the opportunity would still be there for him if his football career didn't work out for any reason.

The burning question was which club he should join. Of course, I would have loved to have signed him for Gillingham, with a view to developing him for a move to a bigger club, but the Third Division just wasn't the right level for a schoolboy international.

Charlton would have been ideal. Not only was it my team, but it was the one he had grown up with as a youngster. Unfortunately, the club was in turmoil for much of the early 1980s, with several changes of both manager and chairman, looming bankruptcy and eventually the decision to vacate The Valley in favour of Selhurst Park. Manager Lennie Lawrence was certainly aware of Gavin, but it wasn't really a sensible option, especially as Charlton had yet to gain their surprise promotion back to the First Division in 1986.

Tottenham and Arsenal were after him and I felt he did need to go to a First Division outfit. However, if he went to a very big club there was always a danger that he could be lost among a large number of talented boys.

QPR looked to fit the bill, especially as they were managed by Terry Venables, already acclaimed as one of the top coaches in the game. Promoted to the First Division in 1983, they were also recognised for developing young talent, including the likes of Wayne Fereday, Ian Dawes, Warren Neill, John Gregory, Alan

McDonald and Gary Waddock.

The only negatives were the fact that they played on Astroturf and the journey that Gavin would have to make to get there each day from Barnehurst. Within a month of him signing in 1984, however, Venables had left to manage Barcelona and three more managers – my old boss Gordon Jago, Alan Mullery and Frank Sibley – occupied the hotseat before Jim Smith arrived to restore some stability the following year.

Gavin found himself shunted about all over the pitch during this period, sometimes playing at full-back and on other occasions up front. It was all part of his learning experience, but fundamentally he was a midfield player. The real question was what kind of midfield player he would go on to become.

Should he concentrate on being someone who could get forward and score goals, as Bryan Robson did, or spray the ball around in the style of Glenn Hoddle? After about 18 months of his professional career we discussed the situation and decided that he needed to specialise in one role or the other. A key consideration was that Robson was invariably in the England team while Hoddle was in and out. The goalscoring midfielder who could get up and down the field was coming into fashion and that was the option Gavin chose to pursue.

That was the easy part. Building up his physique to the level needed to adopt that role was far more daunting. Gavin was five-foot-eight with a decent frame and reasonable legs. He was sharp, but not blisteringly quick, and he needed to find that extra strength. Ince, his old rival for a place in the England Schoolboys set-up, had shot past him in terms of physique and soon became a powerful athlete in the West Ham midfield.

Then fate stepped in. Gavin picked up a stress-fracture injury playing for England U18s in the spring of 1986 and was ruled out for three months. He was ten-stone-twelve and needed to add about ten pounds in muscle. That meant he'd have to endure a lot of pain, but his dedication came to the fore once he had decided to go for it. It wasn't something that could have been done while he was playing matches, as that would have left him too tired to perform at a stage in his career when he needed to be making an impression. But the injury, combined with the looming close season, presented him with the perfect opportunity.

Today many players have their own gym at home, but Gavin's work was done in the garage at Barnehurst with some old weights of mine. Sometimes I'd work with him, but most of the time he had only his Rocky music and a Sylvester Stallone poster for company. It was an exhausting and painstaking enterprise, which he saw through admirably.

The transformation unfolded before my eyes that summer, but it was a gruelling regimen. He couldn't run because of his injury, so all his efforts went into building up his upper body. As well as the physical exertion, he had to eliminate fat from his diet and eat all the right food. In the end, he put on nine pounds. He was successful, although he did lose a little stamina as he now had to carry a heavier load. What he gained was the strength to hold off big centre-halves, which meant that he could now play further forward.

Witnessing this happen first hand encouraged me to recommend similar programmes to other players at Charlton. Jon Fortune and Richard Rufus were two men who made significant strides by working their bodies really hard, both in and out of season.

Gavin now started to score lots of goals for the reserves, many of which I saw while scouting Leroy Rosenior. QPR played their reserve games on midweek afternoons, so I could get over to Loftus Road after training and monitor Gavin's progress at the same time.

Thanks to the generosity of the Gillingham board, I nearly saw Gavin's League debut, which came at the end of November in a home game against Sheffield Wednesday. We were away to Wigan that day, but luckily enough it was a morning kick-off. The directors arranged for a plane to fly me back to Heathrow, so that I could see at least some of the game at Loftus Road.

It was a very nice gesture, which unfortunately came to nothing. When we got to the airport the flights were being delayed by fog and we couldn't get off the ground. I ended up listening to snippets on the radio as we made our way home by road. To make matters worse, Wigan had beaten us 3-1.

QPR drew 2-2, with Gavin acquitting himself well, but although he had a run of appearances at the end of that season he didn't establish himself in the side. Rangers still had a good crop of youngsters and Jim Smith always worked with a number of senior players. Gavin remained on the fringe of his plans.

One morning in October 1987 I casually asked him at breakfast if he'd like to come to Gillingham on loan. He was nearly 20 but hadn't started a League game so far that season and the time was ripe for him to be playing first-team football, whatever the division.

He immediately liked the idea and Jim Smith agreed that it would do him good, so a deal was struck. Any concerns that might have been felt about me signing my own son were soon dispelled as he settled in well, making one of the goals in a 3-0 home win over Bristol Rovers on his debut.

Lesley was in her element with her two men at the same club. However, she spent many a sleepless night worrying that Gavin would call me "dad" instead of "boss" in front of his teammates!

At the end of the month, both Gavin and I were keen to make the move permanent. He'd got a taste for playing in front of a crowd and I knew that he could be a real asset to us. It helped that Paul Taylor, John Gorman and Buster Collins were all desperate to get him in. It was obvious what he could do, but I needed him to be one of the better players at the club so that there could be no accusation of favouritism.

Despite speaking highly of Gavin, Jim Smith saw him remaining on the periphery at Loftus Road and was willing to sell. The fee was £40,000, plus half as much again after a number of games, but for obvious reasons it was the one deal during my time as manager that I didn't conduct. Gavin signed on December 9th, after briefly returning to QPR at the end of his loan. He was taking a gamble with his career by dropping down two levels in the hope we would act as a springboard back up.

I did warn him that there was bound to be a risk that he could get lost at the lower level. On the positive side, the fact that Gillingham had been among the contenders for promotion from the Third Division for a few years meant that we were a team that other managers would watch. The moves made by Steve Bruce, Micky Adams and Tony Cascarino had all proven that.

In the back of my mind was the idea that I might be able to sell Gavin on to Charlton in a year or two for twice the money I had paid. He would cut his teeth with Gillingham, score goals for us and then bounce on to The Valley. We never discussed Charlton explicitly, but it was obvious that if he did well at Priestfield then he could hardly fail to be noticed by our nearest neighbours, who by now were in the First Division.

Things didn't quite work out as I had planned. Three days after Christmas I was sacked. Now Gavin was faced with a dilemma. He was clearly enjoying his football in the centre of midfield, but he was playing for a board of directors that in his eyes – and mine – had treated his father unfairly.

Had he said emphatically at that point that he no longer wanted to play for Gillingham, the board would have accepted his decision. That indeed was his first instinct, but we talked it through and he decided to stay. It was enough for me that he felt the way he did. His decision had to be the best one for his career, not an act of revenge. He didn't have to deal with the directors on a day-to-day basis anyway. He knew Paul Taylor, who had taken over, so that wasn't an issue, and he got on well with the players. What was important was to establish himself as a good midfield player.

I'd always told the family that it was inevitable that they would one day read in the papers that I'd been fired. Football has many good aspects, but fairness is not one of them. It is not enough to be good at the management job, you also need luck. On this occasion, mine had run out.

Gavin had been my last signing and I wanted people to remember him as one of my best. I was pleased with my record in the transfer market while at Gillingham and this was an opportunity to improve it further.

What did become very awkward was the fact that I wanted to continue watching my son play. I didn't see why the hell I should be deprived of that pleasure as well as my job, so I went to see him in the very next game, at Southend on New Year's Day. Gavin scored with an overhead kick. "That's my boy!" I chuckled.

The problem came when I went to see him play at Priestfield. The fans made their point to the board about my departure and I was extremely touched by their reaction, but it was impossible for me to return until feelings had died down.

Gavin and Gillingham played out the season in mid-table, but the team made a terrible start to the following season, losing ten consecutive matches early on. Paul Taylor was sacked and replaced by Keith Burkinshaw. Even so, they were relegated to the Fourth Division for the first time in 15 years.

Gavin was now showing all the qualities of which I had known he was capable. He was also doing it as an offensive player in a struggling side, which was all the more creditable. I have always maintained that it is easier for a defensive player rather than a creative one to shine when in a losing side.

Burkinshaw had used him in more of a holding role, spraying passes around, but still he scored nine goals. The Gills fans showed they valued Gavin's contribution by naming him Player of the Year.

He was catching the eye of several clubs. Now was the time

to tell the Gillingham directors that he wanted to go. He'd served the club well, but he could feel no loyalty towards the board after my dismissal and he was probably less forgiving than I would have been, having more in common with his mother in that respect. I tend to move on a lot easier than they do.

Although Gavin was now 21, I continued to act as his personal adviser. He never had an agent as such. This arrangement worked well, as he knew that I always had his best interests at heart.

Harry Redknapp, the Bournemouth manager, came in for him and there were one or two others making enquiries. I rang Lennie letting him know the fee, but Charlton didn't follow it up, so Gavin went to Dean Court. The Kent outfit received £250,000, which in those days was a huge return for a club of their size. I had just taken over at Maidstone, but travelled down to the South Coast, saw Harry and completed the deal with a minimum of fuss.

At the same time as Gavin left home he married his fiancée, Amanda, so 1989 was a busy summer. Now he had a Second Division stage on which to perform, but although he did well personally the season ended in relegation. It was a body blow, especially as there had been no indication this was going to happen during the campaign. A major factor in joining Bournemouth had been to step up a level. Although he had enjoyed working under Harry, he now had to request a transfer after just one season.

Jim Smith had taken over at Newcastle, but he had been unable to prevent them slipping into the Second Division the previous spring. He'd followed Gavin's progress since leaving QPR and made a bid for him in November 1991. Again I spoke to Lennie, just to keep him in the picture, but Charlton had just followed Newcastle down from the top flight and they were still stranded at Selhurst Park. The money to back up any interest they might have had simply wasn't available.

The fact that Newcastle were keen was special anyway, particularly for my dad, so I was torn. It seemed so far away, but it was a wonderful opportunity for Gavin. Even so, he took some time to make up his mind. It meant that he and Amanda would be five hours away from their respective families.

He signed for £350,000 at the end of November, the day after my father's birthday, which was a neat coincidence. Once again he did well and this time he was given licence to get forward more, scoring seven times in 27 games, despite the fact that Newcastle remained stuck in mid-table. However, Jim Smith was under pressure and eventually left in March. It was the third time Gavin had lost his manager within a short time of joining a club.

Jim's replacement was Ossie Ardiles and the Argentinian's commitment to attacking football was to be good news for Gavin. Newcastle became an exciting team to watch, despite – or perhaps due to – the fact that the emphasis on attack left them vulnerable at the back. They were involved in some fantastic games, including one with Charlton that went down in SE London folklore, as the Addicks came back from three down to win 4-3 at St James' Park.

Gavin was ever-present in a side for the first time in his career and finished top scorer with 19 goals – 16 of them in the League. Many of them were outstanding strikes and it seemed at the time that about three-quarters of his efforts on goal were finding the back of the net. Despite this the team was struggling. They had some good players, but many of them were finding it difficult to perform in front of the demanding Geordie fans, who didn't expect to be watching a side fighting to stay in the Second Division. They had been used to seeing outstanding players over the years and expected good footballers to be put before them, but Gavin at least was able to rise above the situation.

The home defeat by Charlton in mid-January had been watched by only 15,000 of the faithful and a disastrous 5-2 reversal at bottom-of-the-table Oxford United followed. That was the final straw for the Newcastle board, who foresaw another relegation. They sacked Ardiles and replaced him with Kevin Keegan, already revered on Tyneside for helping restore Newcastle to the First Division as a player in 1984.

The home crowd immediately doubled to almost 30,000, as the Geordies turned out to welcome back their hero, although it would still be a struggle to survive. Gavin had been doing well enough already, but Keegan's arrival was further motivation for him. He was undoubtedly the player in the squad most similar to the way Keegan had been himself. Gavin was sometimes up front, sometimes in midfield. He was dedicated and he had boundless energy. He would run until he dropped. In short, he possessed all the attributes that Keegan admired. The new manager was also an inspirational figure, who commanded great respect for what he had achieved in his own playing career.

Shortly after Keegan's arrival, Gavin scored a superb goal against Swindon at St James' Park. He caught the ball on his foot, controlled it with his thigh and then volleyed it, all in a split second.

It was a stunning goal by any standards, and it particularly stuck in the mind of the Swindon manager, Glenn Hoddle. His enthusiasm was no doubt shared by his assistant John Gorman, who had known Gavin since he was 12. Newcastle won 3-1. The game was also notable because Keegan abruptly walked out after it, only to return by the following weekend.

Newcastle were in a terrible plight, but the adversity provided one of my proudest moments. It came at Derby County with three matches to go. It was a game they had to win. I managed to get to the Baseball Ground a minute before kick-off and ended up behind the goal with the Newcastle supporters, a one-off experience for me. I was used to being in a more detached environment, sitting in the comfort of the directors' box.

Everything went wrong for the Magpies that day, starting when Kevin Brock gave away a penalty and was sent off. He was the kind of player who never did anything untoward, so it was an indication of the way things were going for them. Derby were going for promotion and they were 2-0 up at half-time. To make matters worse, Newcastle were reduced to nine men when they had a second player sent off.

They were now playing a 4-3-1 formation, with David Kelly on his own up front and Gavin supporting him at every opportunity. He ran and ran in an effort to overcome the impossible odds and I still can't imagine how he managed to sustain it. Incredibly, he pulled one back and for a while the unthinkable seemed possible.

In the end Newcastle had a third player sent off and the eight men lost 4-1, but in football terms I felt as proud as I have ever been. The fans around me were fantastic and I felt very emotional, partly from being among the Geordie diehards but also from watching such an extraordinarily gutsy display from my own son. It was a performance of immense heart, as well as skill, and it was definitely fitting that I had watched it surrounded by the passion of the Newcastle fans. Passion was what it was all about.

Keegan used the events of that day to generate a revival. His side beat Portsmouth 1-0 at St James' Park in their penultimate match and then went into the final game, at Leicester, needing to win to be certain of survival. But the situation was complicated by the fact that their opponents were still in contention for the second automatic promotion spot, trailing second-placed Middlesbrough only on goal difference.

Gavin scored the goal that put Newcastle ahead, intercepting

a back pass and calmly beating the goalkeeper, only for Steve
Walsh to head an equaliser in the last minute. Nobody knew if a
draw would be enough for Newcastle, but within a minute they had
gone back in front with a freak goal, everybody missing the ball as
it was played into the box and allowed to trickle over the line. As
it turned out, Brighton and Plymouth both lost and were relegated.
Newcastle would have stayed up even if Leicester had got the
winner, but no one could be sure of that in those dramatic final
moments at Filbert Street. When the referee blew his whistle, the
ecstatic visiting fans streamed on to the pitch in celebration.

Gavin was as delighted as everyone else, but he was now out
of contract and no closer to his dream of playing in the top
division, which was about to become the Premiership. His career
had definitely taken off, but the teams he played for had
consistently gone backwards. On the positive side, he had made a
name for himself now and was established as a £1m player.

Billy Bonds was interested in taking him to West Ham, but he
was having difficulty coming up with the cash. The fee would have
been decided by tribunal, always an additional risk. Keegan was
hell-bent on keeping Gavin. He saw him as his key player. When
the squad reported back for training in July, Gavin was super-fit.
Seeing him in pre-season made Keegan even more determined to
re-sign him.

This time I made no phone calls, but I did receive one. I was
back at Charlton myself and knew we could never meet Gavin's
wages, never mind the fee. As fate would have it, the interested
party was Lennie Lawrence, now boss at Middlesbrough, who had
just been promoted to the Premiership in his first season in charge.
After all those times when he couldn't take Gavin to The Valley, he
now wanted to sign him. The shirts were still red and the shorts still
white, but they belonged to the wrong team.

Gavin longed to play in the Premiership, but his heart was
still in Newcastle. With hindsight it looks as if it should have been
an easy decision to stay on Tyneside, but the Magpies had been in
the doldrums for a number of years and there was no guarantee
that they would emerge from them in the near future. Boro were
traditionally the poor relations, but with Sunderland also outside
the top division they were suddenly the region's top club.

My view was that we should go to Ayresome Park, talk to
Lennie and get a feel for the place. I had a sneaky feeling that Gavin
would know instinctively what he should do. The meeting went

well. Lennie was great, their chairman was fine and everything they said about the football side was agreeable. We didn't go into the financial aspect in any detail. Whenever I went with Gavin the conversation would revolve around how the team would play and where he would fit in. We had a walk around the ground and after a very pleasant couple of hours set off back to Durham in the car. Gavin just said: "No, it's got to be Newcastle." But I had already known what his decision was going to be.

Once again he was taking a big risk. He was turning down the chance to be in at the start of the Premiership, with all the Sky money pouring in. But somehow Middlesbrough just couldn't compete with Newcastle in terms of atmosphere and tradition. The fact that Keegan wanted him to be part of his team so badly was a big factor in Gavin's thinking.

The negotiation with Newcastle that followed was wonderfully honest on both sides. Gavin could have exploited the situation by making out that he was tempted by Middlesbrough's offer. Instead, he told Keegan upfront that he had decided to stay. All he wanted was the best deal that the club could offer him. The matter was signed, sealed and delivered within 24 hours.

Gavin was well looked after and when Newcastle started the following season with 11 consecutive wins it already looked like the right decision. They duly won promotion and Gavin had another super campaign, this time scoring 16 goals, despite missing part of the season through injury.

His presence at Newcastle also played a small part in the departure of Robert Lee from Charlton that September, at a time when the Geordies had just overhauled the Addicks at the top of what was now the First Division. Gavin was making a public relations appearance in Newcastle with Keegan when the story appeared on evening newspaper placards in the city that Boro were in for Lee. Gavin rang me and put Keegan on the line.

Kevin wanted to know if it was true that Lee would be going and asked me for some background on him. I had to say that he was an outstanding player and could only recommend him, even though from a management point of view we would be very sorry to see him go. At the time I thought Robert was an exceptional talent, but he went on to do even better than I anticipated. He had the ability to score goals and make things happen in the last third of the pitch, but for us he was playing a lot on the right side of midfield, which possibly limited his effectiveness.

Following that conversation, Newcastle came in and pipped Middlesbrough at the post for the second time in about a month. As with Gavin, the final outcome owed much to Keegan's influence, especially as Lee knew Lennie Lawrence as well as anyone. But Robert's choice may have been made slightly easier by the fact that the Tynesiders had won their opening seven games.

Lee had already spent four seasons in the top flight with Charlton, but when Newcastle clinched promotion to the Premiership, it meant that Gavin had finally arrived on the biggest stage just a few months short of his 26th birthday. His only previous games in the top division had been his 17 League appearances as a youngster for QPR, but ten of them had been as a substitute. The gamble he had taken in signing for Gillingham in 1987 had taken five and a half years to pay off.

Gavin's preference had always been to reach the big time with a London club, and Charlton would have been his first choice, although West Ham might have been an option in the years he was out of contract. However, he had acquired star status while with Newcastle. He'd been selected to play for a Football League representative side and was soon to be called up by Terry Venables to attend an England training day, so he was considered to be on the fringe of the international set-up.

Events that summer, however, dictated that he was not destined to play Premiership football for Newcastle and again it was a situation from which Keegan emerged with credit. What led to Gavin's departure was the arrival of his son Jake, who was born without a right hand.

As soon as Amanda went into labour, Lesley and I jumped in the car and drove straight to the North East. Since nothing untoward had shown up on the scans and there had been nothing in her pregnancy to suggest there would be any complications with the baby, a negative thought had never entered my head. After many hours in the waiting room, Gavin called me aside to say that the baby was a boy. But there was a problem. We were completely shell-shocked by what he told us.

It was a very emotional time for all of us and all I could think about were the things that Jake, as he was named, wouldn't be able to do in later life. He wouldn't be able to take part in sport, he wouldn't be able to swim. Suddenly I was acutely aware of everything that I did with my own two hands and how I took it all for granted.

Amanda was amazing. After 48 harrowing hours of labour, it was she who assured the new grandparents that little Jake would learn to cope. How right she was. Jake does everything and anything. All our worries for him have just faded away. He is an incredible swimmer and earned his bronze medal before most other kids of his age. He's tall and strong, and he seems to have inherited his maternal grandfather's passion for DIY, at which Gavin and I are hopeless. He plays centre-back for his Sunday team and is improving each season. In fact, he even played for Charlton's U8s when he was younger, which gave this grandad a particular thrill. Three years later, Amanda gave birth to my beautiful granddaughter Ava, completing their family circle.

Gavin makes no secret of the fact that he is a Christian and his faith was a source of strength to him when Jake was born. Lesley had been educated at the Roman Catholic St Stephen's Primary School in Welling as a girl and she started to attend a local church when Gavin was about 18. He accompanied her to some of the services and his interest developed from there.

If you are a prominent footballer you have to make a choice about how open and active you are going to be about your religious beliefs. On rare occasions he was on the receiving end of some light-hearted stick from opposition fans when it first became public, but certainly nothing unkind. Since then Christians in Sport has developed a much higher profile and Gavin is just one of many who do so much for the game and support numerous charities.

In Jake's early years, it was understandable that Gavin and Amanda wanted to be nearer to their immediate family. Keegan didn't want to lose Gavin, but he understood their dilemma. Glenn Hoddle had just taken over at Chelsea and, given his interest in Gavin, there was a deal to be struck. I was able to talk to both sides and they were a little bit apart financially, but ultimately managed to agree a fee of £1.25m.

Things came to a conclusion towards the end of July, when Gavin was a week short of receiving a sizeable lump-sum payment. Despite the fact that he had earned it, Gavin said that as he had asked to move south he would be willing to waive it. The deal was duly completed and Keegan still gave him the money.

Kevin's empathy and sensitivity in a very delicate set of circumstances will never be forgotten by our family. He knew that Gavin was genuine in his motives for wanting to leave and his contract at Newcastle ended on the same note of honesty as it had begun. I can't stress too much the extent to which an act like Keegan's restores one's faith in human nature. It demonstrated that football doesn't have to be all about big business.

I look back on that set of negotiations, including the talks we had with Glenn, with a smile on my face, because they were a classic example of football people doing their best for a young professional. It was a complete contrast to the way some deals are conducted today, with the involvement of agents, some of whom may have little interest in their client's long-term career or long-term happiness.

We had lengthy discussions on how Gavin might fit in at Chelsea and what tactics Glenn was likely to deploy. This doesn't go on enough nowadays and yet it is so important. It's essential in determining whether a transfer is going to be successful in the long run. You often find that if this discussion takes place at all it will be after an agent has agreed the financial aspects, which is jumping the gun really.

An agent might argue that he could have secured Gavin a better financial deal than I did, but I think I had the advantage since the people I was dealing with knew that I understood the game and didn't mess around. It enabled me to cut through weeks of bluff about finances, which is where agents probably think they are earning their money. You can put together a contract very quickly when necessary, but maybe players would then start to question exactly what they are paying for.

Gavin was on fire during that first year at Stamford Bridge and scored eight goals in 37 League matches, plus six in the FA Cup run that culminated in a Wembley final against Manchester United. He got the only goal in the sixth round against Wolves and followed that up with both strikes as Chelsea beat Luton Town in their Wembley semi-final.

I was still going to see Gavin as often as I could and I was usually accompanied by my dad. We enjoyed a marvellous day at the semi-final, and I also got a great deal of satisfaction from seeing Tony Cascarino in the spotlight, all those years after he had signed for little old Gillingham.

Cas had carved out a successful career, although he was now entering his twilight years. Charlton were interested in him at the time. I thought he could still do an effective job for us in the First Division and he was set to be available on a free transfer at the end of the season. Things went awry in March when Tottenham came

Above: My first Gillingham side. This 1981/82 line-up includes my assistant Paul Taylor (middle row, first left), with defender Steve Bruce next to him

Left: My first and only game for Tampa Bay Rowdies, an indoor league match against Atlanta Chiefs

The 1989/90 Maidstone squad included future England star Warren Barton (back row, third left) and my former Charlton teammate Les Berry (middle row, fourth right)

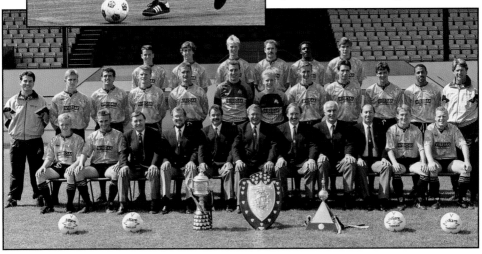

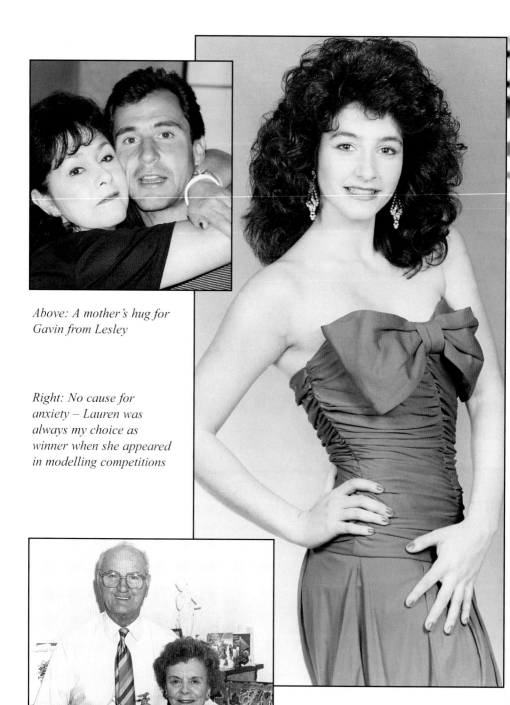

Above: A mother's hug for Gavin from Lesley

Right: No cause for anxiety – Lauren was always my choice as winner when she appeared in modelling competitions

Left: My parents, Tom and Lydia, celebrating their golden wedding anniversary in 1989

Tom Morris

Above: The veterans make their debut at Welling United in October 1992. Television comedy actor and Charlton fan Karl Howman is on my right

Right: Sharing thoughts with Newcastle United boss Kevin Keegan at Upton Park

Left: Lesley tries to go incognito in Barcelona following the miserable failure of the veterans' wives to remember the words to the Red, Red Robin

Above: Proud father – with Lauren on her wedding day in September 1995

Above: Family album: Gavin's wife, Amanda, and Lauren's husband, Andy, with us on a night out. Right: With Valerie at her daughter Lisa's wedding. Left: Out on the town!

Left: Directors Michael Grade and David Sumner present me with a salver to mark my second testimonial, in 2000. Grandchildren, Celine, Jake and Ava lend support. Below: Lesley and I with my committee of John Rooke, Neville Maw, John Hayes, Gary Allen and Terry Carrigan

Bottom: The bench erupts at Villa Park in 1999 as Danny Mills makes it 4-3 in the last minute to keep us alive

Tom Morris

Paul Marriott

Above: Captain Courageous – with former Charlton skipper and Republic of Ireland midfielder Mark Kinsella

Right: Gavin gets the right kit on at last, on his Charlton debut in 2001

Below: Wembley hero Clive Mendonca was forced to retire prematurely through injury

Tom Morris

Empics

Above: Champions at last – celebrating in the dressing room at Ewood Park in 2000 with Curbs and Mervyn. Right: Hales, Powell and Flanagan are reunited in 2004

Above: We must be winning!

Right: Alan Pardew, then Reading boss, and I found ourselves in neighbouring hotels in Las Vegas in 2003

Winning team: Mascots Ava, Jake, Celine and Shania out on the pitch with their grandad before the Newcastle United game in October 2004

Left and above: The proud grandmother, Lesley, and our two children, Lauren and Gavin

in for him. Chelsea asked £250,000, which was criminal from the player's point of view, given that he would have been available as a free transfer in six weeks' time.

Hoddle was understandably reluctant to give him away to another London club. Glenn was undeniably proven right when Cascarino made the first goal at Wembley for Gavin, a volley, and then had a hand in the second, which was a one-touch bender. They were both excellent goals and it was a magical day on which everything seemed to go right. Cas went on to have a good World Cup with Ireland in the USA and was then snapped up by a French team with whom we just couldn't compete financially at the time.

At that point the devaluation of the FA Cup that has taken hold in recent years hadn't really kicked in. It was still the schoolboy dream to play in the final and, for me, scoring the winning goal was as good as it can get in the game. Gavin had done it for Chelsea in the semi-final and he had also scored the only goal in both their Premiership meetings with Manchester United that season, so the scene was set for him.

The noise was absolutely deafening as I watched the blue shirts of Chelsea walk out alongside the red and white of United at Wembley. Fireworks were exploding and the atmosphere was electric – everything you would expect of a Cup final in the national stadium. Lesley was craning her neck to see her son and I should also have been searching for the young man wearing number eight, but instead I looked to my left at my 79-year-old dad, who was anxiously waiting to see his grandson emerge on to the hallowed turf. I remember wondering how clearly his old eyes could see the events below us. It probably didn't matter. Simply knowing that his own kin was about to appear in a Wembley final was enough.

The script demanded a storybook finale for Gavin and soon the moment arrived. The ball came to him and he dip-volleyed a shot over Peter Schmeichel, but it smacked against the crossbar and rebounded to safety. That proved to be his one and only opportunity in the game. The chance had fallen to the right man, but on this occasion it didn't quite happen for him. It was still 0-0 at half-time, but then United got the breakthrough and went on to win 4-0. However, it wasn't that clear-cut a game for an hour.

Overcoming this disappointment, Gavin continued to do well at Chelsea and the following season he captained the side in the semi-final of the Cup Winners' Cup. They lost 4-3 on aggregate to eventual winners Real Zaragoza, after a valiant attempt to overturn a 3-0 deficit from the away leg.

Unfortunately for Gavin, Hoddle left in 1996 to take over from Terry Venables as manager of England and Ruud Gullit was installed as Chelsea's new player-manager. There was also an influx of major foreign stars, such as Gianluca Vialli, Gianfranco Zola, Roberto di Matteo and Dan Petrescu, meaning competition for places became that much more intense.

The previous season Gullit had lined up alongside Gavin, but as manager he appeared to see no necessity to maintain relationships with his players or explain his decisions. One he made was to leave Gavin out of the side from the start of the 1996/97 season. Gavin eventually went to talk to him, only to be told that he would be unlikely to play more than ten or 12 games a season, in contrast to the 28 Premiership games in which he had been involved the previous year. Given that he was just short of his 29th birthday that was never going to be an acceptable proposition, even though it would have been financially rewarding. So it was that he asked for a move. As a result of his request, he was excluded completely.

Gullit wasn't the first manager to leave out an unsettled player in such a way, but he didn't display any sensitivity or psychology in the way he dealt with problems in general. It seemed to me that if he couldn't manage someone like Gavin effectively, even to the extent of having one half-hour conversation about the best way forward for both of them, he was unlikely to find long-term success as a manager. I wasn't surprised that it proved the first of many disputes that he had on the man-management side of the job. Alan Shearer and Robert Lee, among others, fell out with Gullit when he later took charge at Newcastle.

Once again it was the wrong time for Charlton, who were not yet in a position to spend serious money in the transfer market. QPR probably weren't either, as subsequent events demonstrated, but it was they who came in with a £1m offer in November. Rangers had just been relegated from the Premiership and were gambling on an early return, with Gavin's Chelsea teammate John Spencer moving to Loftus Road for £2m at the same time and a club record £2.75m going on Stoke City's Mike Sheron the following summer.

The club was being over-extended and during the following years they slipped backwards and were eventually relegated to the Second Division in 2001. Gavin did well for Rangers, winning their player of the year award, but he was back playing with a struggling club and I could only respect the way he responded to the challenge.

There were several changes of management at Loftus Road, with a succession of players being offloaded to reduce the wage bill. Gavin's own value in the transfer market was depreciating as he moved into his 30s, yet he was on such a good contract that only a Premiership club could have afforded to sign him.

The last move of his career saw him finally join Charlton on loan in the summer of 2001. Alan Curbishley had always held him in high regard, and we began our campaign with an injury crisis, while Rangers were now desperate to cut their wage bill to reflect their new Second Division status. Gavin was now 34, but after seeing him in a pre-season game against Celtic, QPR manager Ian Holloway assured me that my son could still play in the Premiership.

I was in a peculiar situation. Gavin was coming in as a squad player and wouldn't be an automatic selection in the way he had always been at Gillingham. He was in competition with a number of younger midfielders, but once again his performances left his credentials to play at the top level in no doubt. He made his debut as a substitute in the opening game against Everton, a decision from which I had to distance myself. In the next game, at Ipswich, he had to go man-for-man with Matt Holland, who would later sign for us, and did a very professional job in a 1-0 win. He was in great nick, his attitude was spot-on and it was rewarding for me to see him finally run out in the red shirt of Charlton. The dream had come true, fleeting though it turned out to be.

After the Ipswich game, Curbs wanted to sign Gavin for 18 months. He just needed to get a few games under his belt to prove his fitness. Unfortunately, in the process of pushing himself to show that he was worth the longer deal, he picked up an injury. It would have been nice if he could just have seen out that season in the Charlton colours, but at least he did make it to The Valley in the end.

He made three more Premiership appearances as a substitute, the final one at Highbury in an historic 4-2 win over Arsenal, one of the most memorable matches in which Charlton had ever been involved. Even though he didn't play a major part in events that day, it wasn't a bad way to conclude his playing career at the top level.

It was to Gavin's credit that after five years out of top-flight football he was able to pick up the pace again so quickly, however briefly he was called upon. As I knew from my own days in the old Third Division, it's inevitable that you slip into the mentality of the lower level when you have played there for a while, but he was able to re-adjust.

Eventually he returned to Loftus Road and saw out the 2001/02 season, concluding 18 years in the professional game. As he likes to point out, that is one more season than I had. His career panned out very differently from mine. Gavin is a more impetuous character than I am and was probably never going to be a one-club man. He took his own path and that only serves to make me all the more proud of everything that he has achieved.

My son had been a text-book example of the modern professional, conducting himself with dignity both on and off the field of play. What more could any father ask? During the course of his career, I had been his manager, coach, adviser and friend, but the role I enjoyed most of all was being his dad.

Chapter Thirteen
COMING HOME

"Would you like to be manager of Charlton Athletic?"

It wasn't so much the question that came as a surprise as the person who asked it. Five months had elapsed since I had parted company with Maidstone United and my interrogator was Lennie Lawrence, still very much the holder of the post he was asking me about. Lennie had called me in for an end-of-term chat at the conclusion of some scouting work I'd been doing for the club that spring and was gazing out through the window of his office as he put me on the spot. I was evasive in my reply, conscious that it might sound as if I was after his job, but five or six weeks later he had gone to Middlesbrough and I was indeed back at Charlton after an absence of 12 years. As it turned out, though, my role was to take charge of the reserve team.

The months after I left Maidstone were my first real break from full-time work and gave me the opportunity to reflect on what I had achieved in the game. I became more philosophical about life in that period and took advantage of the time available to see more of Gavin's games. After Lennie approached me to do some scouting, I would go into the Charlton training ground at Sparrows Lane, New Eltham, most Fridays for a chat with him or Arnie Warren, the general manager and chief scout. It gave me an insight into the set-up.

I was up in Durham in early July when the news broke that Lennie was on his way to Middlesbrough. It wasn't long before Arnie was on the phone asking me to come down to help with the coaching of the youth team. The previous youth coach, Colin Clarke, had also left. Alan Curbishley had been coaching the first-team squad the year before, with Steve Gritt in charge of the reserves, so it was logical that they looked after the senior players while the process of selecting Lennie's successor unfolded.

From the outset it was more or less assumed that I would be among the applicants and, given my background, I was likely to be one of the favourites. Returning while the appointment was being made put me in a strange situation, but it was a chance to be involved at the club. After a few days, Steve and Alan told me that they were each applying as well, so we were all in the same boat and just had to get on with our temporary jobs while we waited.

After a fortnight the board decided to appoint Steve and Alan as joint first-team coaches, with Arnie Warren looking after the financial aspects, as well as the scouting. I would take the reserves, with John Cartwright eventually appointed as youth coach.

There is a part of me that believes in fate and that things work out for the best. What happened to Charlton over the following years justified the board's decision, although Arnie was unable to take the role that was initially envisaged for him because unfortunately he soon required major heart surgery. I was unsure about the decision to go for a joint managership. Even if two people work very closely together, someone has to be in charge. But certainly no two men could have handled the situation better than Steve and Alan, and I was impressed with how well they were able to operate. The structure originally proposed by the board was probably too complicated, but Arnie's misfortune allowed Steve and Alan to take on a more appropriate level of responsibility. This was formalised when Arnie retired at the end of that first season and their title was upgraded to joint manager.

For my own part, I was very happy in the years that followed. A reserve-team job at another club would not have appealed to me at that stage, but I thought the timing was right to be back at Charlton and it was a role in which I could be totally relaxed. It had taken me a very short time to get a feel for the place again, so I was there in the background for the new managers, with a lot more experience than they had at that time. I like to think that I helped as much as I could in the early days, but they had to develop their own style of management and arrange things according to their own ideas.

My new role also gave me opportunities that would never have been available had I been under the pressure that went with a manager's job. In particular, I was able to spend a lot of time with my father in the last years of his life. We would travel up together to watch Gavin play for Newcastle, which might mean getting back in the early hours of the following day. I could still get up and do my job the next morning. These quieter years of my career were also the most significant in Gavin's and I saw many of his games, enabling me to fully enjoy his success.

The demands of management mean that you are bound to miss out on family life. I don't believe that you can measure career achievement and satisfaction against that. Ultimately, your personal relationships are always more important.

I was now mixing with the players far more than I had been as a manager and those who had played under me at Gillingham and Maidstone would probably not have recognised me in my new role. Team spirit was a key ingredient at Charlton in the early 1990s and I did my best to nurture that by encouraging the banter and looking for different ways to add fun elements and levity to the weekly routine.

Money was short, with the first team now playing at Upton Park and the directors working hard to put together a financial package that would allow the club to complete the return to The Valley, which had first been announced two years earlier.

I'd been very disappointed by the original move to Selhurst Park in 1985. Owing to my involvement at Gillingham, however, I didn't really have time to dwell on it in the same way as the long-suffering fans who had to make the journey. In the years that followed I sometimes travelled past the old stadium on the train and it was heartbreaking to see The Valley deteriorating each time.

Now we were apparently going back, but I must admit that I thought I would only believe it when it happened. In the meantime we had to get on with playing at West Ham. This too felt wrong, but at least we knew it was likely to be short-term. Oddly enough, players are probably the people within a club who are least affected by the venue. It isn't the same for them as it is for the fans, the administration staff and even the stewards, because half the matches in their career are away from home. They have to adapt. Many fans and staff will never travel to an away game, so they are only familiar with the club's home ground.

In the short term, it's possible to have a side that is suited to playing away from home, but over a period of time there is nowhere like your own home stadium, where you can build up long-term support. This is proven by the statistics.

In the early years I would usually attend the home games and be in the dressing room, maybe having a word with the odd individual. I needed to keep in touch with the first team, so that I could make my own judgement of the players who were coming in and out of the reserves. For the away games I would tend to be off scouting, something for which I assumed more responsibility after Arnie's retirement.

Alan and Steve portrayed a united front and that extended to their dealings with me, so I was never put in the impossible position of having to take sides between them. Any differences they may have had were handled in private within the confines of their office. The fact that they had a similar level of experience and seniority may have made it easier for them to have a balanced partnership.

They also had to set a clear distance between themselves and the squad, which was complicated by their age and the fact that they were still playing. I think I helped them do that. In my position I was available to listen to the complaints of the older players who were upset when they weren't in the side and those of the younger ones who felt they weren't getting the breaks they deserved. In effect, I acted as a buffer.

The first year was more of a holding operation while the directors sorted out the longer-term future of the club, but after a shaky pre-season the team bounced back and only missed out on a place in the promotion play-offs on the final day. Key to this was the signing of experienced professionals Garry Nelson and Steve Gatting just before the first League match, and Alan Pardew in November. These three became part of a group of senior players who over the next few years were very important in keeping Charlton going until the good times came along – people like John Bumstead, Colin Walsh, Bob Bolder, Simon Webster and Keith Jones. None of them had been at the club throughout their careers, but they had what I call Charlton hearts and were totally committed to the cause.

The part these men played in stabilising the club cannot be overstated. They were all strong characters, who had a positive influence and provided a rock-solid foundation in a really difficult period. They received decent financial rewards themselves, but they also paved the way for those who followed them to receive much more significant sums in wages. I worked very closely with this group and I very much respect and admire what they did for the club.

We were fortunate also that the young players who came through – Anthony Barness, Steve Brown, Richard Rufus, Shaun Newton, Scott Minto, and later Lee Bowyer, Scott Parker, Paul Konchesky, Kevin Lisbie and Jon Fortune – had all been brought up the right way in terms of accepting what Charlton was all about.

Robert Lee had by now emerged as the star player. I loved playing alongside him in training sessions and benefiting from his quick football brain and exceptional skill. However, he was one player whose full potential I underestimated. I also thought he was playing slightly within himself. He did the bread-and-butter things, in terms of keeping possession, but he seemed to me to take it easy when things were frenetic in the first half, then come to life when the game had settled. I'd never seen a player do that as if it was part of a plan. With other players I was confident I knew what they could achieve. Although I thought Robert was destined for greater things, I never saw him going as far as he did. I felt he could play at the top level but not for England. Once he got back to the bigger stage, he kicked on again and his long and distinguished career is there for all to see. He was a tremendous player and a terrific person too.

Work finally restarted at The Valley in the summer of 1992 and everything that happened in the following season was overshadowed by the great event of going home, which finally took place on December 5th, with a 1-0 victory over Portsmouth. Before that, however, came a sharp reminder of the old Charlton that I had known so well, when we were forced to sell Barness to Chelsea and Lee to Newcastle, despite the fact that the Geordies were our main rivals at the top of the table at the time. This trend would continue with the sale of Webster and Minto in the following two years and you could not fault the directors for it, but inevitably it made the job of building a successful team more difficult.

The return to The Valley was a magical, nostalgic occasion, all the more so for those of us who had previously known it as home. I was part of the parade of former players on the pitch before kick-off and it was a day for reminiscing with ex-teammates and so many of the supporters I had known over the years. However, we always knew that we had to win the match to make the day complete. Fortunately, the exhilarating atmosphere lifted the team. The fans always play their part, but this crowd cheered every move and it seemed inevitable we would get the ball in the net one way or another. An early goal from Colin Walsh proved decisive.

Of those who played that day, only Steve Gritt had been part of the Charlton squad that had left SE7 in 1985, but the players understood the monumental achievement that going back to The Valley represented and responded accordingly. We had trained there in preparation and very soon it seemed like home again, even though the dressing rooms were housed in a Portakabin and the facilities were very basic. The return created good vibes around the club and the redevelopment of the ground over the following years generated an atmosphere of optimism and progress that had a positive effect on everyone.

Morale was also something I kept very much in mind as I worked with the players on a day-to-day basis. Someone key to that in the first couple of years was Alex Dyer, a two-footed striker with great individual skills, who was invaluable around the building during the week. He was a popular, bubbly character with a great sense of humour and sometimes I'd ask him to take the warm-up as a way of varying the routine. He would get the players doing different things or on another occasion he would simply enliven a particular session with a funny comment at the right time. Although dropped a number of times, he showed great character and resilience and managed to combine being an entertainer within the ranks with being professional at all times, much in the way that Dennis Booth and Phil Warman had done in the 1960s and 70s.

One year I organised a competition to see who could do the most dips on the parallel bars in the gym, in order to raise money for a reserve-team night out. I also announced that I was the undefeated champion at this, so if someone could beat me I would put a few quid into the pot. If not, the players would have to pay to watch the grand final. In fact, my own prowess was less distinguished than I had suggested, so behind the scenes I had to put in quite a bit of training to justify my claim.

My two biggest rivals turned out to be Linvoy Primus, our young centre-half, and John Vaughan, the goalkeeper who had been part of the Cambridge team that beat Maidstone in the play-offs. Primus had a seriously muscular physique and he was adopted by Alan Pardew, who looked after his training, but Vaughan looked the natural winner. He had monstrous arms. I continued to bill myself as "unbeatable", but I was beginning to have second thoughts. Secretly, I was praying for divine intervention.

The showdown took place one morning before training and all the players came in early to watch it. Linvoy made a grand entrance like a professional boxer, wearing a black satin cloak and surrounded by supporters like Carl Leaburn, with *Simply The Best* pounding out on a tape machine. Garry Nelson took charge to make sure that all the dips complied with the rules. Linvoy did 48, Vaughan about 45, but I managed more than 50, backing up my boast. I then bet the players that I could manage 75 and overall we raised about £600 towards a night out. It was all good fun and the important thing was that it got the banter going between the players and fostered the right atmosphere.

Another innovation that became an integral part of the weekly routine for many years was the Yellow Jersey Award. This took place at the team meeting each Friday and would go to the person who had dropped the biggest clanger during the previous week. Originally it was confined to mistakes on the training field, but it soon became extended to slip-ups in any context, with the players making the case for it to be awarded to each other. Everyone won the yellow jersey at some stage, including Curbs and myself, much to the lads' delight. In later years, people like Steve Jones and Mark Bright really entered into the spirit of it. You had to be able to take stick, because the mistake that you had made would be exaggerated out of all proportion. It was a pity that as we developed as a Premiership club this particular ritual came to an end, but until 2000 it helped maintain team spirit and humility among the whole squad.

The training ground was run on a shoestring budget in the early years, with Johnny Yarnton looking after security, his wife Barbara and Jeanette Tipp doing the catering, and Jackie Monahan in the office upstairs. Johnny was then and remains a great Charlton fan and because of his commitment he was willing to be there at all hours, always talking the club up to parents of youngsters for no other reason than that he believed in it.

Jeanette's initial task was to make a few sandwiches and drinks for the apprentices. Now she and Tony Brown, the chef, organise an extensive lunch menu for all staff at the training ground. In conjunction with our sports scientist, they make sure the food is highly nutritional and that the players are able to have the correct breakfast and lunch every day. It's all a far cry from grabbing a Mars bar and a bag of peanuts on the way home from a morning session, as tended to happen not so long ago.

In the early 1990s, our resources at the training ground were severely stretched. People like John Rooke and Mick Cole were helping out for sheer love of the club. They later joined the staff and became an integral part of the set-up.

Part of my role as reserve manager was to help develop the youngsters coming through from the youth set-up. I was fortunate in that John Cartwright's very specific ideas about working with young players meant that by the time they came to me they were as comfortable on the field as they could possibly be. John's emphasis was on producing skill and technique to such an extent that the goalposts could have been on the halfway line for all the difference it made to him. Winning didn't come into it.

On occasion, the reserves were involved in some gross mismatches. I recall having to play Shaun Newton at left-back against the Arsenal winger Jimmy Carter. He was a very difficult player to handle, enormously quick and clever on the ball, but Shaun marked him out of the game. I only ever envisaged Shaun as a full-back, although he broke into the first team as a midfielder and performed admirably in that position for us in the First Division. He had tremendous pace but no trick, and I thought with the game in front of him as a defender he could have gone further still.

I'd had my first insight into Shaun's talents and those of the other younger players in my first two weeks, while I was in charge of their training. We did a variety of activities in that first fortnight and I'd put up a tenner for the best overall performance. When I announced that the winner was 16-year-old Richard Rufus, he was very wary of coming up to get the money, thinking it must be a trick. He was cautious by nature, but perhaps in a central defender you want someone who is wary of being thrown any kind of dummy. He was a colt-like figure in those early years, lean as a bean, but he had a massive heart and wanted to win everything.

In those first two weeks he had shown me his desire to make the grade and 95 per cent of the time it is the players with that kind of determination who go all the way. Others who have greater ability but lack grit may fall by the wayside. You often hear people say that a certain talented individual was "unlucky" not to have made it at a club, but unless a player also has the necessary resilience and desire then he will very rarely come through. These qualities were there in Richard Rufus and later in Scott Parker. I have often used these two as examples of players who would go as far they possibly could in the game, although in Richard's case injury intervened. Coaches have often been wholehearted players themselves and knowing what was required for them to succeed they can spot the necessary attributes in youngsters. The players who don't have the right mental attitude get brushed aside.

Darren Pitcher was a good example. He was never a great footballer, but he gave 100 per cent once he got into the Charlton side and established himself. He needed flair players like Robert Lee and Scott Minto around him, as much as they needed him to do the hard physical work. Someone else, like Andy Salako, had much more natural ability, but lacked the extra determination. He failed to make the breakthrough. Then when his chance had gone he wanted another, but it was too late. Unfortunately, it also went wrong for Darren after he scored the winning goal in the FA Cup at Blackburn in 1994, culminating in what became a bad career move to Crystal Palace.

I always arranged a hard Friday for the players who weren't going to be involved at the weekend. This was something that really put their character to the test. They would already be disappointed that they weren't in the first-team squad, which meant that they had no game to look forward to. Now they also had to work at a time when their mates who were playing would be taking it easy in preparation for the match. On those occasions you could tell the ones who found it a chore to knuckle down.

Two players who appeared more regularly in the reserves than they would have liked were Paul Gorman and Kim Grant, both of whom were strikers. Each was capable of scoring some sensational goals, but their performances were too erratic for them to become established in the first team. I had seen this type of player so often. They had the potential to make the grade for a short time but couldn't sustain it.

There is room in the game for this kind of player and more so now that there are five substitutes allowed. This means that you can have someone wearing down the opposition defence for 70 minutes and then bring on the player who can produce the unexpected to finish the job by netting the winner. They may be players who are popular with the crowd because they are exciting and also men your opponents don't want to see in your side. You don't necessarily want to start them, because they can put you under pressure, by giving the ball away cheaply or not closing down the opposition. That puts extra responsibility on the rest of the team, who invariably prefer playing with the more reliable strikers. The latter may be short on flair, but they do their job within the team structure.

Paul Gorman's non-League background with Fisher Athletic had no doubt left him with some rough edges, but with Kim Grant it was about mental strength. Kim was a likeable chap who developed his upper body and leg muscles so that he could compete, but he found it hard to accept being substituted when he felt he didn't deserve it. That is a real test of a player's resilience. The public don't quite realise when someone like Garry Nelson or

Chris Powell clocks up 600 appearances just how many setbacks they will have had along the way.

The characteristics of reliability were epitomised by our regular first-team forwards in those early years, Nelson and Carl Leaburn, although the latter's selection must have caused more controversy over the years than that of anyone else in the club's history. Most players are the subject of debate at some stage in their career, but with Carl it seemed to be an issue from the day he had made his debut in 1987 to the moment he left for Wimbledon in 1998.

He was an obvious target for attention for two reasons. One, because he was so tall, at six-foot-three, and had the longest legs that I have seen in the game. Two, because he was a striker with a very poor goalscoring record. However, he did many other things for his teammates and when he wasn't in the line-up he was missed. He was very strong in the air and crucial at set-plays at both ends of the field. Sometimes he might not even touch the ball, but his physical presence unsettled the opposition. If you put him at the near post when defending, he killed off that area as surely as a giant centre-half.

Carl was naturally powerful and he could hold the ball up, with good control for a big man, and bring other people into the game. We used him as a battering ram, to create openings for other strikers or players coming from midfield. In training I've seen him hold off Simon Webster as if he didn't exist, and Simon could get through most people. Ironically, his best performances always came when he lost his temper. Then he became unplayable.

His teammates always appreciated him, but he was not a particularly good finisher on the ground, being hindered by his long levers, so he would tend not to go for goal with the ball. Football crowds have always liked forwards who are direct and look to go in on the goalkeeper the moment they gain possession. Actually, hitting the ball when you are running with it, in the way that Bobby Charlton made his trademark, is one of the hardest things to do in the game. It's much easier to get power on a shot when the ball is played back to you or passed sideways.

Carl played to his strengths and the crowd didn't like it. They wanted to see someone like Paul Gorman or Kim Grant heading for goal, with the anticipation of a shot at the end of it. He became an easy scapegoat when the team wasn't scoring enough and in fairness the fans had a point, because the purpose of strikers is to score goals.

He did start to score more often after the change of managership in 1991, but I looked at him and wondered if he could be converted into a central defender. As a manager I'd always looked for a centre-half who could get me six or seven goals a season. I found that they tended to get them in tight games, such as local derbies, when their bravery in the box paid off. If Carl had been a youngster, I would have tried him there, but he was rarely in the reserves and we didn't have the money to replace him as one of our first-team strikers, even if we had wanted to do so.

To Carl's credit he didn't hide from the critics and he was important to the foundation work that was done in the early and mid-1990s. He was always involved in the yellow-jersey debate and part of the general banter of the dressing room. He was never loud, but played his part and would help any younger player coming into the side. He'd had to take a lot of stick and could relate to anyone who found themselves in a similar situation. My only criticism of him would be that he didn't have the desire to finish with his feet. Had he developed that he would have become a major force.

The 1994/95 season was memorable for me as I went close to steering the reserves to their first Football Combination title since 1950. There is no reliable way of forecasting the league standing of a reserve team, because of its unpredictable make-up. Your main aim is to help youngsters come through, teach them good habits and try to keep them buoyant while waiting for their chance of a break. The hardest thing is to motivate the senior players who have come out of the first team and get them playing to the best of their ability. You don't want them to risk injury, but at the same time you need them to be going in for tackles and headers.

If you are not strong enough as a side then you are not going to win matches however keen you are, so league position isn't the major measure of success. There is a great deal of satisfaction for a coach in achieving a draw against an obviously superior side or even in an individual performance that shows a young player might one day be a contender for the first team.

Of course that didn't mean that I wasn't disappointed when we lost to Spurs in the final match and forfeited the title in the process. A fair number of supporters travelled across to St Albans to see the vital game, so it had sparked interest among the fans as well. The crucial blow came when Steve Brown hurt his knee in a five-a-side the day before. I knew that I didn't have enough height to deal with the side that Spurs, who took the title, would field. A draw would have been enough, but we couldn't do it without Brownie and finished third, with Southampton overtaking us as well.

One advantage I'd had in my side that year was the emerging talent of Lee Bowyer, who turned 18 in the January. In spite of the reputation he would subsequently attract for his exploits outside the game, Lee was a coach's dream. His lust to train and play was second to none. He was prone to retaliate, even in a practice match, as he did once against teammate Paul Linger. I immediately pulled him off the field and made him sit by my feet. He hated this because he had to watch his team lose and was helpless to intervene. A fine would have been a more bearable punishment in his book.

At least I tried to instill that discipline into Lee so that he wouldn't continually be getting himself into trouble on the pitch. It was obvious that he was going to have a big future. When he established himself in the first team the following season, his ability to cover every inch of the pitch made him a major asset. He was a good goalscorer, but no matter what kind of session I put on in training his imagination, skill and mobility shone through. He was the epitome of the modern midfielder.

If 1994/95 was relatively eventful for the reserves, it proved notable for the first team in that it was the last under the joint managers. This had as much to do with changes in the boardroom as it did with a mediocre season in the First Division. The team had finished seventh, 12th, 11th and 15th under the combined leadership, but I think the consensus of opinion among the fans was that there had been enough stabilisation and, with the ground beginning to take shape, it was time to forge ahead.

As reserve coach I had a surprising amount of contact with the directors and would even attend board meetings, but this Charlton board had made a point of being accessible to everyone. Roger Alwen had been among the first to work for a return to The Valley. He was indefatigable and it was fitting that as chairman he had been able to lead the club back. Martin Simons, who had been one of the major players in getting back to The Valley, would sometimes have a pint with the supporters in the Royal Oak round the corner after a game, and the fact that he could do that was testimony to the sense of common purpose around the club. It was also important that the board had a high degree of visibility, because of what had gone on in the past. He had formed a highly effective partnership with Richard Murray, who brought greater business acumen and a cool head, but an equal commitment to the cause. The two of them were investing substantial sums of their own money in this period to keep the club afloat. The former skipper Derek Ufton provided continuity from the old days and football experience, while Richard Collins had helped the club survive its financial traumas in the mid-1980s. As time went on they were joined by the US-based Mike Stevens, who brought fresh ideas, enthusiasm and, not least in importance, more financial backing.

There were significant positional changes on the board in early 1995, with Martin Simons assuming the chairmanship of the football club and Richard Murray taking the chair of the recently created plc. A direct consequence was the decision that summer to end the joint managership, with Alan Curbishley assuming sole charge and Steve Gritt leaving the club. The partnership had worked as well as anyone could have foreseen, so I was surprised when the split came. Steve was certainly unlucky. Although Alan had probably emerged as the stronger of the two, any public distinction was slight and it had been a successful relationship. It transpired, however, that Richard shared my own initial view that a partnership was ultimately unworkable and he wanted to deal with just one manager.

Steve's departure was difficult for some fans. He had the greater history with the club and maybe the natural expectation was that either both men should go or neither of them. However, it's hard to imagine that the club could have been more successful if the partnership had continued, or if Alan had also left.

The change didn't make a huge difference to my job. Les Reed came in from the FA as first-team coach and I found him a very easy person to get on with and work alongside, and at the same time we enlisted Ted Davies as chief scout in order to spread our net a little wider. However, it did prove a significant stage in Charlton's reconstruction. The team seemed to gain momentum from the switch and after that we were always looking upwards. Suddenly my dream of nearly 40 years earlier to help the club regain its top-flight status began to look a more realistic prospect.

Chapter Fourteen
NEVER TOO LATE

Late in 1977 the *Evening News* asked me to go out for a dinner
with a Charlton supporter who had won a competition they had
been running. During my 17 seasons as a player I met a lot of fans
and I can't say this one made a special impression on me at the
time. We met in Il Traghetto, a restaurant opposite what is now the
leisure centre in Woolwich, and as far as I can recall the paper's
well-known football writer Victor Railton did most of the talking.

Little did either of us realise that 20 years later the same
supporter, who had earned his prize by writing a report of Charlton's
4-1 victory over Tottenham, would become chief executive of the
club. Before then I would get to know Peter Varney rather better in
his capacity as a fund-raiser, and for his support of the charity
matches played by the Charlton veterans team.

I was still at Gillingham when I first formed an ex-Charlton
side to play for charity. However, things really began to come
together after a match at Chiddingstone, in Kent, shortly after I
returned to the club. Brian Kinsey had asked me if I would arrange
for a team to play. It was bizarre. We had a lot of well-known
former players coming along to face a tiny club in what seemed to
be the middle of nowhere. As well as Kinsey, Mike Flanagan,
Colin Powell, Martin Robinson, Steve Gritt and Alan Curbishley
were all involved. I have a vivid memory of Curbs and I parking
our cars and having to make our way across a cow field. This
didn't do much for his suede shoes!

It was so good to get everyone together and a bonus that we
were able to raise money for a worthwhile charity in the process. All
the same, it struck me looking round the dressing room that there
was potential to do a lot more. Most of the players were relatively
young and the standard of football was good. I was still pretty fit
myself at that stage. Maybe we could play on a more regular basis,

closer to The Valley, and raise some substantial sums of money in the process? The club was always being asked to help out local charities. Then, in October 1992, I arranged a game against a team of former West Ham stars at Welling United, in aid of the Greenwich and Bexley Cottage Hospice.

The match took place on a Sunday morning and amazingly 1,300 people turned out to watch. We won 8-4 and it was good quality entertainment. When we walked around the pitch at the end we received a tremendous ovation. It was clear that the fans still related to this group of Charlton players. Some of the goals scored were quite spectacular and it was obvious that everyone had thoroughly enjoyed the trip down memory lane.

There was one unhappy aspect to the day, because Gritty didn't turn up. The idea had been that he would play for Charlton and Curbs would play for West Ham. When Steve didn't appear, we knew something had to be seriously wrong. It was completely out of character for him to let anyone down. Sadly, his daughter Hayley had been taken ill with a brain tumour.

After the tumour had been successfully removed, Steve became involved with the newly established British Brain and Spine Foundation, and asked us to arrange a match to raise funds for that charity at the end of the 1992/93 season. We could now use the newly re-opened Valley, so it became a special occasion for all concerned. The other good news was the willingness of Derek Hales to turn out. I had tried unsuccessfully to arrange for him to play at Welling, but the reception he received from the Charlton fans at the first match back at The Valley had stirred his emotions. For the first time since 1979, the old front line of Flanagan, Hales, Powell and myself was to be reunited. After 15 years I also met up again with Peter Varney, who organised all the match sponsorship.

In many ways, it was the perfect day. We had just under 5,000 people present to see us play a Millwall XI, which included Harry Cripps and Barry Kitchener. Mick McCarthy, who would go on to manage Millwall, Ireland and Sunderland, was also playing and kicking Hales whenever he could. Afterwards, Derek was left sitting in the dressing room nursing cut knees. This hadn't prevented him getting a hat-trick. I managed to get the first goal, with a header, and the more times I described it afterwards the more powerful it became. When I saw it on video later I had to tone down my version of events. It wasn't from quite as far out as I'd thought!

One thing that I didn't need to exaggerate was the extent of interest from the Charlton fans. There was an enduring affection for that 1970s team and especially the old forward line. Fans loved bringing their kids to see the players whom they used to watch, as well as the chance to see the current management team in action.

After that things really took off. Taking charge of the veterans was time-consuming but a lot of fun. I would raise a laugh by repeating to the players the sort of remarks that they had heard from their respective managers in their first-team days. The hard part was getting the side together. I assembled a squad of 18 players, so that at least 12 of them would always be available.

I became very aware of the enjoyment that can be derived from reminiscing about games and players from the past. Even as someone who has mixed with professional footballers for more than 40 years, I am still in awe of many of those I watched during my formative years. The great players I come across today don't hold the same mystique for me, even though some of them have breathtaking ability.

The core of the original veterans team was made up of 1970s players. Although they might not have been hugely successful years for Charlton, it was a period of excitement at the club and one that left the fans with many fond memories. Over time, of course, the veterans squad developed to include more recent players. In fact, it got to the stage where I was jokingly assessing older players like Colin Walsh, Phil Chapple, Alan Pardew and Bob Bolder as prospects for the vets while they were still in the first-team squad.

There was a logic to this, because at the other end of the scale we were now seeing boys as young as five or six. There was no reason why players should have to end their association with Charlton once they reached their early 30s. The fact that they didn't disappear entirely at that age provided continuity for the fans and added to the concept of the club as a community.

A team from the Spanish club Espanyol came over to play us at The Valley in October 1996 and provided a real test, having already beaten an Arsenal XI a couple of days earlier. The players were accompanied on the trip by their wives and partners, and the men arrived wearing blue jackets and grey flannels like a top professional side. They'd taken the Arsenal game very seriously and kept the ball in the corner in the last few minutes as if they were playing a vital league match. We beat them 4-3 and it was the best veterans game that I have seen or been involved in.

At the post-match function, our president Steve Sutherland

challenged the Spaniards to a return fixture. They eagerly accepted and Varney soon had his fund-raising hat on. We flew out the following June, with an Eynsford team led by Gary Allen joining us as our main sponsors. After we had played Espanyol, Eynsford linked up with us in a four-team tournament with sides representing two smaller Catalan clubs, Terrassa and Sabadell.

The match with Espanyol ended in a 1-1 draw, meaning we had won 5-4 on aggregate, although how we did it I'll never know. We then drew 1-1 with Sabadell the next day, but beat them 6-5 on penalties. Next we had to play Terrassa in the final of the tournament, but this was to be our third match in as many days and of course more than a few of the players had been out drinking to all hours. We were also carrying a number of knocks and before the game the entire team was sitting slumped in the huge changing rooms in the depths of the Olympic Stadium wondering what on earth we were doing there. I started by doing a roll call of the fit players.

"John Humphrey . . . "

That was about it. But I looked around the dressing room and what I saw was a bunch of strong characters, among them Alan Pardew, Bob Bolder, Colin Walsh, Steve Gritt, Humphrey, Curbs and Richie Bowman. We were going to win that game no matter what. Most of the other side were in their early 30s, but character and determination doesn't decline with age and it was still within our players to pull off a result.

Mike Bailey, who was 55 by now, had limped into the restaurant the previous evening and appeared to have no chance of taking part in the final. Much later, as we were walking back to the hotel in the early hours of the morning, we were arguing about where Gritty should play in the game. Mike felt we needed his defensive qualities at the back, I was determined that he should play up front. Trailing behind us were our wives, Barbara and Lesley, who must have been wondering when these couple of old football dogs would finally lie down.

Mike left me with one parting shot before going to bed: "My groin's feeling a bit easier. I'll give it a late fitness test tomorrow!"

"Great, I'll see you in the morning," I replied, smiling at how a couple of bottles of wine could cure a strain so effectively. But I knew that Mike would somehow rally himself to play at the back the next day if it was humanly possible. He passed his fitness test and was absolutely brilliant in the game.

Our wives were there to give us their wholehearted support. Lesley had been rehearsing with them for hours. Dressed in the red and white of Charlton, they were ready to put the Dallas Cowboys cheerleaders to shame. The stage was set for their big moment. Unfortunately, their dance routine was a shambles and not one of them could remember the words to the *Red, Red Robin*. As the vets and the opposition posed for the pre-match photograph, the wives – led by Janet Bumstead and now completely out of control – sprinted across to sit on the laps of the dark, handsome, and certainly more youthful, Spaniards. They had defected!

They soon returned to their husbands when their men were victorious, defeating Terrassa 2-1, courtesy of goals from Gritt and Pardew, with our Eynsford friends cheering every moment.

Mike Bailey was absolutely in bits afterwards. He had a black eye and could hardly walk, which probably didn't go down well with Barbara since he was due to go on a family holiday straight afterwards. It summed up the spirit that footballers have within them. He had been my captain when I started my career and now he was again. It was like turning the clock back for Mike and me.

In many ways what happened that day was meaningless to anyone other than ourselves, but it was great to see the Charlton spirit rekindled in that team. They were playing simply because they enjoyed the game – just as they had at the outset of their careers.

The trips abroad became an annual event and that in turn led to Peter getting even more closely involved. During a ten-year period, more than £130,000 was raised for the Hayley Gritt Research Fund through the veterans. Varney's contribution always had another facet, too. While we were waiting to clear customs on the way to face Espanyol, he sat down with a group of Spaniards and persuaded them that Lesley, with her jet-black hair and dark brown eyes, was a famous ex-flamenco dancer, returning to the country to perform. As we came through he started a round of applause and everyone else joined in. Lesley and I were left looking around us to see who the celebrities were. Suffice it to say we had our revenge later. But that's another story.

It wasn't until September 1997 that Peter joined the full-time staff at Charlton, initially as managing director and then chief executive. It was the season that we got promoted to the Premiership and we needed someone of his calibre to look after the business side of the club on a daily basis because the financial side of things was about to be transformed by our elevation. The commercial aspects of the club had to be taken to a new level if we were to compete effectively. We needed someone who would be forward-thinking and ambitious for Charlton. Peter's background meant that he was able to raise money and persuade people to invest. Here we had a man whose heart was in the club – and it showed.

The chief executive's job at Charlton is problem-solving on a grand scale and to do it you must be someone who gets an adrenalin rush out of succeeding in that. It helps that he has a very dry sense of humour. He is not only an employee but also a supporter, which allows him to understand that the club's success is measured by the performance of the football side.

Of course it makes a huge difference commercially if the first team is doing well and Peter was fortunate to join the club at just the right time. Lee Bowyer had established himself in the first team in 1995/96, scoring 14 goals from midfield in 52 matches. He was fast becoming one of the most sought-after young players in the country, but he was still a teenager. It was probably too much to expect him to sustain his level of performance all season. We faded in the closing weeks and only just made the play-offs, then lost the home leg of the semi-final 2-1 to Crystal Palace. Although we didn't feel it was impossible to overturn the deficit at Selhurst Park, the home side scored an early goal, making it very difficult for us. Nonetheless the season had been a vast improvement on the previous one.

Lee did make the step up to the Premiership that summer, when Leeds United paid £2.8m to take him to Elland Road, which kept the club on track financially. It also opened the door to a signing that proved to be sensational. Having watched Mark Kinsella play for Colchester United a number of times, I saw him as an excellent prospect and was instrumental in getting him to join us in pre-season for a trial. He was 24, yet had already played more than 200 games for the Essex club.

It was a stroke of luck that nobody had taken a risk on signing him before, but the longer he stayed at the lower level the more people probably questioned whether he could make the step up. He didn't have great pace and he was slightly on the small side, whereas the modern midfielder tends to be more of an obvious athlete. I disregarded this in part because I had taken to heart something Brian Clough had said, which is that you should never judge a player by his style of running. John McGovern had had a terrible running style, but Clough had made him his captain and with great success.

We needed to take a look at Mark before we committed ourselves, only because it is helpful to be able to make direct comparisons with the quality of your existing squad. Twenty minutes into his first training session with us it was clear that he'd have no problem playing in the First Division. I'd felt the same about Tony Cascarino and Colin Greenall. It was plain that Mark knew what was going on around him. He had two good feet and a panoramic football brain.

Disappointingly, we didn't manage to capture him straight away because of a dispute with Colchester about the fee, but we got a second bite of the cherry in September when Gillingham started to show an interest. He turned out to be one of the club's best signings of the 1990s. The fact that he was a bargain at £200,000 seems obvious with hindsight, but the money at issue was important to the club at the time. During my Charlton days we had always had to keep a tight hold on the purse strings, so I accepted that we had to buy as cheaply as we could and get the best bargain on any deal.

Kinsella became the catalyst and mainstay of the side. He was remarkably consistent and capable of being in the game constantly. He could pass, tackle and get goals, some of them spectacular. He became the darling of the crowd. The fans knew that he had the power to inspire and so did the other players. Off the pitch he was a quiet man, but on the field all the vocabulary he needed was in his boots.

Charlton was the right move for Mark at that time. He had been the kingpin at Colchester and slotted into the same role at Charlton. Kinsella relished that situation. He soon became the captain and he responded well to the role. Charlton was good for Mark and Mark was to be good for Charlton. He would be ever-present in the next three seasons.

Richard Rufus was also in the side by now and improving by the year. As much as I like centre-halves who come out of defence and play, it's crucial to have someone in your line-up whom the opposition fear. Richard was certainly someone that I wouldn't have wanted to play against. He was quick, aggressive and uncompromising.

In my mind I still thought of myself as an attacking player and football as a creative game, but Richard must have got up in the morning thinking about tackles he was going to make and shots he was going to stop. That way of thinking is alien to me, but it is so vital to have players of this mentality in your team. When I had worked with him in his early years, I had tried to concentrate on honing his destructive instinct. He had more ability than people realised, but he never lost that single-mindedness about defending.

In February 1995, David Pleat asked me to be his assistant as he took charge of a Football League U21 representative side to play a one-off game in Italy against a team drawn from that country's Serie B. One of the originally selected squad had to pull out at the last minute and I suggested to David that we should replace him with Rufus. I was a bit nervous about how he would perform, since I'd gone out on a limb to get him involved. There was still a rawness about him and I knew that in Italy a moment's recklessness could easily get him a red card. I was coaching the defence on that occasion. David always preferred working with the forwards. Richard made one rash challenge early on, but after that he played really well and he certainly impressed David. He showed he had both the attitude and the adaptability to go all the way.

Players often grab headlines because of what they do on the ball, but I gauge players on their effectiveness wherever they play on the field. I wouldn't judge a winger by how many step-overs he does, but on how successful he has been in making goals and putting crosses into certain areas. Sometimes players excite the crowd but don't produce the end-product. In Richard's case the end-product was that he invariably destroyed the opposition's moves. Very few players got the better of him.

By the second half of the 1990s we had a man at the back who opponents didn't relish playing against and someone in the middle who was always in the game. In the summer of 1997, Curbs paid Grimsby Town £700,000 for a striker fated to become a legend at the club within one season. It was, of course, Clive Mendonca.

Clive was possibly the first Charlton striker since Derek Hales who the fans felt would take every half-chance that fell to him. He quickly won their trust, so his misses tended to be forgotten and his mistakes were quickly forgiven. He was highly professional, in training and in matches, and an outstanding finisher who lived for goals. He wasn't particularly good in the air and his left peg was undistinguished. When it came to his right, however, he had ice in his veins. Some strikers need to be within eight yards of goal when they shoot, but in Clive's case you could extend that to 20 if he got the ball on his right foot. He could disguise a shot, too, looking one way and hitting the ball across the goalkeeper into the other corner.

Technically, he was better than Hales, but Derek's fantastic pace allowed him to get across and in front of people. Hales could hit all kinds of balls and his strength allowed him to get into dangerous situations. His speed would have given him an edge as a goalscorer, but Clive offered the team more in terms of build-up play. In 1997/98 he scored 23 times in 40 First Division matches and his contribution was decisive on numerous occasions. Once he was signed, the spine of a successful team was firmly in place. Charlton were rarely out of the top six from October onwards.

With Carl Leaburn looking to leave The Valley and out of the team in the first part of the season – he returned to the side but left the club in January – Mendonca's early strike partner was Steve Jones. He had been signed from West Ham the previous year but played only twice because of injury. Jonesy had a big heart and an ability to run the other side of defenders that we didn't have elsewhere in the side. He could suddenly open a game up for us and turn a lost cause into a goalscoring opportunity.

He was quite an amiable man, but his lack of professionalism in training annoyed me. He would be slack with his passes or miscontrol the ball and didn't seem bothered about it. One of our regular sessions was piggy-in-the middle. Two players would have to intercept the ball as it was passed around the centre of a circle made up of the others. Whoever gave it away would have to go into the middle. More often than not it was Jonesy. As a result, he would come in for a certain amount of good-natured stick, from Mark Bright in particular.

One day on the way to Oxford I sat next to Steve on the coach and got to know him a bit more deeply. He was very much aware that technically he wasn't as good as some of the other players.

As a result of this conversation, I introduced something that I called the Steve Jones Shooting School while the piggy games were in progress and put him in charge. This was something he was good at. Not only did he enjoy doing it, it also gave him lots of practice in an essential area of his game. I started to feed him lines for the Friday morning sessions to decide who should get the yellow jersey. As time went on he became more and more confident, both on the field and around the other players. He became an accepted member of the squad and was respected for what he did.

In March 1998 it was decided that we should go on a mini-break to Spain for four days to refresh the troops and hopefully galvanise team spirit. Peter Varney immediately arranged sponsorship and the first-team squad flew out, along with Curbs, Les

Reed, Varney and myself. Soon after we landed, the three coaches were deep in conversation at the front of the team bus, discussing sprinting routines and the use of weights to increase a player's power over short distances. Peter, who was listening, suddenly threw down the gauntlet to Les by stating: "I could beat you in a 100m sprint – and I don't use any weights."

Les laughed off the challenge, but he was repeatedly goaded by Peter and eventually succumbed. The big race was set to take place after the final training session. I pulled Les aside and quietly advised him to shorten the distance to 60m. The first-team coach paid no heed. He was confident he could annihilate the managing director, who at the time was boasting an over-generous waistline.

All the players lined up at the finishing post. Those who were backing Reed stood to the left. Those backing Varney were on the right. Only Steve Brown was on the right – he was closing in on his testimonial year, so it appeared a wise move. I blew the whistle to start the race. Reed led at 60m, but the long-legged Varney came through. I wish I could say "like a blur", but actually it wasn't that fast. Peter passed the winning post first, although Les threw himself over the line in a desperate attempt to win the day. Chaos ensued. Reed was still hotly disputing the decision as a delighted Brownie counted his winnings.

Peter had helped to fuel team spirit and the level of banter within the camp increased even more. When he returned to his hotel room that evening, his furniture had been rearranged, his shoes were stuck to the ceiling and the infiltrator had left a single bristle on his tooth brush, although very generously two teeth remained on his comb. The victim swore he would seek revenge, but with 20 suspects it was always going to be a tricky crime to solve. He never discovered the culprit, but I have a theory that the cunning Varney exacted retribution nonetheless. One by one the possible candidates disappeared from the club between 1998 and 2004. Even the faithful Brownie got it in the end. It's believed the evidence is still in a safe in the chief executive's office – labelled "unsolved".

The latter part of 1997/98 campaign was marked by the dramatic emergence of goalkeeper Sasa Ilic, who came from nowhere to play a starring role in the closing months of the campaign. What made the Australian-born Serb's rise through the Charlton ranks so spectacular was that the previous year he had been turning out for St Leonards Stamcroft in the Southern Division of the Dr Martens League. When he first appeared at

Sparrows Lane in pre-season, we were only paying him expenses.

I could see his potential, but initially I couldn't give him more than the odd game in the reserves. Then Graham Hobbins, the general manager at Welling United, approached us to see if we could lend them a keeper for one match. Having only just come from non-League football, Sasa was a bit crestfallen when I put the idea to him. He agreed, but something told me that he wasn't right about it mentally. I phoned him on the Friday night and warned him not to go if he thought he was too good to be playing for the Wings. I knew that if he went there with the wrong attitude he would have a poor game and that would rebound on him when I reported back to Curbs. To Ilic's credit, he responded to that advice, played very well and then took part in a second match for them in midweek in which he was equally impressive.

He got into my reserve side against Millwall in mid-December and again acquitted himself well. Then we went to Southampton, where he had a very young side playing in front of him. The kids worked hard, but the Saints were so much stronger than us that we were hard-pressed to get even a single shot on goal. Sasa put in an unbelievable performance. He saved everything that night, including about half a dozen one-on-one situations. Afterwards, I did something very unusual for me, walking into the dressing room and announcing: "You've all worked hard, lads, but I think we've all got to thank Sasa for getting us a point." I very seldom single out an individual in a team, but that night it was "Southampton Reserves 0 Sasa Ilic 0".

We signed him in January and he continued clocking up clean sheets for the reserves. I never coached him. I just saw this incredible ability and confidence that was visibly growing. I knew he liked hard work, so I put on drills that had him diving from post to post almost non-stop. Another goalkeeper might have preferred a slower pace and to do more technical stuff. Not Ilic. The harder he worked, the more he liked it.

I knew that whenever a cross came in, Sasa would come out for it, so I told the other players to get back on the goal line. He was prone to advance long distances and they would only get in his way otherwise. In one match he came out 30 yards and was lobbed, but the ball was hooked off the line by a defender. It wasn't luck. We had planned for that eventuality.

By the middle of February, Ilic had gone six reserve games without conceding a goal. The senior team was doing well in the

First Division, but a 3-0 defeat at Stockport County gave him the opportunity he needed. He replaced Andy Petterson for the following midweek match at Stoke City – in which he did finally concede a goal, in a 2-1 victory – and was ever-present for the remainder of the season. That wasn't the end of a remarkable story. After conceding a modest seven goals in his first eight games for Alan Curbishley's side, he embarked on another faultless sequence of nine matches at the most crucial stage. Six of Charlton's final seven First Division fixtures ended in wins and the other was a goalless draw, at Birmingham City on the final weekend.

We needed to win at St Andrews and two other results to go in our favour to get automatic promotion. Sasa was having a blinder, but at half-time events elsewhere were going against us. I said to him in the dressing-room that I hoped he wouldn't have so much work to do in the second period. He had completely the opposite view: "I just want them to keep coming at me," he insisted.

His ego was growing fast. There are good sides and bad sides to that, but when players feel invincible they can perform Herculean feats. Eddie Firmani told me that he had a similar feeling in his first spell at Charlton. He just knew he was going to score and it was only a question of where he chose to put the ball. Great players may have that feeling for the majority of their career. The more mortal ones have it only for a certain period. This was Sasa's time – and it was to Charlton's benefit. Almost inevitably, Ipswich failed to beat him in either leg of the play-off semi-final. Unfortunately, he couldn't carry his form over to Wembley, even though he made the crucial penalty save. He may not have deserved to be hailed as a hero for his performance on the day, but there was a measure of justice about it because of what had gone before.

As for the reserves, they continued to flourish without him. From November to April we recorded 11 consecutive clean sheets and scored 26 times without reply, winning the Football Combination with seven points and an unfulfilled fixture against QPR to spare. A 1-0 win over Arsenal at The Valley in March drew a bumper crowd of 7,583 – more than had seen many of the club's home League games in the early 1970s and 80s – due largely to a range of pre-match entertainment aimed at families.

Times were certainly changing at The Valley and my own role would be no exception. Wembley would transform everything.

Chapter Fifteen
PREMIER CLASS

After Sasa's save, the celebrations went on for days.

I was very much aware that this was our moment and that it had been so long in coming, not just for me but for the supporters who had kept faith all those years. Mark Kinsella went up the famous steps to collect the play-off trophy, but the real prize was the return of top-division football to The Valley after 41 years.

Curbs was never going to do a Bob Stokoe – galloping across the pitch to hug his players as Bob had famously done after his Sunderland team won the FA Cup in 1973. He enjoyed the moment to the full, but didn't allow his emotions to run away with him. Even at that stage of his career, such professionalism was what we'd come to expect from him.

We were told to stay out on the pitch for as long as we could so that the Sunderland fans would disperse and reduce the congestion around the stadium. None of us had a problem with that. I eventually walked off behind the hat-trick hero, Clive Mendonca. He was the happiest man on the planet at that moment. It was the absolute pinnacle of his career, but a small bunch of Wearsiders tried to spoil his joy by threatening his family as he headed for the tunnel. What effect it had is hard to say, but at the time he seemed upset by their comments. He had grown up in their community and still had relatives living locally, so that gave their bile some weight. Overall, the Sunderland supporters responded with great dignity and sportsmanship to the defeat. They were a credit to their club.

There was champagne in the dressing room, but everyone was shattered. I've seen more jumping around after an average home win. Richard Murray had arranged for the club to use some television studios, just off Wembley Way, as a base for the day. We walked there, with some of the players carrying the trophy through the remaining supporters. It was like a scene from an earlier era. We came across a group of fans slumped by a wall. Some of the faces were familiar, but they were too drained – emotionally and physically – to even get up to greet us. I knew exactly how they felt.

After receiving the congratulations of the families, club officials and the fans who had been invited, we boarded a coach back to the hotel for a more formal reception. There were speeches and it was a pleasant occasion, but the mood was lower key than one would have expected. The strains of the day were catching up. We did have one very familiar gatecrasher. Derek Hales, whose son Leigh was with the club as a trainee, was there to share the jubilation. There was also a cake to mark director Derek Ufton's 70th birthday. I don't suppose he could have chosen a better present.

The following night there was an open-top bus parade from The Valley to Woolwich Town Hall, where the club was granted the freedom of Greenwich borough. Nothing like this had been seen at Charlton for 50 years and it was an unforgettable experience. The streets were lined with supporters and everywhere I looked it seemed that I could see faces I recognised. The diehards deserved what had happened more than anyone and I'm sure they were the ones who were uplifted the most.

I'd known big crowds at Charlton when I was watching the team from the terraces in the 1950s and even played in front of some in the early part of my career. Over the years, the lack of success had seen them dwindle to the extent that you wondered whether the later generations would ever return. Suddenly here they were and the club was rejuvenated. It was like a religious revival.

What made the Wembley thriller so big was the fact that it was covered live on television, nationally and internationally. Nothing was ever the same after that day and in terms of the way football finance was going, with much bigger Sky deals in the pipeline, it was exactly the right time for us to make the leap.

The pressures of the Premiership may have forced Curbs to restructure the management team regardless, but my own role changed following the departure of first-team coach Les Reed that summer. Les had brought sound coaching practice into the club gleaned through his years with the FA. He is a very likeable man and I got on very well with him in the three years he was with us. Success is often about getting the right blend and his background and approach made a distinct contribution to what we achieved. He chose to move back to a more structured and predictable working life by rejoining the FA, although until the play-off final his departure had been a closely guarded secret between himself, Alan and the chairman. It must have been very strange for Les to be part of the promotion party, knowing that he'd be leaving anyway.

After seven years in charge of the reserves – and 18 years after I'd first been offered the job by Mike Bailey – I became assistant manager. It was probably a more fitting title for the role that I had been carrying out and we needed a three-way split of first-team responsibilities in the Premiership. I had enjoyed being my own man in terms of the reserves, as I could give my own team talks and manage the side within certain limitations. I missed having that level of autonomy, but the timing was right to move on and concentrate on helping Alan with the senior team.

I continued the link with the reserves and the youngsters in my new role and tend to bounce around the different levels, but my main priority is the first team. I'm out on the coaching field each day – focusing more on individuals and groups since Les left – and I liaise with the scouting network and the energetic Jeff Vetere. I also deal with the wide variety of issues that relate to the football side but don't warrant the direct attention of the manager. I like to work in tandem with Alan so that I know I am doing what he requires and can anticipate how he would want me to play things.

Curbs and I didn't know each other in 1991, whereas I'd played with Gritty, so ours is a relationship that has slowly developed as the seasons have passed. The important thing is that he knows he can trust me. Over the years we have spent countless hours discussing different matters so that has naturally brought us closer, especially since 1998. I probably know 95 per cent of the time what Alan will think and I try to react accordingly.

Mervyn Day came in as first-team coach to replace Les. He'd been a successful manager himself at Carlisle United and as well as playing at the top level he'd had some behind-the-scenes experience of the Premiership as a goalkeeper coach at Everton. He and Alan had played together at West Ham, so there was already a strong bond between them. It was important that Curbs could feel confident and relaxed about the man who came in, especially as we were moving into new territory on the field. Mervyn has proved to be invaluable. As well as being a first-class coach, introducing imagination and variety into his sessions, he's intelligent, reliable and very well organised. Away from the training ground, golf is his passion. When he smashes a "Day Special" off the tee, you know you are up against a formidable opponent.

Our first Premiership game was away to Newcastle United. We drew 0-0 at St James' Park, despite having Richard Rufus sent off before half-time. From then on we didn't have too much to fear, although we would have to play with the accelerator pressed down to the floor all the time. Unfortunately, we hit a horrendous run in mid-winter, losing eight consecutive matches. It is something that can happen in the Premiership and it went on a fraction too long for us to pull ourselves round at the end of the season.

One player who did not survive the experience of the Premiership was Sasa Ilic. He started off OK, but then got clattered in a game at Chelsea in October. His head went back like that of a boxer on the end of a punch. Sasa was the sort of person who wanted to play again the next day, although he had to be rested for a designated period of time under the rules governing head injuries. I believe he still came back too soon. Shots began going in from distance, which suggested that his reflexes weren't quite the same. Then his confidence went and he started making mistakes. He'd also lost the confidence of the fans. If he had four good games and then made a mistake, it was the error that they'd remember.

I have a soft spot for Sasa because I had spent a lot of time working with him and saw his enthusiasm and desire at a time when he was relatively unknown. His story was the comic-book cliché of the trialist who turned up at the training ground and ended up playing at Wembley, but his reign was short-lived. Technically he had his faults and he was too swashbuckling for a goalkeeper. You need defenders thinking in a different way when they have to cater for an eccentric keeper behind them. Given a choice you would always go for someone like Dean Kiely, whom we signed in the summer of 1999. I'd seen him play for York City many years earlier and thought then that he had everything that was needed. He is the opposite of Sasa – totally consistent and he rarely does anything unusual. Reliability is everything in a keeper and Dean gave us much needed stability.

Mendonca scored another hat-trick in the club's first Premiership home game, a 5-0 thrashing of Southampton, but his season was plagued by injury. He had played a critical part in the history of the club, but he never really got the chance to test himself among the elite. And then suddenly his career was over.

In any promoted side, there will be players who can make the step up and others who have to move on if the team is to establish itself at the higher level. Steve Brown was one of the former. He was a player who had shown great character in overcoming a knee ligament problem that had threatened to finish him in 1992 when he was still only 20. He was playing well in the reserves but had already been in discomfort for some time when Paul Gorman fell on his knee in a small-sided game during training. Steve had to undergo a major operation, but he made his comeback, played well and proved himself. He was then offered a monthly contract for the following season, which meant that he was on a free transfer if he chose to leave. Steve is a very easy-going guy, but this was too much of a disappointment even for him. He felt he had proved himself already.

Physio Jimmy Hendry alerted me to the fact that Steve had walked out. I chased after him and persuaded him to stay. His heart was still at Charlton and I told him that he had the chance to show that he deserved a two-year deal. If his performances merited such a contract then the club would come back to him with an offer, which is what happened. He went on to become an excellent player, stayed another ten years and earned a testimonial.

Brownie's best position was centre-half, but he ended up playing at right-back for some time and he was also a superb goalkeeper. Someone with that kind of adaptability is worth their weight in gold at any club. He lacked a bit of pace and was probably thicker set than most modern centre-halves, but he was totally dependable. He was also one of the cleverest I've seen in that position, second only to Steve Bruce. He would demonstrate his guile when he came under pressure in the air. Another defender in the same position might jump up and power the ball away with a 30-yard header, but it would go straight to the opposition. Brownie would appear to make less decisive contact, but he would flick the ball off to his own full-back. He had an uncanny ability to break up an attack and find a red shirt with one touch of the ball. This is invaluable as the first link in build-up play.

Brownie played an unlikely starring role in the most dramatic match of our first Premiership season. Despite our involvement in the dogfight at the bottom of the table, the campaign had produced some wonderful memories. The feast of football served up by the players during the 4-2 home win over West Ham United in October was one of the highlights. Nothing, however, compared to the penultimate match, at Aston Villa.

Southampton were playing Wimbledon at Selhurst Park that Saturday afternoon. If the Saints picked up three points then we had to do the same in order to keep our hopes of staying up alive for the final weekend. Alan Pardew, who had left the club three years earlier, had been doing some scouting for me. I asked him to go to the Southampton game and keep me in contact with events. Even as I was on the bench concentrating on the action at Villa Park, I was clutching my mobile phone and hoping that he would ring with good news. Up to the 79th minute, we were leading 3-2. The electronic scoreboard flashed up "Wimbledon 0 Southampton 0". But what happened next was almost unbelievable. First, Julian Joachim equalised for Villa. A minute later, our keeper – Andy Petterson – was sent off. Immediately after that the phone rang: "It's 1-0 to Southampton," yelled Pards. "You've got to win now, mate."

With Brownie on the bench, we were reasonably confident that we didn't need a substitute goalkeeper as well, but these were extraordinary circumstances in which to hand the gloves to an outfield player. As he put them on, he was rolling his eyes and shaking his head, repeating: "Oh, my God! Oh, my God!" I went across to the terrified substitute and calmly instructed him: "Brown Dog, tell the other players we have to win. Southampton are 1-0 up."

All he could say in reply was: "Oh, my God! Oh, my God!" I don't think he took in a word I said. You have to know Brownie to understand this behaviour. He was a player who always gave 100 per cent and was tough as teak. He had great skill and was the best emergency goalkeeper I'd ever seen. But he didn't think so. His first job was to deal with a direct free-kick from 19 yards out – the result of Petterson's foul. A stinging low shot was parried away to safety. He also made a couple of other saves. Then suddenly there were only two minutes left. Curbs was yelling from the touchline to throw caution to the wind. We had to score or we were down.

The drama continued when Villa's Steve Watson followed Petterson up the tunnel after bringing down Martin Pringle 20 yards out as our Swedish forward closed in on goal. I didn't have a clue who would be taking the free-kick. Before I could think about it, the phone rang. For an instant, I thought the Dons might have equalised.

"Southampton just scored their sec . . ." But I wasn't listening. I had dropped the phone and was leaping over the advertisement hoarding in front of me. Danny Mills had crashed home the winner. It was deflected, but who cared? We were still in the Premiership. A couple of minutes later, the final whistle blew. I picked up my phone and ran on to the pitch, convinced that we were destined to survive. After all, I'd seen it happen so often before.

This time, however, there was no reprieve. Southampton won

their last match and we lost to Sheffield Wednesday at The Valley. My good friends Dr Lewis Berger and his wife Ileana were over from Florida to watch the final game. Lewis couldn't believe that we received a standing ovation from the home crowd as we did a lap of honour at the end. He questioned: "Are you sure that you've been relegated, Keith?" Yes, I was sure, but I also knew that we had given the Premiership our best shot and would have a good chance of returning. In the effort to survive we had signed quality players like left-back Chris Powell, midfielder Graham Stuart and striker Andy Hunt. They helped to make us a real force when back in the First Division the following season. It was a setback, but not a disaster.

We did lose Mills that summer to Leeds United for a club record fee of £4.375m. Considering that we had paid Norwich City only £250,000 for him just 15 months earlier, it was an outstanding piece of business. With due respect to all full-backs, we knew that we could find a replacement at a lower cost. If we had been forced to sell Mark Kinsella, as might have happened based on his performances in that first season, it would have had a much more severe effect on both the crowd and the team. Curbs brought in Greg Shields from Dunfermline. He did all right, but then got injured. The ever-reliable Brown and then Anthony Barness, another sound character, filled in and offered us something different in the role. John Robinson and Shaun Newton were still there as the two wide men, which was important. And let's not forget the 25 goals scored by Andy Hunt.

Robbo had been at the club since 1992 and by now had become extremely popular with the fans. His willingness to run all day and produce a stream of crosses made him very effective. With him on one side and Shaun on the other, we became renowned for our outstanding wing-play.

Scott Parker was on the fringe of the first-team squad by now, but his obvious potential didn't protect him from the dreaded Yellow Jersey Award. There are too many yellow-jersey stories for me to tell in this book, but I'm sure Scott won't mind me mentioning the time he won it as a young pro. After taking his girlfriend out to a Chinese restaurant, he was telling the lads how good the food had been and added: "The animated duck was different class."

His mischievous teammates were on to the slip in an instant and he won that week's award by some distance. Thereafter, I'm sure that Scott always had an aversion to aromatic duck.

Another victim was Mark McCammon, a six-foot-two striker

who lived in fear of being nominated. Most weeks he would be in the running. At the end of one training session on a foggy day, my group of players was heading back towards the building as the mist thickened. Mark had been sent to retrieve a ball that he had kicked over a boundary fence and disappeared from sight. Suddenly, I heard a muffled cry: "Help, Keith! Help!"

I ran across towards the fence only to discover him with one foot jammed into the top of the railings and the other barely touching the ground on the park side, where the ball lay. He was all but split in two and in considerable discomfort, but his first words were: "Don't tell the lads – they'll give me the yella!"

"Sorry," I replied. "I can't promise that."

I released him in the end and, come Friday, Mark had to take his medicine like a man. It was just as well I had heard him, because the visibility was almost down to nil. Needless to say, the lads cracked up as the story was told – and somewhat embellished – by the judge. I was always the judge!

Early in the 1999/2000 campaign we embarked upon a partnership arrangement with the Milan club Internazionale. Director Bob Whitehand and I travelled to Milan. I represented the management team and Bob was there on behalf of the board as we tried to form a link that would benefit both clubs, but Charlton in particular. It was a thrilling experience watching great stars like Ronaldo, Roberto Baggio, Christian Vieri and Alvaro Recoba train.

Bob and I met Inter's Giuliano Terraneo, with football club chairman Martin Simons and chief executive Peter Varney joining the discussions at a later stage. Although we were never able to sign players who could have improved our team, the relationship did give two Charlton youngsters – Michael Turner and Alex Martin – a chance to sample life in Milan. Certainly, Michael was a better player for the experience. Overall, however, it was a frustrating exercise. As we improved, the Milan club's fortunes began to fade. Players we wanted from them were invariably in their starting 16.

Bob employed his bubbly personality and enthusiasm to set up the deal and on the last night of our stay we were both enjoying a meal and a glass of wine when Peter and Martin walked into the restaurant, having missed their flight home. It was international fashion week and there were no hotel vacancies available anywhere in the city. I agreed that Martin could sleep in my room and Peter went to Bob's. Martin had enjoyed several glasses of wine by the time we were ready to turn in. I slipped between the bedclothes at the furthest point of one side of the bed, while the chairman chatted away non-stop as he paced up and down the room in his underwear. Eventually he jumped into bed, with me still keeping a respectable distance between us and the sheet pulled up to my chin.

Within seconds, Martin was snoring louder than a Boeing 747. For the next four hours I lay there motionless, finally falling into an exhausted sleep around 5am. Martin slipped away, refreshed, to catch an early flight back to London with Peter. It was only afterwards that a good friend of mine gave me a tip that would have helped me out that night. Had I kissed Martin on the forehead as soon as he started snoring, he would have been the one staying awake all night and I could have enjoyed a sound night's sleep!

This was only one of the things to happen in the 1999/2000 season that could not have been predicted or even imagined. Beginning on Boxing Day with the 2-1 defeat of Crystal Palace at The Valley, we won 12 consecutive matches. It was a phenomenal sequence – not even matched by Arsenal in their unbeaten 2003/04 championship run. However good a team may be, it needs luck to achieve such unbroken success at a professional level.

When we did lose, at home to bottom club Swindon, it was a freak goal that beat us, but with so many points in the bank it was now just a question of getting over the line. By the time we beat Queens Park Rangers on the last evening of March, we were a mammoth 16 points clear, with seven matches to play. We didn't win again that season and staggered over the finishing line. We had been flat out for a long time and ran out of energy.

On the Friday evening of April 14th we took on Huddersfield Town at The Valley, live on Sky. We had been within nine minutes of promotion at Nottingham Forest the previous week, but results had turned against us. However, with only four more games to play, victory over the Terriers would be enough to get us up. Curbs. Merv, Peter and myself had decided to have a weekend in Bournemouth, together with our wives, to celebrate our return to the Premiership. We lost 1-0, but the arrangements had been made so we travelled anyway. On the Saturday, Ipswich Town moved into third place by winning at Stockport County. That brought them to within 11 points of us and kept the Charlton champagne on ice.

What should have been a special weekend away was now a low-key affair, the highlight of which became a late-afternoon visit to the local cinema. I chose the movie – Erin Brockovich, Curbs bought the sweets, Peter volunteered to buy the tickets and Merv was is in charge of the soft drinks. Simple.

All the drinks were loaded into Merv's arms, with Peter unhelpfully adding an extra few to make the pile unsteady. A slight trip later and the foyer floor was awash. One of the best keepers in England during the 1970s and 80s had just dropped the lot. Varney tried not to laugh, but anyway was too busy arguing with the cashier that he had been short-changed. The cashier turned out to be right. Her arithmetic was better than that of the chief executive, who prides himself on his financial wizardry. At last we made it to our seats. It was quite crowded and the film had already started.

Curbs then opened a gigantic bag of sweets. He pulled too hard on the top and they flew everywhere, peppering the unsuspecting audience whose attention was fixed on the screen. The elderly gentleman seated behind Alan asked him if he would be kind enough to sit down. The eight of us were now on all-fours trying to retrieve what goodies we could, but dozens of Maltesers were rolling towards the front row. Fortunately, none of our motley crew was recognised in the semi-darkness and after watching the excellent film we slipped discreetly away into the night.

The following week, after the frustration of only drawing with Portsmouth at The Valley on Good Friday, we were finally able to celebrate the great moment. Curbs was at Tottenham, Mervyn was at QPR, and I was at Crystal Palace. Ipswich lost at Loftus Road, which was enough to confirm our promotion, and we were all instantly on our mobiles congratulating one another. But it wasn't quite the kind of celebratory weekend we had planned.

The majority of the Charlton players who had gone down in 1999 were part of the squad that came back up. They were humble enough to go to Walsall and roll up their sleeves. They didn't think they were too good. The First Division was still quite fresh in the minds of most of our players, but now they'd had a taste of the Premiership, so that was a real incentive for them to knuckle down.

One thing the relegation season had taught me was that we needed a different kind of player to survive. We'd signed the former Liverpool and England midfielder John Barnes from Newcastle in January 1999. It was terrific just to have him within the club, even at 35. He had a level of ability that I hadn't seen at Charlton before. Defenders would get very tight on him, but he could still change his mind about a pass in mid-movement of his foot.

Barnes added something tangible and made me aware that more was necessary if and when we got back into the Premiership.

We had all the heart in the world, but we had to have players who could win games. They might not be able to help us draw when the going got tough, but a player with a bit of magic would get us three points at home, which is very difficult in the Premiership. In that first season, we had won only four matches at The Valley.

Those we found in 2000 included Claus Jensen, a Danish midfielder, and Jonatan Johansson, a Finnish winger converted into a striker. South African central defender Mark Fish came slightly later from Bolton and he played the ball out from the back in a way that we hadn't done before. It made a difference, because in our second Premiership season, we racked up 11 home wins, five draws and only three defeats, finishing a highly impressive ninth. We now frightened teams when they came to The Valley, but crucially we retained our work-rate. It resulted in the club's highest position at the end of a season since 1954.

The 2000/01 season was a hugely satisfying one, but it was also marred by two events that put the highs and lows of football into perspective. Returning from Denmark after our final pre-season away game, Alan received a call that would devastate everyone at the club. Pierre Bolangi, an academy left-back, had drowned at an Army training centre in Aldershot. Only a few weeks earlier, Pierre had travelled with the first-team squad to its pre-season base at Woodbury Park, helping out and endearing himself even more to every professional and member of staff. It is fitting that as we walk into the reception area at the training ground each day, we see a photograph of his smiling face. He will never be forgotten.

One month later, Richard Murray's wife Jane was stung by a wasp while eating breakfast at home and suffered an anaphylactic shock, causing massive brain damage. She would remain in a coma for nearly three years, before passing away in July 2003. At the height of his club's achievements, the chairman had to cope with this dreadful personal loss, although the esteem in which they were both held by fans and employees alike meant that the grief extended throughout Charlton Athletic.

I have a vivid memory of Jane from my 50th birthday in 1995. Lesley had organised a surprise party at Gavin's house, to which she invited all the directors who were serving on the board at the time. Not one invitation was declined. Where else but Charlton would you find a board of directors who would attend a birthday party for the reserve-team manager? As Gavin opened the door, Jane's was the first face I saw. She was beaming and yelling "Surprise!" as she sat on the stairs in front of Richard. It was also my great pleasure to partner Jane in a doubles tennis match with Richard and Mike Stevens, our American director. Her warm and effervescent personality will be remembered forever.

The season turned on a 5-0 defeat at West Ham on Boxing Day. Mark Kinsella had done magnificently well for us, but he needed a knee operation and came out of the side after that game. The team that went to Manchester City four days later deployed Bulgarian international Radostin Kishishev on the right side of midfield, with Paul Konchesky and Andy Todd coming into the defence alongside Mark Fish and Richard Rufus. South African international Shaun Bartlett started only his second game for the club up front and Scott Parker came into central midfield alongside Jensen. This pairing, in particular, was to be a fruitful one. We won 4-1 at Maine Road and embarked on a nine-game unbeaten run.

I had worked quite closely with Scott from the time he came into the club. He went into the reserves at a young age and like Konchesky, who was part of the same year group, made his senior debut at the start of the 1997/98 season, aged 16. The first time he played for the reserves we beat Swindon 1-0 away and I was very critical of the team at half-time and full-time, but Scott stood out. He showed an ability to tackle players twice his weight and size. It wasn't really part of his play. He was someone who twisted and turned on the ball, but he nailed a couple of tackles that surprised me and that stayed in my mind. He had set out to make an impression.

He did well in pre-season when he was 17 and 18 and that seemed to indicate that he should be considered for the first team. However, when the pack settled and other people were fit, he would find that the more experienced players were starting. This was the period when he was knocking on my door to express his disappointment. He felt he was ready to play.

Dougie Livermore phoned me up in late October 2000 and asked if Scott could come on loan to Norwich City. Curbs and I felt that the experience would be good for his development. He did very well at Carrow Road, although he was taken off a few times.

Scott's loan period was coming to an end anyway, but we recalled him and I was very much for putting him in the side. I knew that he could take on the ball-winning role in Kinsella's absence. Everyone needs to bring that special something to a side. Parker was exciting, but he didn't get enough goals to be an attacking midfielder. He didn't quite make enough chances for others, as

Jensen did. He couldn't pass the ball and do the link-up play like Kinsella. His niche had to be that of ball-winner and I told him so. He came into the team at Maine Road and did that specific job. After that, there were no doubts. The speed with which he covered the pitch to stop opponents and the qualities that he suddenly brought into his game were quite stunning. I knew he could tackle, but against City he was like a Scud missile homing in on its target.

He was now fast becoming the main man in midfield. By the summer of 2002, Parker and Jensen was the preferred pairing in the centre of the field and Kinsella left for Aston Villa.

Scott improved dramatically in the three years after he broke into the side, and the impact he was having in games was apparent when we went to Arsenal in November 2001. The Gunners cut us apart at the start of that match. We were 1-0 down and if it had been 5-0 that would have been a fair reflection of the play. Two free-kicks from Konchesky changed the game before half-time. Steve Brown headed us level from the first. Then we got a second goal when their keeper punched the ball into his own net under pressure from our summer record signing Jason Euell. The Arsenal players were in total shock coming down the tunnel for the break, with Thierry Henry complaining about the treatment he had received from Parker.

We were already playing five across the midfield with only one man up front, so our tactical options were limited. Curbs' half-time team talk was totally positive. Incredibly, we then went out and got two more fine goals, one each from Jensen and Euell. Johansson even had a chance to make it five. Arsenal did get a penalty to make it 4-2, but what had gone on in the first half was a distant memory and we were fighting tooth and nail. It became one of the great Charlton victories. Very few teams get four goals at Highbury. There were many things about that game to relish.

Despite having lost Richard Rufus to injury in the second game of that 2001/02 season, we climbed as high as seventh in the table by the time he made a memorable return at Tottenham in March. Unfortunately, we only picked up three points from the final eight fixtures and finished the season 14th, with 44 points.

The way the fear factor operates in the Premiership, there's relief within almost every club when the supposedly safe 40-point threshold is reached. Whether it caused us to lose a psychological edge or not, we tailed off that year. Something similar happened the following season, when we took only four points from the last ten games, slipping from sixth to 12th. My personal view is that in both cases it was a combination of the fixtures, injuries and tiredness. What happened in 2003/04 was rather different.

Scott Parker was carrying all before him in the first half of that season. A run of five wins in six games – the other was a 1-1 home draw with eventual champions Arsenal – took us into fourth place at the beginning of November. We fell off the pace slightly but then beat title contenders Chelsea 4-2 at The Valley and won 1-0 at Tottenham over Christmas to regain fourth spot, which we retained for six weeks. This was as high as Charlton had been in the league since I'd started watching them.

Scott was hugely influential in this period and as good as an extra man in the centre of the field. If a striker came deep to collect the ball and then turned and started running at our central defender, the Scud missile would come from nowhere and nullify the danger. This lifted the crowd and allowed the centre-half to come away with the ball without having to make a tackle, so he could then start a breakaway attack. Scott did that so many times for us.

He was a player who took rollickings on the chin. He wanted to listen and learn. As a former midfielder himself, Curbs had helped him improve his all-round game. In his younger days Scott had been quiet, but he had now become a well-rounded personality and good company. The crowd loved him. His disciplinary record was not the best, but we needed him to play with the passion and desire as if every tackle was his last.

Unfortunately, his contribution to our season came to an abrupt end during the January transfer window, when Chelsea stepped in with an offer. The timing couldn't have been worse. He'd just won his first England cap and we were in with a realistic chance of finishing fourth, which would have meant a place in the Champions League. Chelsea wanted him there and then. The deal probably wasn't going to be on the table at the end of the season. They wanted someone they could play in the Champions League and the FA Cup, as well as the Premiership, to help give them three possible routes into Europe the following season.

He had been such an exceptional professional from a very young age that it would have been perfect if he could have left Charlton with the cheers of the crowd ringing in his ears and the good wishes of everybody in the building. It didn't happen that way, but once he decided he wanted to go it became an impossible situation for the club. The fee was £10m, an enormous amount of money for Charlton, but the board didn't want to accept the offer. In the end, they had no choice.

Despite what happened, I have nothing but positive feelings for Scott, because when he pulled on a Charlton shirt he gave of himself like no other. I will only remember him as the brave, skilful player who inspired us for three years. He was always a pleasure to have in the side and around the training ground. I believe that he should have stayed with Charlton for another 18 months. It would have helped his England future. However, he made his decision, which I respect. Only time will tell whether or not it was the correct one.

It was inevitable that Scott's departure would have an impact on the team, but it had taken more than one player to catapult us up the Premiership. The performance at Birmingham City in November epitomised the team spirit that had developed. Matt Holland put us in the lead with a fine header from a Jensen corner. There was some inspired football being played, but it was a very aggressive game. Just before half-time, Herman Hreidarsson split his head open and a nasty gash appeared above his eye. By the time Alan and I reached the dressing room from the directors' box, Hermann was with the Birmingham doctor. Blood was streaming down his face and I was doubtful that he would be fit to return for the second half. Curbs obviously needed to know as quickly as possible whether he could carry on. The doctor seemed to think the wound was too wide to stitch there and then. Hermann just grabbed his arms and instructed: "Just sew it up, man." You don't argue with the Hermannator.

The Icelandic defender strode back into the dressing room, his face ashen grey, blood stains covering his face, neck and shirt, and visibly shaking. Scott and Claus were sitting together and looked at him in absolute awe. At that moment, I'm sure they both went a shade whiter. "Do you think he'll be OK?" I questioned Curbs.

"Yeah, he's as tough as they come."

"No, I'm talking about Claus!" I quipped.

Curbs gave me a wry smile before embarking on his last-minute half-time talk. We went out for the second half and were magnificent. Claus and Scott seemed to be even more inspired by Hermann's effort. I'm sure that if this injury had happened to me, I would have been out of action for at least a week.

Alan Pardew and I formed a strong friendship towards the end of his playing days at Charlton. We kept in touch as his coaching career took off and he would often be on the phone for the odd tip or two. So it wasn't a complete surprise that when my protégé left Reading to take over the reins at West Ham the telephone rang.

Pards asked me to join him at Upton Park. Naturally, I was very flattered. No matter at what stage of your career you may be, it's a good feeling to be wanted. He understood when I declined the offer. The ties that bind me to Charlton prevented me accepting. I have the utmost respect for Pards and am certain that, with a little luck, he will one day become a top Premiership manager.

We finished seventh at the end of 2003/04, disappointing only insofar as we had been higher for much of the winter. In reality it was an incredible achievement for us and Charlton's highest final placing for 51 years. The single most important relationship that has helped us prosper to this extent is that between plc chairman Richard Murray and Alan Curbishley. It has been the cornerstone of our success. Richard has driven the club forward at a remarkable rate over the last ten years. Although he is someone who has chosen to remain largely out of the limelight, he has shown incredible foresight and energy to keep us on course.

Alan has become a top Premiership manager. This does not happen by accident. He has demonstrated an ability to learn and improve himself every season. Although he has very clear opinions of his own, he has never hesitated to talk to Sir Alex Ferguson, one of the coaching staff or even one of the players in his quest to resolve a problem. He has a rare willingness to gather all the information before coming up with a solution. It is not unusual for Mervyn, Alan and myself to sit in his office for three hours at a time discussing tactics for a forthcoming game. He will take on board any suggestions and only reach a decision after full consideration. This is not an easy thing to do because of the variety of opinions bound to be expressed, but he has retained the humility necessary to do it.

In the last year or so, Alan has become even more determined to advance Charlton further and further up the league. He knows the burden of expectation rests firmly on his shoulders.

On the Friday night before an away match, the three of us will dine together. Lengthy discussions take place about the team and other club matters. By the time the coffee arrives, it is not unusual for Curbs to have Merv and I creased up with laughter at one of his many football stories. These are the rare moments when he is able to relax completely.

Alan now has an outstanding record that puts him high up the list as a potential England manager. I do believe that one day he will be asked to fill this role.

Chapter Sixteen
BACK TO THE FUTURE

My story is nearly up to date. Today we are at home to Newcastle
United in the Premiership. What makes it a unique occasion for me is
that my four grandchildren will be among the mascots who will walk
out with the team in a special strip to commemorate Charlton's
centenary year. They are the awesome foursome. Jake is my first and
only grandson – I'm so proud of all his achievements and he has such
a wonderful disposition. Ava is my oldest granddaughter, with her
dark brown eyes, delightful honey-coloured hair, and is a joy to be
with. Then, of course, there is Celine, with her gorgeous blue eyes,
porcelain skin and a nature that makes me want to buy her the world.
Completing the quartet is little Shania, with her flashing smile, eyes
to die for – and what a personality! I can't wait to see them all.

My son-in-law Andy has offered to drive me to The Valley.
Unfortunately, he remains an Arsenal supporter despite my efforts to
convert him. Andy often gets left out of the football conversation
when Gavin and I get carried away at our family gatherings.
However, he more than gets his own back when he annihilates us on
the golf course. As far as table tennis is concerned, the former
England youth international gives us a 12-point start and still
hammers us out of sight. And Gav and I used to think we were good!

I arrive earlier than usual and walk straight out on to the pitch
to have a few words with my old pal and Valley groundsman, Colin
Powell. Paddy has been very smug for the last month since reading
on Charlton's website that he was rated a £10m player while I had
a £1m valuation in a game of fantasy football based around the
club's history. He will never let me forget it.

I head up to the north-west corner of the ground to have a quiet
five minutes on my own before the crowd begins to arrive. As I sit
halfway up I look down at the pitch and still can't get over how
much The Valley has changed since I signed as a pro in 1962. I gaze

around this wonderful stadium, with 27,000 seats, numerous lounges, executive boxes and all its other marvellous facilities. In my mind I see the old terracing that I ran up and down so many times in my youth, the crush barriers and the clumps of weeds growing through the cracks in the concrete. What a difference!

Many past moments flash into my thoughts. There's Paddy making the goal of the season for Derek Hales to smash home. Mike Flanagan scoring his hat-trick against Spurs and another against Chelsea. The pain of Paul Went crumbling to the ground as big John Toshack shatters his cruciate ligament. Peter Reeves making bone-shuddering tackles with such precision on Rodney Marsh and Tony Currie. And there, in one second, Mark Penfold catching a ball on his chest with such great skill as only he could do. Then moments later seeing his shin fold in two as he broke his leg in a crunching tackle with Don McAllister, the Spurs full-back. Colin Walsh's special goal, Chris Powell jumping out at the end of the game and Paolo Di Canio's sumptuous skills. I don't need videos. So many of these games, goals and incidents are firmly imprinted on my mind.

Memories. Nostalgia. That's what it's all about. Well, not quite. Newcastle are the visitors today. I must get down to the tunnel.

Curbs, Merv and myself have a small room linked to the home dressing room. Alan is already sitting there looking over the last few scouting reports. Mervyn arrives. He is always organised. He writes out the teamsheet. It's a 4.05pm kick-off, so at 2.30 we move next door to join the players, who are beginning to change.

Mark Zambarda and Darren Page are now at full-throttle giving massages. Wayne Diesel and George Cooper are overseeing all strappings to ankles, knees and wrists, while Doc Fraser is prepared for any last-minute emergencies. The music is now turned up full blast. It's a good time to seek refuge in our little room. Alan is very concerned about Craig Bellamy's runs and my main fear is that Lee Bowyer will slip his marker and get in on goal. We have a final few minutes of discussion on these two matters. There is a knock at the door and a young academy boy arrives to meet the manager, with his parents in tow. Merv takes out the teamsheet, returning five minutes later. Hermann Hreidarsson is given the task of marking Alan Shearer at corners and free-kicks – not a contest for the faint-hearted.

At 3.10 we re-enter the dressing room. I turn the music off. Thank heavens for a bit of peace and quiet. I have a few words with

Kevin Lisbie and Shaun Bartlett and a quick chat with Jonathan Fortune about how important the first 15 minutes will be in his battle with Shearer. Curbs writes up the Magpies team and their formation on the flip-chart. The team talk begins and about ten minutes later Merv goes over all the free-kicks and corners for the very last time. Everything is marked on our gigantic board so that the players are continually able to check on their duties.

Fitness coach Nick Davis now calls for the lads to go out for the warm-up routine. Merv and I go out on the pitch to keep a general eye on the players and offer any last-minute words of advice. The ground is beginning to fill up and the adrenalin is just starting to pump. There is ten minutes to go before kick-off. Back in the dressing room, the music is blaring once more as each player moves around doing his final bits and pieces, wishing each other good luck with a shake of the hand or a hug. The bell rings and the linesman calls for us to go to the tunnel.

Reserve coach Glynn Snodin – a great character – is just outside the dressing room and he gives the lads a last-minute gee-up. They run out to the familiar strains of the *Red, Red Robin*. Alan, Merv and I look at each other: "It's an important game this one, Keith. We go seventh if we win." We close the door to our little room. It's funny that for the last six years we've said how important each game is. We walk down the tunnel. The atmosphere is superb.

I clap the fans at the north end and see the familiar faces whom I acknowledge in the west stand. As I approach the bench, my four little grandchildren run off the pitch and I'm asked to pose for a photograph with them. Lauren and Amanda look on with pride as their children smile for the camera. I glance up into the stand and see my sister Valerie, still keeping a watchful eye on me. Lesley is in her usual seat and seems to be having some last-minute banter with Karl Howman and his dad, Fred. Gavin is working in a studio to do commentary on the game. Every one of my family has a great vantage point, but as I look up at the grey skies I hope that my mum and dad have the best seats in the house. They would be overjoyed to see their great-grandchildren as mascots at The Valley, in a game against Newcastle United, of all teams.

As I wait for yet another 90 minutes to unfold, with all the drama and passion that goes with it, I am as excited by what lies ahead as I was in 1962. I have been truly lucky to have had this feeling as player, coach and manager for 42 years. And I'm as certain now as I was at the outset – for this there is No Substitute.